GREAT CAMPAIGNS

The First Air Campaign

GREAT CAMPAIGNS

THE FIRST AIR CAMPAIGN

August 1914 - November 1918

Eric and Jane Lawson

COMBINED BOOKS
Pennsylvania

PUBLISHER'S NOTE

Combined Books, Inc., is dedicated to publishing books of distinction in history and military history. We are proud of the quality of writing and the quantity of information found in our books. Our books are manufactured with style and durability and are printed on acid-free paper. We like to think of our books as soldiers: not infantry grunts, but well dressed and well equipped avant garde. Our logo reflects our commitment to the modern and yet historic art of book-making.

We call ourselves Combined Books because we view the publishing enterprise as a "combined" effort of authors, publishers and readers. And we promise to bridge the gap between us—a gap which is all too seldom closed in contemporary publishing.

We would like to hear from our readers and invite you to write to us at our offices in Pennsylvania with your reactions, queries, comments, even complaints. All of our correspondence will be answered directly by a member of the Editorial Board or by the author.

We encourage all of our readers to purchase our books from their local booksellers, and we hope that you let us know of booksellers in your area that might be interested in carrying our books. If you are unable to find a book in your area, please write us.

For information, address:
Combined Books, Inc.
151 East 10th Avenue
Conshohocken, PA 19428

Library of Congress Cataloging-in-Publication Data
Lawson, Eric.
    The first air campaign, August 1914-November 1918 / Eric and Jane Lawson
        p. cm. — (Great campaigns)
    Includes bibliographical references and index.
    ISBN 0-938289-44-6
    1. World War, 1914-1918—Aerial operations. I. Lawson, Jane. II. Title. III. Series.
    D600.L385 1966   95-43895
    940.4'4—dc20   CIP

Printed in the United States of America.
Maps by Beth Queman

For our son, Eric

Acknowledgments

Particular thanks go to Robert L. Pigeon, Kenneth S. Gallagher and John Cannan of Combined Books, who made this volume possible; and to Beth Queman, who did a great job on the maps. The staffs of the Norfolk Public Library, Morrill Memorial Library, and the Walpole Public Library tracked down many, many sources for us. Thanks also to Bruce Gudmundsson of the Institute of Tactical Education, August Blume and Richard Bennett of the Society of First World War Aviation Historians, Ward Bpyce of the American Fighter Aces Association, Eric and Carol Miller of the Western Front Association, Steve Rawlings of Clash of Arms Games, Phyllis Quirk at the Robins Air Force Base Museum of Aviation, Jack Ramsay at the New England Air Museum, Carl Koenig and Capt. Clark Luther. Special thanks are due to our parents, Edward and Joan Lawson and Howard and Dorothy Naberhaus, for their support and encouragement. And we owe a particular debt of gratitude to our children, Eric and Grace, who had to live with us through it all.

Contents

Sidebars

Maps & Diagrams

Preface to the Series

Jonathan Swift termed war "that mad game the world so loves to play." He had a point. Universally condemned, it has nevertheless been almost as universally practiced. For good or ill, war has played a significant role in the shaping of history. Indeed, there is hardly a human institution which has not in some fashion been influenced and molded by war, even as it helped shape and mold war in turn. Yet the study of war had been as remarkably neglected as its practice commonplace. With a few outstanding exceptions, the history of wars and of military operations has until quite recently been largely the province of the inspired patriot or the regimental polemist. Only in our times have serious, detailed and objective accounts come to be considered the norm in the treatment of military history and related matters.

Yet there still remains a gap in the literature, for there are two types of military history. One type is written from a very serious, highly technical, professional perspective and presupposes that the reader is deeply familiar with the background, technology and general situation. The other is perhaps less dry, but merely lightly reviews the events with the intention of informing and entertaining the layperson. The qualitative gap between the last two is vast. Moreover, there are professionals in both the military and academia whose credentials are limited to particular moments in the long, sad history of war, and there are interested readers who have more than a passing understanding of the field; and then there is the concerned citizen, interested in understanding the military phenomena in an age of unusual violence and unprecedented armaments. It is to bridge the gap between the two types of military history, and to reach the professional and the serious amateur and the concerned citizen alike, that this series, **GREAT CAMPAIGNS,** is designed. Each volume in **GREAT CAMPAIGNS** is thus not merely an account of a particular military operation, but is a unique reference to the theory and practice of war in the period in question.

The **GREAT CAMPAIGNS** series is a distinctive contribution to the study of war and of military history, which will remain of value for many years to come.

Introduction

Only a decade before the Great War began, airplanes did not exist. *The First Air Campaign* recounts the remarkable development of the airplane as a weapon of war in an entirely new battlefield—the sky. And, while the airplane was revolutionized, so too did the airplane revolutionize war. The technology of flight evolved dynamically. New types of aircraft reached the front, tipped the balance of air power in their favor, and were obsolete within a month. In the course of the First World War airspeeds doubled, maximum altitudes and climb rates tripled, typical engine horsepower increased fivefold, machine gun fire rates went up ten times, and bomb loads increased a hundredfold!

The concepts and applications of air power developed during the First World War remain the basis of air power strategies today. By 1918 there were specialized types of aircraft for strategic bombing, aircraft carrier based fighters, seaplanes for anti-submarine patrol, interceptors, ground attack craft and reconnaissance planes. Tactics developed in World War I became the basic dogma of air fighting. Maneuvers like the Immelmann turn, barrel roll, falling leaf and wingover became the required repertoire for a pilot. Terms like close support, contour flying and formation flying all date from the First World War. The first air war also created a new category of warrior, the fighter pilot. Death dogged these brave souls as they ventured into the unknown. Life expectancy fell to 21 days for a front line pilot. No wonder an early aviator wrote in his diary, "I've lived beyond my time already....Here I am, 24 years old, I look 40 and

I feel 90. I haven't a chance, I know, and it's this eternal waiting around that's killing me.... Oh, for a parachute!"

The world's first aerial campaign changed the face of war forever. This is the story of how it happened.

CHAPTER I

Wright Makes Might

When my brother and I built the first man-carrying flying machine we thought that we were introducing into the world an invention which would make further wars ... impossible.
—Orville Wright

*E*arly one morning on the beach at Kitty Hawk, North Carolina, a cold stiff wind blew across the dunes. The "Flyer," a contraption never before seen, a flying machine that would change the course of history and the future conduct of war, lay on a long wooden rail in the sand. Orville Wright, bicycle builder turned aeronautic scientist, lay prone on the lower wing. His pioneering brother Wilbur held the lower right tip of the forty foot wings, balancing the flying machine on the take-off rail while its tiny home-built engine, connected by bicycle chains to the two propellers, warmed up. Releasing the tether that held the Flyer still, Wilbur ran beside the Flyer until it lifted off the rail into the wind, propelling Orville forward. A local lifeguard captured this moment in a photograph. The Flyer rose ten feet off the ground and flew straight for 12 seconds at an airspeed of 30 miles per hour. Buffeted by gusts, the Flyer came down 120 feet from its take-off point. It was the first time in history that a machine had risen into the air under its own power to carry a man in flight. Next it was Wilbur's turn. He used the forward elevator control to pitch the aircraft upward or downward, and moved the control yoke he was lying on to twist the wing tips. This "wing-warping" was used to aid recovery if the plane tilted left or right. A crude rudder mounted to the rear automatically counterbalanced the drag caused by the wing-warping control. On the fourth flight of the day, Wilbur kept the Flyer under control in the strong gusts for 59 seconds to travel 852 feet. The day was December 17, 1903. In little more than a decade, this new marvel of science, which the Wrights believed would be an instrument for peace, became a weapon of war that inflicted death and destruction on a scale never before seen.

Though a remarkable new technology had been born on this historic day, it went virtually unrecognized and poorly reported. Only a few local newspapers carried the story and fewer readers believed it. The Wright brothers took a methodical approach to perfecting their aeroplane. They built a second craft in 1904 that made 100 flights near their home in Dayton, Ohio. Then their Flyer #3 attracted some attention when it flew for 38 minutes over 24 miles on October 5, 1905. European governments sent military representatives to examine the flying machines, but the Wrights refused their advances, hoping to offer their ideas to their own country first. However, the United States Army twice rejected the Wright brothers that year, painting them as just two more dreamers seeking government funding. The disheartened Wrights ceased flying for the next two years. Meanwhile, the French sent Captain Ferdinand Ferber with an offer to purchase one aeroplane to scout for the French Army in the impending Moroccan Crisis. The Wrights wisely urged France to immediately seize this new aerial technology because it would grow rapidly should the European climate break into an arms race or a war. Their foresight is evident in their letter of November 4, 1905: "With Russia and Austria-Hungary in their present troubled condition and the German Emperor in a truculent mood, a spark may produce an explosion at any minute. No government dare take the risk of waiting to develop practical flying machines independently.... To be even one year behind other governments might result in losses." ...Ferber forwarded the Wrights' plea to his superiors but was greatly disappointed by their cool reception. With the decline of the Moroccan Crisis, the French Army lost interest in the Wrights and retracted their offer. But Captain Ferber never lost interest. He wrote several treatises on aerodynamics, gliding and the mathematics of flight and their use for the military. Ferber acknowledged his debt to Wilbur Wright with the statement, "Without this man, I would be nothing.... my experiments would not have taken place."

Although governments and armies officially turned a deaf ear to heavier-than-air aviation, other aviation pioneers in France and America leapt to action. As early as 1902 the American Octave Chanute went to Paris to lecture on the Wrights' Kitty Hawk experiments with gliding and wing-warping control concepts. Many future aircraft designers attended the talks and pursued these principles. Captain Ferdinand Ferber built a glider based on the Wright design, and Gabriel Voisin copied the Wright glider for the founder of the Aéro Club de France. Applying power to these designs required development of light gasoline engines, and Ferber aided Leon Levavasseur in creating his Antoinette engine. The Brazilian coffee heir and famous dirigible experimenter Alberto Santos-Dumont mounted one to his "canard" airplane (so named because it looked like a duck in flight), and flew 50 meters straight on October 23, 1906—the first recorded heavier-than-air flight in Europe. Henri Farman, a Parisian born of English parents, achieved the next milestone on January 13, 1908. Combining the best materials available, Farman put a 50 hp Antoinette engine on a pusher biplane built by the Voisin brothers (Gabriel and Charles) and flew one full kilometer in a circle. American motorcycle maker Glenn H. Curtiss followed Farman's exploits closely. Curtiss, a member of the Aerial Experiment Association, a group of American and Canadian aviation pioneers formed by the inventor Alexander Graham Bell, flew his June Bug one kilometer at a speed of 39 mph on July 4, 1908.

This new activity coaxed the Wright brothers out of seclusion, and their first move was to readdress the military authorities of the United States and France. After President Theodore Roosevelt persuaded the U.S. Army to accept the Wright's fourth request, Orville set off for Fort Myer, Virginia, to demonstrate the airplane to the U.S. Army while Wilbur went to Le Mans, France, to start a new European company to sell their planes in the summer of 1908. They soon set their reputation

Maurice Farman M.F.7 "Longhorn,"also called the "Flying Birdcage."

straight by establishing remarkable new world records on two continents for altitude (100 meters), distance, flight duration (two hours and eighteen minutes), flights carrying a passenger (6 minutes 24 seconds), the first woman passenger (who simultaneously introduced the cinched at the bottom "hobble skirt" to Paris fashion), and the first military passenger. Regrettably the first death in an aerial accident also occurred when Orville's army passenger, the U.S. Army's military liaison with the Bell group, Lt. Thomas Selfridge, died in a crash September 17. The Wrights proved they truly were flyers, not "bluffeurs," as one French newspaper dubbed them.

Aviation development sped up after these demonstrations. In the next year Wilbur Wright established the first commercial aerial school at Pau, France. This school later became one of the largest pilot training centers for French and American aviators during the Great War. Orville Wright came to Europe after recovering from his Fort Myer accident and set up a company and the first flying school in Germany at Johannisthal, the future seat of nearly every major German aircraft company. Orville took Crown Prince Frederick Wilhelm on a flight that confirmed the excited prince's interest in aeroplanes. Then the brothers went off to Italy to establish another school. The Wright's exhibitions with their Model A biplane exhilarated crowds

Blériot monoplanes were used as scouts by French infantry and cavalry corps in the first months of war.

across Europe. The year 1909 also saw great feats by other aviation pioneers. In England, A.V. Roe made the first hops by a British designed plane on British soil in June. Louis Blériot flew his little Type XI monoplane across the English Channel on July 25, showing that Britain was no longer an island protectable by its navy alone. The first international air races began in August at Rheims, France, where Henri Farman set the distance record at 112 miles, Hubert Latham in an Antoinette won the altitude contest at 508 feet, and Glenn Curtiss won the first coveted Gordon Bennett trophy for the fastest aircraft at 47.65 mph (around a twenty kilometer course). Curtiss went on to win the Italian air meet in Brescia where he took the famous Italian poet Gabriele D'Annunzio on his first flight. D'Annunzio told his countrymen of the exhilaration and glory of "conquering the elements" in the air, saying that "until now I had never really lived."

The proven successes of the airmen finally convinced some in the military world to get involved with heavier-than-air flight. After Orville's cross-country flight of ten miles at over 42 miles per hour carrying the future head of the U.S. Air Service Lt. Benjamin Foulois, the United States War Department purchased the first successful military aircraft on August 2, 1909. Officially

Count Ferdinand von Zeppelin, visionary of air transportation and dirigible manufacturer.

it was called Aeroplane No. 1 of the Heavier-than-Air Division, U.S. Aerial Fleet, U.S. Signal Corps. The Wrights were awarded $25,000 plus a $5,000 bonus for breaking the speed requirements. In France the following month, immediately after the Rheims air meet, the French Corps of Engineers purchased two Wright Model A biplanes, two Henri Farman biplanes, and one Blériot monoplane. A French artillery commission also purchased two two-seater Wright biplanes, three Farmans, and two Antoinette aircraft to adjust artillery from the air. The French purchases sadly coincided with the death of the man who stimulated military interest from the beginning, Captain Ferber, who died when his Voisin rolled over while taxiing on the ground.

German interest in heavier-than-air aircraft was greatly hindered by their conviction of the superiority of lighter-than-air dirigibles. Even though Germany spent 8 times as much on aviation as France in 1910 and 80 times Britain, nearly all of the funding went to development of military dirigibles and balloons. Of the world's successful dirigibles then in existence, the majority, 14, were in Germany, only five were in France, two in

Purchased from Germany, this Parseval non-rigid airship added to Britain's small fleet of airships before the war.

Italy, and one each in Britain, America, and Russia. Count Ferdinand von Zeppelin, the most prolific dirigible producer, captivated both the Kaiser and the German public with his airships. Since 1900 he had been developing his aluminum-framed, hydrogen-filled rigid airships at Lake Constance in southern Germany, and sold several to the German Army. The Zeppelin airships had exceptional load carrying capacity and range that the military thought would be optimal for bombing or reconnaissance. Germany also sponsored development of the Schutte-Lanz rigid airships, the Parseval non-rigid dirigibles (blimps), and the army's own Gross-Basenach semi-rigid military designs.

But aeroplanes were gaining some ground even in Germany. The first German design was a poor copy of the Wright Flyer minus the rudder, and it immediately crashed on its first flight in 1910. The head of the German General Staff, Helmuth von Moltke, saw value in the heavier-than-air planes. He recommended that the Army train officer pilots and promoted military contests to stimulate German industry. At first only foreign aircraft won these meets, so later only German designs were invited for evaluation. The first truly successful plane came from the Austrian designer Igo Etrich. Etrich created a bird-like

Early-war German Taube, as preserved at the Owls Head Transportation Museum in Maine. (Author photo)

airplane design in 1910 named the Taube or Dove. Its curving monoplane wings were actually shaped after the zanonia seed. The original Taube used early wing-warping control but some manufacturers of the plane substituted ailerons. Germany at first did not accept the Taube, having at one point banned all monoplanes as dangerous, but after the German Rumpler company began producing Taubes in large quantities they soon became the standard military plane. Taube copies were produced by numerous German manufacturers right up to the beginning of the war. The new aircraft companies of LVG (Luftverkehrs Gesellschaft) and Albatros later produced biplane designs by Ernst Heinkel which surpassed the performance of the Taube and won the military contests of 1912 and 1913 with speeds of up to 69 mph. Oddly, one of the requirements of the conservative German military contests was to limit engine horsepowers to 100 hp or less!

Across Europe in Russia another flurry of aerial ingenuity flourished in relative isolation. Remarkably, Russian enthusi-

Igor Sikorsky's "LeGrand," the prototype for Russia's giant Ilya Mourometz bombers.

asm for aviation came right from the top. Grand Duke Aleksandr Mikhailovich persuaded the Tsar to create an aviation branch for the military in 1909, and to buy foreign aircraft including Blériot, Voisin, Farman, Wright, and Curtiss. By 1911 international air meets were held in Russia and military and civilian aviation schools were well established. Large aircraft manufacturing firms like the Dux Company and the Russo-Baltic Works built French designs under contract as well as the designs of the Russian pioneers. Several firsts came out of Russia in 1913. In September Lt. Peter Nesterov performed the first successful loop above Kiev weeks before the French stunt pilot Adolphe Pégoud made his famous loop-de-loop. Aircraft designer Igor Sikorsky flew the largest multi-engined plane in existence aptly named the Grand. Sikorsky followed the Grand with the Il'ya Muromets that flew 16 passengers in luxurious surroundings powered by four 100 hp engines in February 1914.

The British were late starters in the aerial arms race. Britain's earliest aerial pioneer A.V. Roe was rejected by the Imperial War Office which "saw no possibility for using aeroplanes for war purposes." The first British officer to fly was Capt. Bertram Dickson of the Royal Field Artillery, who used his own money

Louis Béchereau's sleek 1912 Deperdussin Monocoque Racer broke world speed records before the Great War and foreshadowed later fighter plane designs. **(National Air and Space Museum)**

to buy a Henri Farman biplane in France. Inspired, Dickson wrote an official memorandum for the Committee of Imperial Defense on the future value of aviation, stating prophetically, "In the case of a European war between two countries, both sides would be equipped with large corps of aeroplanes, each trying to obtain information of the other, and to hide its own movements. The efforts which each would exert in order to hinder or prevent the enemy from obtaining information ... would lead to the inevitable result of a war in the air, for the supremacy of the air, by armed aeroplanes against each other. This fight for the supremacy of the air in future wars will be of the first and greatest importance." A skeptical War Office took heed in February 1911. The army ordered the formation of an Air Battalion of the Royal Engineers: "a body of expert airmen" to conduct "the training and instruction of men in the handling of kites, balloons, aeroplanes and other forms of aircraft." This organization was commanded by Capt. J.D.B. Fulton (who learned to fly at his own expense with his own Blériot) and consisted of five aircraft: a Blériot, a Wright, a Farman, a de Havilland, and the Paulhan pusher biplane. On April 13, 1912, this aviation organization was renamed the Royal Flying Corps (RFC) by royal edict. A naval wing of the RFC was created to absorb the naval aeroplane pilots released when the Admiralty quit aviation following its failures with lighter-than-air dirigibles. The naval wing was officially separated as the Royal Naval

Air Service (RNAS) just months before the war began in 1914. Dickson, instrumental in driving British military aviation forward, became the first victim of a mid-air collision during a meet in Milan in 1912. He succumbed to his injuries a year later.

In Italy the military visionary Giuilio Douhet urged his government to accept the value of aviation. He forecast aerial warfare, writing, "the sky is about to become another battlefield no less important than the battlefields on land and sea," and "in order to conquer the air, it is necessary to deprive the enemy of all means of flying, by striking at him in the air, at his bases of operation, or at his production centers. We had better get accustomed to these ideas, and prepare ourselves." Not only had Douhet presented a clear analysis of air tactics in the next war, but foresaw strategic bombing as well. In fact, Italy used the airplane in war early on. During the war in Tripolitania (Libya) between Italy and Turkey, the Italians made several aviation firsts flying nine aircraft and two dirigibles from the obscure desert towns of Benghazi and Tobruk. On November 1, 1911, Lieutenant Gavotti flew his Taube monoplane at 700 feet over an encampment of two battalions of Arabs. He pulled a small bomb from his bag and tossed it over the side, resulting in the immediate dispersal of the Arabs and reportedly several casualties. The Italian Army's new Farman biplane performed other bombings and aerial reconnaissance that first week of November. Aerial photography and tests of Marconi's wireless receiver were also carried out operationally. Before the war ended in 1912, the Ottoman troops started firing back at the planes with noticeable success. Captain Montu was the first airman wounded in battle, hit by ground fire from 1,800 feet below. The French and the Spanish also used planes in North Africa to reconnoiter the activities of the rebellious tribesmen in Morocco. The French dropped grenades and steel darts called "flechettes" on the Moors while the Spanish dropped German Carbonit bombs from their Austrian built Lohner planes.

The uses of the airplane in war were tested in a number of other small conflicts. To protect Texas from being violated during the Mexican Revolution in 1911, a Wright biplane went with troops to patrol the border. With Lieutenant Foulois in the observer's seat, the plane made numerous reconnaissances around Laredo, Texas, in the first operational use of an aeroplane. It was not until November 1913 in Mexico that the first aerial dogfight took place. Dean Lamb, an American soldier of fortune flying for Pancho Villa, was over the enemy entrenchment just south of Arizona to drop his pipe bombs when he met a plane piloted by another American, Phil Rader. Rader fired the first shot with his revolver and the two planes circled for fifteen minutes trying to shoot one another down until their ammunition ran out. In the Balkan Wars of 1912 and 1913, all countries involved used a handful of aircraft for observation and some homemade bombing. Never was there any report of airmen firing at one another in this conflict.

Airmen experimented with arming aircraft on both continents prior to the Great War. Major Jacob Fickle of the U.S. Army fired the first shot from a plane in August 1910 with his Springfield rifle from the seat of a Curtiss biplane. In France, Gabriel Voisin strapped an ominous 37mm cannon to his plane for photographers, but it never left the ground. Commander Cleland Davis of the U.S. Navy patented a more compatible form of recoilless cannon that fired a counterweight out a tube to the rear of the gun while firing its shell through the barrel. A year later Col. J.E. Capper of the Royal Engineers lectured that while the key role of British aeroplanes is reconnaissance, "I would require them to be armed with some light form of shooting weapon, as it … may be required to fight an enemy's aeroplane, either to secure information themselves or to prevent him obtaining any." In June 1912 Lieutenant-Colonel Isaac N. Lewis of the U.S. Army presented his new light machine gun design at the aircraft testing field in College Park, Md. The gun, in a Wright Model B, shot at a ground target from 250 feet. This first aerial use of an automatic weapon received such an insulting response from the military board of review that Lewis went off to Europe to sell his ideas like so many other Americans. Back in Britain, the RFC fired a Maxim heavy machine gun from Geoffrey de Havilland's prototype for the F.E.2. The heavy, unwieldy, belt-fed gun that generally required a two-man crew on the ground, was mounted in the front cockpit of this pusher biplane called "Fighter Experimental No.2." In the next year a 1½ pounder Vickers cannon was fitted to the nose of the plane for potential ground attack or anti-Zeppelin work. Further experiments in 1913 with the Lewis, Hotchkiss, and Vickers machine guns led to the first production model of a "Fighting Biplane," the Vickers F.B.5. This pusher powered aircraft became famous as the "Gunbus" in the early days of the war.

The year preceding the Great War saw some experimentation but little implementation of machine guns on tractor driven aircraft. The French developed armed and armored designs but only a few ever flew, like the Deperdussin TT monoplane with its armored shield mounting a Hotchkiss gun for the standing observer to shoot above the propeller arc. Raymond Saulnier designed a synchronizing mechanism on his Morane Type N monoplane whereby a mechanical bar pulled the gun trigger on command from the rotating engine. Ironically, the war interrupted development of the device. At the German LVG company, Swiss engineer Franz Schneider also designed another type of synchronizing gear but it too was overlooked by the military.

A glimpse of the future of naval aviation occurred on November 14, 1910. An 83-foot downward sloping ramp had been rigged on the bow of the U.S.S. *Birmingham* anchored off the naval base at Norfolk. The daredevil exhibition flyer Eugene Ely flew a Curtiss pusher biplane off the front of the cruiser and landed safely across the harbor on land. Two months later in San Francisco Bay, again flying a Curtiss, Ely safely landed on the stern deck of the battleship U.S.S. *Pennsylvania*. The plane was stopped on the deck tail-hook style by arresting cables designed by another exhibition aviator, Charles Willard. Glenn Curtiss tried another experiment in San Diego which the Navy found more palatable. He attached floats to his "hydroaeroplane," took off from the water and landed beside the U.S. Naval vessel which then hoisted the plane aboard. This launched Curtiss into his successful series of seaplane and flying boat designs. Large numbers of his early "flying boats" were purchased by Russia for her Baltic and Black Sea fleets. The Royal Navy also became interested and bought the design of the flying boat "America," planned to be the first plane to cross the Atlantic.

Europe was gearing up for war by 1914. The war machines of each country were numerically and technologically superior to

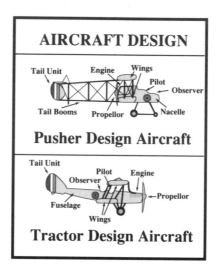

anything ever seen before, yet each country felt they had the advantage to achieve a swift and easy victory over their foe. The airmen hoped to play a key role in bringing about this victory, spurred on by military theorists and sensational civilian authors. In *The War in the Air*, published in 1908, H.G. Wells wrote of great sky battles between fleets of airships and hundreds of one-man flying machines. The spark that sent centuries of imperial European grandeur down in flames came on June 28, 1914. The progressive Archduke Franz Ferdinand of the Austro-Hungarian royal family was assassinated by a Serbian terrorist in the quaint Bosnian town of Sarajevo. This started a chain reaction among European nations entangled in interlocking treaties, ententes, and mutual defense pacts. Austria sought retribution from Serbia and planned an invasion. Russia mobilized its forces against Austria-Hungary to defend fellow Slavs in Serbia. Germany mobilized against Russia to aid her Austrian ally, but also planned an initial invasion of Russia's western ally, France. The French planned an attack into Germany to fulfill her entente agreements with Russia and to retrieve the provinces of Alsace and Lorraine. Britain agreed to support France, but most swiftly spun into action when the German Army invaded neutral Belgium in its sweep toward France. Nations prepared for a short victorious campaign that would be over before the leaves fell, and surely by Christmas. Few foresaw the end of an age, and a way of life.

As death rolled across the continent, many sought to join the fray. The frail Georges Guynemer rushed to the French recruiting office to enlist, but was refused because of his poor health. A young German cavalry officer named Manfred von Richthofen rode his horse into the Polish forests to scout for the enemy. In Turkey, the young Irishman Edward Mannock inspected telephone lines for a British phone company. In England, James McCudden, a mechanic in the Royal Flying Corps, prepared aircraft for their trip across the English Channel. An African American prize fighter in London, Eugene Bullard, hurried to Paris to join the French Foreign Legion. Back in the States, Norman Prince took up flying and dreamed of forming an American volunteer flying unit for the Allies. At Princeton University, freshman Elliott White Springs read in the newspaper of the troubles in Europe. Racecar driver Eddie Rickenbacker kept his sights on winning the next Indianapolis 500. Not one of these young men knew that they were about to be immortalized in the history of aviation and modern warfare.

Pushers

The "pusher" aircraft design is as unique to the first air campaign as triplanes and rotary engines. Pusher designs draw their lineage directly from the Wright Brothers' Flyer which, like a powered boat, had its thrusting propellers mounted behind the lifting surfaces to push the vehicle forward. The engine that drove these pushing propellers was mounted roughly in the center of the aircraft between the wings and just behind the pilot seat. The short body of a pusher is called the nacelle, enclosing the pilot and engine, while the tail surfaces were held by an open framework of booms extending rearward from the wings, outside the arc of the spinning propeller. While the rudder and control surfaces of most pushers were mounted at the extreme rear of pusher aircraft, the elevator to control climb and dive of the Wright Flyer (and the later Farman M.F. 7 "longhorn") was mounted well forward of the wings.

Pusher designs proliferated in Europe where they competed with the novel "tractor" designs of Blériot, A.V. Roe, and Sopwith. The more streamline tractor planes had their engine and propeller mounted at the front of a long "fuselage" body to pull the craft forward. Several interesting hybrids also arose: the Caudron G III with its small nacelle but tractor mounted engine, Caproni bombers with both pusher and tractor engine mounts, the German Gotha bombers with conventional fuselages but engines mounted pusher-fashion on the wings, and the unusual SPAD A.2 which was a standard tractor aircraft with a small nacelle "pulpit" for the gunner precariously rigged just ahead of the spinning propeller. The pushers, however, were viewed as the more traditional and safer design by the French who placed great emphasis on Farman and Voisin types early in the war. When confronted with the Fokker Scourge, the British also embraced the pusher design. Lacking the synchronization technology for many months, pushers allowed the British to attack enemy planes with a forward firing machine gun unobstructed by the spinning propeller. Starting with the Vickers F.B.5, they produced the F.E.2, the D.H.2, and lastly the F.E.8 fighters.

Pusher type aircraft suffered from a few major detractions. Excessive drag and wind resistance slowed the aircraft. But the most problematic characteristic showed up when a pusher plane experienced a forced landing or crash. The heavy engine, bolted right behind the pilot seat, broke loose, plummeted through the nacelle, and crushed or pinned to the ground many crewmen. Living with this constant hazard elicited the popular airmen's verse:

"Take the cylinder out of my kidneys,
The connecting rod out of my brain,
From the small of my back take the camshaft
And assemble the engine again!"

Ferdinand von Zeppelin

Count Ferdinand von Zeppelin (1838-1917) had a roller coaster career: a rollicking ride full of thrills and chills, crashes and burns, ridicule and adulation. Born in 1838 to an aristocratic family, Zeppelin sailed to America as a 24 year old junior officer intent upon observing the armies engaged in the American Civil War. Granted a military pass after a personal visit with Abraham Lincoln, Zeppelin did indeed move freely among the Northern armies. Later he traveled west and in St. Paul, Minnesota ascended in a balloon with "the famed aeronaut" John Steiner. Zeppelin wrote "While I was above St. Paul, the idea of aerial navigation was strongly impressed upon me, and it was there that the first idea of my Zeppelins came to me."

Zeppelin returned to Germany and spent 20 years rising through the ranks to Brigadier General. But aeronautics remained his first love. In 1887 Zeppelin submitted a report titled *Possibility of Airships* to King Wilhelm I of Prussia. In this report Zeppelin stated that for military purposes airships must be maneuverable, able to remain aloft for a minimum of 24 hours, and capable of carrying heavy loads of men, ammunition, and supplies. He predicted that "airships could accomplish the shortest journeys across mountains, across the sea, or between any two given points." Shortly thereafter in 1890 (perhaps coincidentally, perhaps not) Zeppelin was summarily dismissed from the military. Shaken and disturbed, Zeppelin buried himself in the science of ballooning. Many thought

like one outspoken critic who said, "That poor man is deranged. He is Count Zeppelin, and he wants to fly through the air." Yet, after three years of studying and testing, Zeppelin petitioned for government funds to build the first airship. The Kaiser was not impressed. He said of Count Zeppelin, "Of all Swabians, he's the biggest jackass." But Zeppelin would not be dissuaded. When turned down by the Kaiser in 1894, he said: "I do not blame anyone for considering me a fool, but I feel that it is my duty to go on with my work steadfastly and to hold to my idea, which I know is right."

In 1898, funded with contributions from the German people, Zeppelin received a patent for a "steerable air vehicle with several carrying bodies arranged behind each other" and building began. Unfortunately, the unmanageable *Luft-schiff-Zeppelin One* (*LZ 1*) was a public relations disappointment when it first flew in 1900. Zeppelin believed the main problem—poor steering—could be overcome. But financial problems ensued. Eventually *LZ 2* was built in 1905. But it crashed on its maiden voyage and was damaged beyond repair. But *LZ 3*, produced in 1907, flew for 8 hours! That same year the Reichstag voted to subsidize airship construction. People were amazed and delighted, resulting in a Zeppelin Craze. Even the Kaiser came around, saying, "I thank God, with all Germans, that He has deemed our people worthy of you. May it be permitted to each of us, as it has to you, to be able to say in the twilight of our lives, that we have served our dear Fatherland so beneficially." In 1908 Zeppelin formed the Zeppelin Airship Construction Company with three separate units—passenger, military, and naval—in Friedrichshafen.

In 1909 Zeppelin founded DE-LAG (Deutsche Luftschiffahrts A.G. or German Airship Corporation), the first commercial passenger air travel company ever. Fifty dollars bought a ticket to Hamburg, Dusseldorf or Frankfort, round trip, at a top cruising speed of 45 mph! It cost much more than the price of a first class train ticket, but was quite an elegant way to travel. By 1913 almost 1000 flights per year were flown, although many flights were canceled due to weather.

In 1914, with the advent of the First World War, all Zeppelins were taken over by the military for war purposes. Eventually they proved too slow and flew too low for their bombing and reconnaissance missions. Zeppelin immediately volunteered for active service at the outbreak of the First World War, to be the admiral of a fleet of airships, or perhaps command an airship on a bombing raid over England, but his offer was denied. He did help direct the construction of the airships during the years of the war. But it was others who perfected Zeppelins for military purposes. Zeppelin himself never concentrated on his airships' worthiness for military usage. He always called his airships "Special Ambassadors of Peace and Good Will." Instead, he believed "the crowning effort of my career (would be)...to be the first to pilot an airship across the Atlantic....I want to sail on a peaceful mission when I go to America. My greatest ambition has not been to create a machine of destruction....Zeppelins were suited to far greater purposes than to be used as mere instruments of warfare." Zeppelin foresaw "that aerial travel will become the quickest and safest method." By 1917, Zeppelin felt that "airships were already antiquated weapons in warfare and...the aeroplane and not the airship will control the air in the future." Only days later Zeppelin was dead. His last words were, "I am very tired and would like to sleep."

CHAPTER II

1914
The Wrong Stuff

Aviation is fine as sport. I even wish officers would practice the sport, as it accustoms them to risk. But, as an instrument of war, it is worthless.

—General Ferdinand Foch, Allied Supreme Commander

When the Great War erupted in August 1914, airmen of all combatant nations scrambled to their squadrons with great enthusiasm but with equally great uncertainty. Aerial warfare was a complete unknown. Never before had armies gone to the battlefield with fleets of aircraft at their disposal, and the role of these flying contraptions remained poorly defined and their effectiveness completely undetermined. Reconnaissance was their designated purpose, but most generals of the ground army refused to believe that the information obtained by any single plane could compare in value to that achieved in a classic cavalry probe. Aviators soon found that they were not only fighting the enemy, but also for respect within their own ranks. New missions were developed largely at the initiative of the flyers, and became official practice only after being substantially proven in battle. Effective equipment for dropping bombs from aircraft had not yet been developed. The number and quality of aircraft were insufficient. While the ground war witnessed the largest number of soldiers ever to fight on the continent, only a mere handful of flying machines ever mobilized. And the few fighting airplanes available did not stand up to the rigors of war. The young flyers sought feverishly to take the battle into the

31

clouds where only a few pre-war visionaries had dreamed it could occur. They refused to be just a quaint auxiliary unit of the army. When the sky received its first baptism of fire it was no longer the pure and peaceful realm of ages past, but was destined to become a battleground as bloody as any on land or sea. The opening months of the conflict proved to be a struggle for the airmen both to discover their own potential and to prove to their countrymen the importance of fighting this new war in the air. These first few airmen would change the face of war forever.

The first actions in the air took place while the ground armies were still mobilizing. Just hours after the declaration of war on August 3, a lone German Taube monoplane circled over Lunéville on a reconnaissance. It dropped three small bombs on the French town, causing quite a stir. Days later the Zeppelin Z VI dropped a few improvised bombs on the Liége forts before being put out of service by shots fired from the ground. French aircraft took to the sky to observe the disposition of the German armies in Alsace. They observed troop movements along the French front but missed the great scythe to the north seeking to mow down Belgium.

No flyer was killed until the second week of the war, on August 12. Oberleutnant Reinhold Janow went down in Belgium when his Taube was hit by rifle fire from the ground. Ground fire, both enemy and friendly, was the only major danger to the airmen. The average infantry soldier shot at anything flying overhead since he could not identify the types of planes. German troops were responsible for finishing off at least one Zeppelin while French infantry shot down their own dirigibles *Conté* and *Dupuy de Lôme*. Troops routinely fired on their own aircraft for the first several months of war until adequate national insignia appeared on planes.

History's first military aviators flew to war in machines that were barely improved over what the Wright brothers had flown in the pioneer era. Their machines represented the whole spectrum of pre-war experimental designs. There were biplanes with pusher propellers like the Wright Flyer, monoplanes with a single gracefully curved birdlike wing, and a few tractor powered biplane designs with the engine and propeller up front

Early in the war, ground troops, like these Belgians, fired at any low flying plane.

pulling the plane through the air. All planes were built merely of wooden spruce sticks, covered with clear doped linen fabric, and held together by a maze of wire bracing. When a pilot asked a mechanic how to check if all the wires were correctly set, he was told to "let a bird loose in the center of the wires, if it gets out then a wire is missing." These "birdcages" were invariably powered by either a spinning 80 hp rotary engine or a stationary 100 hp water cooled inline engine. The maximum speed was between 60 and 80 mph, slow compared to aircraft that came later in the war. Most planes carried two men with the observer seated in front of the pilot. This afforded a slightly obstructed forward view for the pilot and a terribly obstructed downward view for the observer, but it was the traditional seating arrangement used by sport planes of the day. No planes were armed, though some of the crew carried pistols or carbines. The risks of flying these pioneer aircraft under war conditions were enormous. These early aircraft were as fragile as a child's plaything. Accidents in flight and upon landing were common. The

Rotary engines, like this 7 cylinder Gnôme Monosoupape, had the crankshaft mounted to the aircraft while the entire block with propeller hub rotated around it.

stresses of moving with the advancing and retreating armies, the repeated flights over enemy lines, and the potshots from the ground also reduced the number of planes available. Reserve aircraft and spare parts were essential for the air arm, but the multitude of different aircraft types in each army made supply extremely difficult.

The airmen of 1914 were adventurers and daredevils, not fire-breathing warriors. Some were thrill seekers drawn by the novelty of flying who transferred from the cavalry or artillery services. Others were chauffeurs and mechanics selected by the army for their experience with modern technology. But many of the flyers were civilians who had learned to fly before the war, wealthy sportsmen and competitive aerial exhibition pilots, who had enlisted in time of crisis. Their training in military flying was minimal as there were no instructors with military experience. They learned on the job to spot ammo dumps and troop concentrations. The aviators were a select breed from day one, a small fraternity of the air that would grow in numbers and diversity.

The air forces of all the combatant nations mobilized rapidly to scout for their respective armies. Germany called up 230 aircraft (half the total aircraft in the country) for active service in their 33 field squadrons, but only 180 planes and 12 airships were in condition to go on campaign with the fighting troops. German armies were well equipped, however, with many Drachen kite balloons for fixed position observation. France planned to mobilize 162 aircraft spread across 23 squadrons, but only 136 planes and 6 dirigibles were serviceable when the war broke out. Britain's Royal Flying Corps (RFC) could call up 179 planes and the Royal Naval Air Service (RNAS) 91 various land and seaplane types, but only a quarter of these were able to cross the English Channel and fight in France. Russia's 39 aviation sections produced 244 aircraft and 14 dirigibles ready for war, but many of these were considered less than first rate, and the lack of spares and replacements hindered their usefulness. Austria-Hungary had the fewest planes of the major combatants at the outbreak of the war, fielding only 13 squadrons totaling 48 front line aircraft. Neutral Belgium mustered a couple dozen military planes, but civilians offered their services to aid Belgian aviation as well. The United States had no involvement in the outbreak of the First World War and did not enter the fighting for nearly three years. But when the European conflict erupted in 1914, America, the birthplace of powered flight, possessed a mere 23 military aircraft. The total forces available to the Central Powers of Germany and Austria-Hungary were on the order of 228 planes. The Allied forces of France and England gathered together 210 planes in the west and Russia had nearly as many in the east. But even though the total number of planes on the first day of the war was small, their value grew steadily in size and importance.

As small as the total number of aircraft were, the vast number of different types of planes was mind boggling. The French fielded thirteen different types of aircraft, although each of the French squadrons (escadrilles) was equipped with a single type

Henri Farman H.F.20 in Belgian service, 1914.

of plane. The escadrille designations reflected this: Escadrille HF 1 was equipped with six Henri Farman two seat pusher aircraft, Escadrille MF 2 contained six Maurice Farman pushers, Escadrille BL 3 was equipped with the two seat Blériot XI monoplane, and Escadrille Dep 4 flew Deperdussin model TT's. Most escadrilles allocated to the Infantry Corps contained these types of aircraft, but a few escadrilles were made up of the Voisin, Caudron, Morane Saulnier, Nieuport, Breguet, and REP Robert Esnault-Pelterie planes. The escadrilles servicing Cavalry Corps consisted of three single-seat Blériot XI military monoplanes such as Escadrille BLC 2. The German squadrons were called Fliegerabteilung (Fl. Abt.), and each contained a mixed bag of two-seat aircraft. The vast majority were the graceful dove winged Taube monoplanes, but there were various models produced by over a dozen different manufacturers including Rumpler, Gotha, Etrich, and Jeannin. Some biplanes

French Farman undergoing field repairs.

such as the Aviatik B.I and the Albatros B.II were also scattered among the Fliegerabteilung.

The British Royal Flying Corps made its appearance on August 13 in an historic flight across the English Channel. This force was an amalgamation of 37 airplanes comprising the better part of three squadrons. The RFC No.2 and No.4 Squadrons came across with B.E.2 planes, No.3 Squadron flew French built Blériots and Henri Farmans, and squadron No.5 arrived a few days later equipped with the Avro 504, the B.E.8, and more Farmans—the first expeditionary force transported by air, yet not without mishap. Nearly a half dozen pilots were killed in accidents in the two hour flight from Dover to Calais, and numerous planes were damaged during the transfers across France to Amiens. And like the squadrons of France and Germany, the primary purpose of the RFC was to reconnoiter and scout for the army units to which they were attached. Dropping bombs was an afterthought and only permissible after the primary reconnaissance task was completed.

EYES OF THE MYOPIC ARMIES

As the armies advanced, their way was scouted by the flying

Pre-war collection of British military aviation equipment including the **Astra-Torres** *type airship.*

machines passing close overhead. Individual aircraft went aloft each day to scout ahead of the army unit to which they were attached. For most of the combatants, a squadron consisting of six aircraft was attached to each corps headquarters for use in tactical reconnaissance. They served only to patrol and observe the deployment of enemy forces as an adjunct to the traditional reconnaissance arm, the cavalry. The long range strategic duties were carried out by the squadron attached to an army headquarters, and in the case of the Germans, each army headquarters was additionally assigned one airship. The Germans and the French used airships mostly for night observation and a little bombing. Locating enemy bivouacs at night was not too difficult because the "black-out" concept had not yet been conceived.

Observations were made at heights of only 1,000 feet so that enemy troops could be identified by the naked eye. Ground forces felt no need to hide their activities from the prying eyes above, but these eyes were often too inexperienced to distinguish a soccer game from a melee. French observers flying their first combat missions over Lorraine mistook dark patches of road tar for troops on the march, and reported headstones in a cemetery as tents of an encampment. Yet some reports were so detailed and extraordinary that the old generals in the rear refused to believe in their accuracy. The top military brass, trained on Napoleonic principles with little emphasis on modern technological advances, were neither interested nor supportive of the new-fangled machines which buzzed infrequently overhead and scared their horses. However, the airplane was instrumental in saving the day on several important occasions.

In mid-August the beleaguered Allies were retreating from Belgium into France to avoid being overwhelmed by the *First* and *Second* German armies. The BEF landed in Belgium and moved in force to Mons without being adequately observed by German aircraft or cavalry probes. They put up a strong delaying action at Mons on August 23, but were dangerously close to being outflanked and overrun. The French aviator (and future Chief Air Marshal) Captain Philip Joubert scouted the left flank of the Mons defenders. From about 1,000 feet in the air he spotted hordes of field-gray troops from the German *II Corps* streaming down the roads to encircle the rear of the BEF. Hit by ground fire, he managed to bring his bullet riddled plane back by plugging holes in the gas tank with his fingers. The report Joubert filed was confirmed by a British flown Blériot from No. 3 Squadron RFC. This convinced the British that it was time to beat a hasty retreat. A young mechanic in No.3 Squadron, the future ace James McCudden, said "things began to hum" that day. Another British officer later recounted that the whole British Army "was twice in thirty days saved by a single observer."

Meanwhile, across the continent on the eastern front, the German *Eighth Army* attempted one of history's greatest encirclement maneuvers—Tannenberg. The Russian Second Army under General Alexander Samsonov moved blindly northward into the belly of East Prussia. The Germans under their new leader Paul von Hindenburg planned to crush this Russian force by shifting all available units in the province to the Tannenberg area. The German airman Leutnant Mertens, flying with his pilot Leutnant Canter in a Gotha built Taube monoplane, observed the Russian troops lunging toward Tannenberg with exposed flanks. They landed as soon as they could in the dense woods and sped by bicycle, cart, and commandeered car to inform General Hermann von François of the developing situation. Von François led his *I Corps* so aggressively that he completely encircled and cut off the main Russian forces which allowed for the complete annihilation of Samsonov's army at the Battle of Tannenberg on August 30. Shortly thereafter Samsonov blew his brains out. Von Hindenburg, credited by his nation for the glorious victory, reflected on the contributions of aviation in the victory: "Without the Airmen—we wouldn't have had Tannenberg."

The Battle of the Marne finally validated the importance of aerial observation. By the end of August, the German armies were careening down upon Paris. The French and British forces were in full retreat, falling back toward the Marne river. On August 30 a German Rumpler Taube flown by Lt. Hindelson dropped two small bombs on the capital city with the warning "The German Army is at the gates of Paris; you have nothing left but to surrender." Parisians panicked. The French government abandoned the city. But German General Alexander von Klück, commanding the *First Army* on the German extreme right flank, realized that his line was spread too thin. Instead of attempting the encirclement of Paris to the west as detailed in the Schlieffen Plan, he drew his army eastward on a new course to catch the BEF and cut off Paris from the main French forces.

This change in direction was duly noted on September 2 by Louis Breguet, the aircraft designer, who volunteered his services and his latest prototype to the cause of defending the capital. His report of "von Klück's turn" was reconfirmed by planes from Escadrilles REP 15 and MF 16 sent aloft by the French 6th Army aviation officer, Captain Bellenger. The general commanding the French 6th Army did not believe these reports, for they contradicted information obtained by army intelligence which described the Schlieffen Plan in detail. Not to be thwarted by such narrow-mindedness, Captain Bellenger next took his aerial reports directly to the commander of the Paris defenses, General Joseph-Simon Gallieni, and to the BEF commander, Sir John French. Gallieni was a progressive minded individual who had gained an appreciation for aircraft before the war. He had such great faith in Bellenger's aerial observations that he went to the supreme commander of all French forces, General Joseph Joffre, and convinced him to counterattack von Klück. Joffre called together the army commanders and expanded the coun-

B.E.2a's of No. 2 Squadron, RFC, in Flanders.

terattack proposal into the most sweeping reversal of the war with the words, "Gentlemen, we will fight on the Marne!" On September 6 the Allied armies simultaneously made an about face and counterattacked their stunned German pursuers. French and British planes had pinpointed the location of each German force while German planes had been stretched so thin that they missed the sweeping assault of the French Sixth Army against the German flank. With the "Miracle of the Marne," the allied French and British armies turned the tide of the German advance and pushed them back to the north. This action changed the course of the war from a swift and certain French defeat to a long-term world conflict . Following the Battle of the Marne, Sir John French praised the British squadrons for "the most complete and accurate information which has been of incalculable value in the conduct of the operations." The French High Command as well was sold on the value of aviation as the new eyes of the army.

Another valuable adjunct to aerial observation was devised at this time. Through the local cooperation of the French aviators and the artillery commanders within some divisions, a measure of artillery direction from the air was achieved. During the German retreat on September 8, two French aviators spotted a large concentration of German artillery near the town of Thiaucourt. By dropping notes to their own artillery, they managed to call down a barrage which destroyed half the artillery of the entire German *XVI Army Corps*. This feat so impressed General Joffre that he officially cited it in that day's army communiqué. Joffre further defined this new role for aviation by limiting general reconnaissances and assigning the majority of aircraft to serve the artillery units. Each artillery battery received an assigned plane. Communication between flyers and gun crews was problematic and usually involved individually arranged codes. This emphasis on artillery cooperation naturally followed the Battle of the Marne when armies formed more stationary trench lines. The end of the mobile phase of the war required less "scouting" and more "spotting" for artillery duels from fixed positions.

COMBAT IN THE CLOUDS

Although thousands had died on the ground in the first days of war, the skies were a sea of tranquillity. The airmen conducted their business in solitude. When two foes would chance to meet in the air, they would fly quite close to one another to check the identification of each other. Even then opposing airmen carried nothing to effectively threaten one another. Mostly, they just waved! But warfare is not sport, and the aviators could see clearly enough the bloodshed on the ground. Aviators soon developed a more warlike attitude. They sought to deprive the enemy of its aerial eyes and protect their own troops on the ground.

At first pilots carried handguns and rifles on planes. These proved useless in shooting at one object in the sky that was undulating in three dimensions from another equally jostling object. Louis Strange of No. 5 Squadron RFC felt that a machine gun might do a better job, so he mounted a Lewis gun to the front of his pusher biplane. But the gun and ammunition weighed down his Henri Farman so much that he could not climb half as high as the Taubes. His commander had the gun removed. Similarly on the other side of the lines, the German High Command also banned such attempts as a waste of time in October, and only allowed arms to be carried for self defense purposes in the event of a crash landing behind enemy lines.

Some British Bristol Scouts were fitted with rifles or machine guns, fired obliquely to avoid the spinning propeller, by progressive minded flyers like Lanoe Hawker.

The British RFC took matters into their own hands. On August 26, Lt. H.D. Harvey-Kelly led three unarmed B.E.2a aircraft of No. 2 Squadron RFC down upon a startled German Taube. The German dove away, chased by Lt. Harvey-Kelly and his mates. Maneuvering as if they would hit the Taube, they bracketed it and shepherded it to the ground. The Germans fled on foot while Harvey-Kelly landed and set the Taube on fire. This method of obtaining victories briefly became a fad among the RFC squadrons.

French aircraft designer Gabriel Voisin brought the solution to the front in the form of six Hotchkiss light machine guns for Escadrille V 24. The machine guns were mounted on a pivoting fork over the front cockpit of each Voisin pusher biplane. On October 5, pilot Sergeant Joseph Frantz with observer Corporal Louis Quénault in an armed Voisin met a German Aviatik biplane over the front. Frantz maneuvered closer to give his observer a clear shot. When machine gun bullets spewed from the French plane, the surprised German turned away. At first there was no damage to the enemy plane. The French pilot determined that the best way to provide his observer with a good shot was to attack the Aviatik from close behind and along the axis of its flight path. This proved successful, and the Aviatik

Bombs were dropped by hand in the early part of the war, before the advent of bombsights and bomb racks.

fell into history as the first victim of aerial combat from machine gun fire. Frantz and Quénault had launched a new phase of the war in the air, as well as an understanding that maneuver and tactics are as important as armament.

BOMBARDMENT FROM ABOVE

Bombs had not yet been developed for use by aircraft. Artillery shells weighing 4 to 20 pounds sufficed. Sometimes crude fins were applied to prevent them from tumbling as they fell. The French used 90mm artillery shells and some old Aasen bombs left over from Morocco before the war. The bombs were carried on belts around the aviators and dropped by hand over the side of the cockpit. Another early weapon of the air war was the "Bon darts" or flèchettes. These were small steel darts thrown from a coffee can at ground troops. Supposedly, an attack with these darts broke up a German cavalry squadron, but more likely the sound of the engines overhead caused the

Searchlights at Place de la Concorde seek German airships and bombers while the rest of Paris is blacked out.

disruption. While the Allies did drop their bombs and flèchettes whenever possible, they were ordered not to use them except when returning from their primary reconnaissance mission.

The Germans made the first and most vigorous use of aerial bombardment in 1914. Both the Zeppelins, which had been designated for bombing before the war, and airplanes participated in these bombing raids. The aircraft made several raids on French railroad stations, bombed Belfort and Lunéville and several other cities. From just before the Battle of the Marne until mid-October the city of Paris was visited a dozen times by the infamous "five-o'clock Taube." These planes caused eleven deaths and wounded fifty Parisians, as well as attracting much public attention. It was one of the first attempts to demoralize a civilian population by aerial assault. A special bomber force deceptively named "Brieftauben Abteilungen Ostende" (the carrier-pigeon detachment at Ostende) was established on the coast of Belgium to threaten the British on both sides of the English Channel. On December 22, a single German plane

The pre-war **Astra-Torres** *served as the prototype for British naval blimps that later patrolled the coastlines for submarines.*

crossed the channel to drop a handful of light bombs on Dover. It was the first round trip military sortie from the continent to the British Isles. This small action was just a harbinger of ominous future campaigns against the English home front.

The French and British focused their only serious bombing efforts on suppressing the Zeppelin menace. French aviators twice bombed the airship sheds at Metz-Frescaty in the second week of the war and managed to damage one airship. After a Zeppelin raid on Antwerp killed 12 people, the British RNAS stationed in Belgium planned to destroy the airships in their sheds. Twice a flight of RNAS planes bombed the hangars in Düsseldorf and Cologne, destroying one of the Zeppelin raiders in early October. When Belgium collapsed, the RNAS pulled back to Dunkirk and was reinforced with more planes and numerous armored cars. Wing Commander C.R. Samson became as famous for his aggressive aerial attacks as for his daring armored car exploits. Then, with a novel strategic approach to the problem, Winston Churchill, the First Lord of the Admiralty, called for an attack directly on Count Zeppelin's factory in southern Germany. In late November the British secretly transferred a flight of AVRO 504 planes across France to the Alsatian town of Belfort. On November 21, four AVRO's flew the 125 miles across Bavaria to Friedrichshaffen on Lake Constance, home of the Zeppelin works. Diving at the factory through a storm of small arms fire, they dropped several 20 lb. bombs that severely damaged much machinery and barely missed a new Zeppelin under construction.

The Royal Navy also developed a sea based air arm to guard the British Isles against Zeppelins. Three cross-channel steamers were converted to carry seaplanes. H.M.S. *Engadine* carried a couple Short "Folders" whose wings folded for storage, while the H.M.S. *Empress* and H.M.S. *Riviera* carried other types of Short seaplanes. These craft were escorted across the North Sea to the Heligoland Bight just outside Germany's main naval base on Christmas Day. Seven planes were hoisted into the water, took off, and attempted to bomb the Zeppelin sheds at Nordholz. Although they could not locate the Nordholz base, they did manage a useful reconnaissance of the German High Seas Fleet at Cuxhaven. While the seaplane carriers were awaiting the aircraft's return, two curious German naval airships flew over the British force at 2,000 feet to investigate. Zeppelin L 6 dropped several bombs quite near the H.M.S. *Empress*, but beat a hasty retreat in the face of the sailors' gunfire.

BURSTING THE ZEPPELIN MYTH

The German army airships had an undistinguished career in the first months of the war. They were not very effective as reconnaissance tools due to their vulnerability to enemy ground fire. Their inability to rapidly respond to specific mission requests also reduced their use for scouting. By the time a great Zeppelin was readied for flight the strategic situation on the ground often changed and its mission would be canceled. The army airships had been slated since before the war to perform bombing operations on important enemy targets. On the third night of hostilities Zeppelin Z VI dropped eight artillery shells with makeshift leather fins on the fortress town of Liége. Her gas cells were pierced by so much rifle and machine gun fire from the ground that she was forced to crash land in a German forest on her return flight. On August 21, both the Z VII and Z VIII bombed French infantry in Alsace. After releasing their bombs from 800 meters altitude, however, the Zeppelins were hit by enemy and friendly ground fire. Both came down out of control in French territory. In the east, Zeppelins *Z IV* and *Z V* performed substantial reconnaissance by night and day. Then on September 6, the Russians shot down and captured *Z V* during a bombing attack on Mlawa. The other airship on the east front, Schütte-Lanz *SL2*, supported the Austrians at the fortress of Przemysl. Of the dozen airships controlled by the German Army High Command (OHL), three—*Viktoria Luise, Sachsen* and *Hansa*—were old civilian ships from Count Zeppelin's Delag commercial air line.

Perhaps the most successful of the early army airships was Zeppelin *Z IX*, a brand new airship just commissioned by the German army. It flew numerous bombing missions across Belgium and northern France including a five-city raid on August 21 against Antwerp, Zeebrugge, Dunkirk, Calais, and Lille. The Zeppelin was such a nuisance to the Belgian and British defenders at Antwerp that the RNAS decided to take direct action against it. The night after its five-city raid, British aircraft sought out the home of Zeppelin *Z IX*. Based on intelligence reports, they flew to Dusseldorf and bombed the Zeppelin shed which normally housed the *Z IX*. Luckily for the airship, it wasn't home, and the following month it continued to drop another 3,000 kg of bombs on Antwerp and 1,000 kg of bombs on Ostende. This bombing spree finally ended on October 8 when Flight Lieutenant R.L.G. Marix of the RNAS caught the *Z IX* at home. Lieutenant Marix flew his Sopwith Tabloid from the RNAS aerodrome at Antwerp to Dusseldorf and dropped two small 20 lb. bombs on the huge Zeppelin shed. An enormous explosion of flame followed as the hydrogen of the airship erupted, consuming both the shed and the *Z IX* within. Marix himself had a difficult time getting home from his successful adventure. On his return flight ground fire forced him down in Belgium. Luckily a Belgian civilian gave Marix his bicycle and directed him toward the retreating British lines which the young lieutenant barely reached in time for the general evacuation from Antwerp.

CONCLUSION

The first months of the First World War revealed the great importance of the air arm and hinted at ways to use it more effectively. Aviation won the respect of the traditional military leadership and started getting the support it needed to grow. Each nation concluded that more and better planes were necessary. They demanded higher performance aircraft and reclassified the less acceptable planes as trainers. The Germans removed the Taubes and focused on the successful biplanes, the British retired their Henri Farmans, and France surrendered its Deperdussins and Blériots. Combatant nations realized that the war would not be over by Christmas, and ordered the civilian aircraft industry to increase production.

The French led the way by taking a dramatic and farsighted approach. In early October, General Joffre placed Commandant Joseph Barès in charge of French aviation. Barès' predecessor had planned for a short war. He closed the flying schools to provide men and materiel for the front and stripped workers from the aircraft manufacturing industry to outfit the squadrons. Barès reversed all his predecessor's shortsightedness. A progressive thinker and dynamic aircraft promoter who had flown in the Balkan War of 1912, Barès developed a three point plan with the French General Headquarters (GQG) on October 8: First, double the existing air forces to over 60 squadrons. Second, customize these squadrons into specific functions. Thirty escadrilles of six planes each would be devoted to corps level reconnaissance and artillery cooperation. Sixteen escadrilles would be reserved under Army level control for purposes of "pursuit" and reconnaissance. Another sixteen escadrilles were devoted to bombing activities and were directly under the command of the GQG general headquarters. These bomber squadrons were grouped into four group de bombardement units in recognition that bombing was most effective when done en masse. And, thirdly, the Barès plan focused on only four types of service aircraft. The Caudron G 3, a biplane with central nacelle containing an 80 hp LeRhone rotary engine up front, was selected for artillery ranging and corps observation. For general reconnaissance, the Maurice Farman MF VII "Longhorn" pusher

Katherine and Marjorie Stinson, here in their Wright Biplane, trained Canadian and American pilots for the RFC.

biplane powered by an 80 hp Renault engine was chosen. The Voisin LA 5, a pusher biplane powered by a 130 hp Salmson was designated for bombing. And for pursuit, the fast little Morane Saulnier Type L parasol monoplane with the 80 hp LeRhone engine was chosen. All other aircraft types were removed from active service and relegated to training duties. French aircraft manufacturers produced only officially designated types under contract. Engine types were similarly designated and built by contract. This plan was a major step in the right direction.

The Germans also realized the superiority of certain types of aircraft. The elegant Taube monoplanes, the mainstay of the German air force at the outbreak of the war, were obsolete after two months of service. Its broad monoplane wing hindered the observer's field of view and its load lifting capability was small. Only biplanes such as the Aviatik B.II, L.V.G. B.I and Albatros B.II were purchased to outfit the Fliegerabteilung. Germany's airships, incapable of safely performing reconnaissance or bombing duties by day, were a disappointment in the first months of the war. A special bomber unit of aircraft was established to harass the British on both sides of the English Channel.

By the close of 1914, aviation had certainly proven to be more than a sport which just frightened the horses. New and valuable missions for aircraft developed daily. Direct cooperation between airplanes and some ground units was officially endorsed. Aviation had demonstrated its superiority as a reconnaissance tool with the eclipse of the cavalry. It became the only form of observation for trench lines, and special attention was given to artillery cooperation. Bombing extended offensive actions into the enemy's rear areas. Most of all, the airmen wrestled and fought and finally brought the war into the air. The airplane was acknowledged as a legitimate weapon of war. The time had come to use it. As 1914 came to an end, the world's first air campaign began.

National Insignia

Friendly fire was a most disturbing problem during the first days of the war in the air. Aircraft flying overhead had no recognizable markings other than their manufacturer's name and their military serial numbers. National insignia for the planes was quickly adopted by the French and Germans. Other nations followed their lead.

The French used a cockade of red, white, and blue modeled after the round symbol of the French revolution that was made by wrapping a French flag about itself. The center was blue, surrounded by a white ring, and an outermost red ring. The dimensions varied slightly, mostly due to the aircraft manufacturer's practice. These cockades were ap-

plied to the top and bottom of wings and the sides of fuselages while the entire rudder was painted like the national flag with vertical bands of blue, white, and red trailing.

The British first applied national markings to their aircraft in October of 1914. The Union Jack was applied to the underside of the lower wings of all aircraft. However, the large dark crosses of the British flag on a moving object flying at great height looked like a German Maltese Cross. By November the RFC officially adopted a roundel emblem similar to the French cockade, but with red in the center, white around it, and a blue outer ring. Roundels were painted only on the undersides of wings with small Union Jacks on the fuselage or rudder until the summer of 1915 when the entire French scheme was mimicked: red/white/blue roundels at all locations and rudder stripes of blue, white, and red trailing. The RNAS attempted to maintain a unique roundel style throughout 1915 with a large white disk surrounded by a red ring, but eventually copied the RFC system. Later in the war, night fighters obliterated the white portions by painting them black or by widening the red and blue to cover the white.

Roundels became the standard design for Allied insignia. Belgian aircraft used wing roundels like the French cockade but used black in the center, with a ring of yellow and then red. Tail stripes were similarly black, yellow, and red. The Italian roundels were red, white, green, and tail stripes were green, white, red. The Russians first painted horizontal bands of white, blue, and red like the Russian flag on their aircraft. They later adopted roundels of white, blue and red but no rudder stripes. A thin white band often separated the colored bands.

When the United States entered the war in 1917, it adopted a white star insignia on a blue field with a red ball in the center of the star. Tail stripes were like the French and British. Several naval planes began operations with this insignia, but before any army planes reached the front in February 1918 a new pattern was ordered. The U.S. roundel colors were white in the center surrounded by a blue ring with an outermost red ring similar to the Russian roundel. Rudder stripes were at first white, blue, and red trailing, but then changed to red, white, and blue trailing.

The German aircraft immediately adopted the Maltese Cross or "Iron Cross" pattern, painted in black on a square white background. This "cross patée" design was applied to the top and bottom of the wings, to the fuselage sides, and to the rudder. Beginning in the fall of 1916, the large white field was dropped to allow better use of camouflage coloring, and the Iron Cross was outlined by a thin white stripe on most aircraft types. With the 1918 Spring Offensive, Germany moved towards the straight-sided Balken Kreuz, and aircraft already in the field had the curving portions of their Iron Crosses painted over with thick straight white borders. New aircraft were produced with crosses of thin straight black arms which spanned the chord of the wings and the sides of fuselages; a thin white line paralleled the black arm but did not outline its tip. The tail was commonly painted white with the black cross on the rudder.

Most of the other Central Powers nations used back and white crosses and insignia. Austro-Hungarian insignia followed the German pattern, but the naval aircraft often used the vertical red, white, red bars of the Austrian flag on the wings and tail. Bulgarian planes carried the Maltese Cross in black throughout the war. The Ottoman Empire initially used a moon and star on a red square, but soon adopted a solitary black square bordered in white with no details.

Aircraft Camouflage

Aircraft in the First World War exhibited some of the most brilliant and revolutionary color schemes ever created. The war in the air forced the art of camouflage literally to new heights. Aircraft required camouflage to conceal them from fire coming from the ground as well as from enemy aircraft.

The first aircraft went to war in their civilian colors, which was no particular color scheme at all. The cloth covered wings and fuselage of the aircraft were made of plain, unbleached, unpainted linen fabric. A clear shellacking of aircraft dope, which is used to seal the fabric taut and strong, gave most of the planes a tawny off-white color. Different manufacturers used slightly different recipes for this cellulose acetate dope, generating various shades from brown to yellow to gray. Metal engine cowlings and wooden struts were also unpainted and left in their natural aluminum or varnished colors.

By mid-1916 it became obvious that aircraft needed to protect themselves from being observed by enemy planes, so aerial camouflage was introduced. The British started painting the upper surfaces of wings and fuselages with a khaki-green protective color called PC10. This greenish dark color helped conceal the aircraft among the landscape when viewed from above, while the light color of the clear-doped undersurfaces still prevented easy recognition from below of the plane's outline against the bright sky. Another more chocolate colored pigment called PC12 was used primarily by RFC aircraft sent to the middle-east and by some RNAS planes.

Also, beginning in 1916, the Germans began to paint their planes in alternating fields of green and mauve on the upper surfaces and sky blue on the under surfaces. The large fields of each color covered up to half of each wing and control surface. Another type of camouflage used on Fokker triplanes was green streaks across the off-white fabric of wings and fuselage. Since applying these extra pigments to the aircraft added additional weight which reduced performance, and paint materials became difficult to obtain in Germany, a new camouflage printed fabric was created late in 1917. This fabric was printed with a repeating lozenge pattern of five colors—dark greens, reds, and indigo for upper surfaces and light violets, blues, and yellows for lower surfaces. Fokkers often used a four color version with similar repeating lozenge motif. The "lozenge" of color was an elongated hexagonal shape about 5" long. This colorful covering for wings and fuselages broke up the outline of the plane in an attempt to confuse an attacker as to its direction of flight, somewhat analogous to the dazzle-painting of ships. Larger aircraft and bombers were simply painted with large hexagons of color similar to the lozenge fabric, or mostly dark colors for night bombers.

The French pattern of camouflage was perhaps the most classic concept. Irregular patches and curved shapes of earth-tone colors (light and dark browns, greens, and yellow ochre) were used to cover all side and upper surfaces of the plane while the lower surfaces were painted a solid sky blue. French night bombers got a dashing frock of basic black.

Unique coloration schemes appeared on many aircraft from particular manufacturers. The Nieuport company in France and Pfalz in Germany applied expensive aluminum based dopes to their planes, leaving them with a silvery sparkle. The American Liberty DH-4 was painted a greenish khaki-brown on its upper surfaces and creamy-white on sides and lower surfaces. The Austro-Hungarian Aviatik company hand brushed their planes with small dots of color, like an impressionist painting, that blurred into an earth-tone image.

Unit Insignia

Distinctive organizational insignia have always been a proud part of the military tradition. But when combat in the clouds grew so complex that many squadrons were embroiled together, clear unit identification became more necessity than vanity.

The French adopted unit symbols almost immediately. Most of these were illustrations of a particularly meaningful object. The elite fighter squadrons in the Groupe Brocard chose gracefully flying storks, and were known as "Les Cicognes." The Lafayette Escadrille of American volunteers chose an American Indian head. Many of the symbols were humorous, like the flying elephant of a Voisin bombing escadrille that struggled along with their obsolescent lumbering crates.

American aero squadrons similarly focused on imaginative symbols. The 94th "Hat-in-the-Ring" was among the first U.S. squadrons to toss itself into the fighting arena. The night reconnaissance planes of the 9th Aero Squadron had an "IX" drawn like searchlights looming over the trenches. The 13th sported the skeleton of death wielding his scythe. The 96th day bombers had the devil throwing down a bomb. The plucky 95th painted an army mule kicking up its heels, but some nicknamed them the kicking ass squadron.

The RFC attempted to standardize their unit markings with simple geometric shapes painted on the fuselage in white. They used white triangles, straight or slanted stripes, dumbbells, boomerangs on the S.E.5a's of No. 4 Australian Squadron, a hexagon for No. 85, etc. These symbols were periodically traded between units to keep the enemy guessing. The RNAS was a little more risqué in their markings, with the black cowlings of Naval 10's Black Flight triplanes and later the different color stripes for each flight of their Camels, or the sunburst designs of Naval 3.

The most colorful unit motifs were the German fighter groups, called "circuses" by the envious Allied pilots. The first circus, von Richthofen's JG 1, used black and white checkerboards on the planes of *Jasta 3*, snake patterns on those of *Jasta 4*, yellow fuselages for *Jasta 10*, and red for *Jasta 11*. Some Jagdgeschwader used a similar tail color for all members of the group but unique nose colors for each Jasta. *JG II* had royal blue fuselages. In Austria, the fighters of *Flik 51J* sported a six-pointed star emblem.

Personal Aircraft Markings

Plane to plane recognition and communication in the air was purely visual in the first air war. Personal markings were necessary to identify members within the flight or squadron. Letters were most often used on British planes, while French and American planes used numbers to designate each plane. Germans used personal emblems or colors. Flight leaders attached colored streamers to their interplane struts. Many Allied flight leaders painted additional diagonal stripes on their upper wings to indicate their position of leadership. Rickenbacker's SPAD had red-white-blue slants on the wing, Brown's Camel had a broad red chevron, and Ernst Udet went all out with a red and white candy striped upper wing on his Fokker D.VII. Besides the officially condoned markings, the pilots could not be held back in embellishing their own trusty steeds.

Personal emblems of bravado, provocation, or good luck adorned the planes. Charles Nungesser, repeatedly wounded but surviving the war, carried all the symbols of death on his Nieuport 17: the skull and cross bones, a coffin and candlesticks, all on a black heart. George von Hantelmann also had the skull and crossbones emblem on his Fok-

ker D.VII. Canadian ace William Barker had an arrow going through a red heart on his Camel, as did the Austrian ace Friedrich Navratil. The German ace Werner Voss painted hearts and a swastika on his planes. American flyer Eugene Bullard painted a bleeding heart with a dagger through it on his SPAD.

Naming aircraft was common. The Canadian pilots in Naval 10's "Black Flight" named their black nosed Sopwith triplanes Black Prince, Black Roger, Black Maria, Black Sheep, and Black Death. Georges Guynemer named his old buddy "Vieux Charles."

As pilots became intimately accustomed to their own mounts personal aircraft markings became an important ritual. Rudolph Stark, commander of Bavarian *Jasta 35*, wrote of how his squadron took possession of its first six Fokker D.VII's: "We land and put our treasures safely away in the hangars. The painter marks them with the Staffel badge, the arrowhead on the wings, then paints the fuselages with the colored bands that identify the individual pilots. He takes particular care with my machine embellishing my lilac stripe with narrow black edges. Only then do the machines really belong to us."

Flying Princesses: Aviatrices of the First World War

Once upon a time little girls really did grow up to fly combat missions. They lived in a time of miraculous change, technological breakthroughs and modern social developments. Many had the gutsy adventurous spirit usually attributed to boys and learned to fly as well as any man. In the event of war, they dreamed that their accomplishments would be a welcome asset to their beleaguered countries, and that they would write a tale of heroic adventure in the air. But this fairy tale is replete with sex, drugs, unplanned pregnancy, violence, and court-martials ... and not a white knight or happy ending in sight! It's Russia 1914.

Eugenie Shakhovskaya, a 25 year old Russian princess, was the first female fighter pilot in history. She received a pilot's certificate in 1911 and promptly sought active service in the Italian Air Service during the 1912 Tripolitanian War. Her request was promptly denied. With the onset of the First World War Princess Eugenie returned home to Russia and went straight to the top. Writing directly to the czar for permission to serve the Imperial Russian Air Service as a military pilot for such reconnaissance duties as the weather (and the Germans) permitted. Impressed, the czar approved her application and the princess was enrolled as an Ensign of Engineers. In November 1914 she was sent to the First Field Air Squadron on the Russian Northwestern Front. And it was here that her troubles began—on the ground.

Ironically, Princess Eugenie's flying career ended with her assignment to the Front. Here she was repeatedly sexually assaulted, passed from officer to officer. When she attempted to escape to enemy lines she was arrested for treason and faced death by firing squad. Czar Nicholas II commuted her sentence to life imprisonment in a convent because she was pregnant. During the Russian Revolution Princess Eugenie took up the Communist cause and put her Mauser pistol to good use for the Cheka. Drug addicted, the Princess was killed by her colleagues after she shot and killed her assistant for no good reason.

Lyubov Golanchikova, a popular stage actress, also known as Milly More, received her certificate to fly in 1911 at the Gatchina Military Flying School. Flying with Anthony Fokker in Germany in 1913, she established the record for high altitude flight for women. Golanchikova was a test pilot early in the First World War, flying a Voisin, before returning to the stage for the rest of the war. During the Russian Civil War Golanchikova flew sorties and trained Red pilots for the Training Squadron of the Red Air Fleet. After the Civil War she emigrated to New York City and patrolled the streets as a taxi driver until her death in 1961, at the age of 72.

Helen Samsonova was another accomplished aviatrix. She received her pilot's certificate in 1913 at the Imperial Moscow Aviation Association flying school. During the First World War she served as a nurse, a chauffeur, and eventually managed to get transferred to aviation. Here she flew in the 5th Army Corps Air Squadron as a reconnaissance pilot. She was shortly involved in an incident in which she fired a pistol at a fellow male officer (reason not recorded) and was quickly transferred out by her superior officer due to "emotional temperament." During the Russian Civil War Samsonova again served as an observer on reconnaissance and artillery missions. She died in 1958, at the age of 68.

Nadesha Degtereva managed to serve her country and fulfill her dream of becoming a combat pilot by making sure no one knew that she wasn't one of the boys. Apparently, that was the best way to avoid trouble. A teenager from Kiev, she disguised herself as a boy and used a male friend's medical certificate to enroll for military flight training. At the aviation park she was pronounced fit and qualified to fly in combat. Degtereva was posted to a reconnaissance unit on the Galician front, piloting two-seaters. On one of her missions deep behind enemy lines in the spring of 1915, she and her observer became embroiled in a fierce dogfight. Bullets from the Austrian fighters pierced her arm and leg and riddled her aircraft. Though wounded, she fought her way back to her own aerodrome and safely landed the crippled plane. Her real name and gender were discovered when she reached the hospital. Degtereva found instant fame as the Russian press regaled the masses with the story of the young girl who was wounded in action in an aerial dogfight. The army was less happy about the story, and shipped her off to the Caucasus Front.

Hélène Dutrieu, nicknamed the "Girl Hawk of Aviation," was the first female pilot in Belgium, and served briefly as a reconnaissance pilot during the First World War. Beginning her flying career in April 1910, she astounded all of Europe with daring stunts and record breaking flights. As well known for flying braless (corsets were too restrictive) as for her achievements, she not only held women's world records for altitude, distance, and endurance, but she won the 1911 Italian King's Cup racing against fourteen men.

But at least the Russians and Belgians afforded a few women some minimal opportunities. The Italians, Germans, English, French, and Americans banned women from all war-related aviation work. Nellie Beese, Germany's first female flyer was almost killed when colleagues at her civilian flying field tampered with her plane's steering mechanism. She survived such harassment and later opened a flying school in Berlin and taught many male flyers. Hilda Hewitt, the first Englishwoman to fly, similarly instructed fighter pilots during the First World War. In France, Marie Marvingt, a flyer and nurse, tried to begin a special aviation branch for emergency medical service during the First World War. Unfortunately, her ideas met with universal skepticism. The French military was decidedly uninterested.

The American Stinson sisters (Marjorie and Katherine) were rejected by the army air service even though they had been training Canadian pilots for years by the time America entered the war. The Stinson Flying School of San Antonio,

Texas (nicknamed the Texas Escadrille) was a family operation and the two sisters taught over 100 Canadian airmen to fly from 1915 to the autumn of 1917. Many went on to serve during the war in the Royal Flying Corps and Royal Naval Air Service. It wasn't long before the United States banned civilian flight training, forcing the liquidation of the school. Denied the opportunity to serve their country in the armed forces, the sisters, nicknamed the "Flying Schoolmarms," found other ways. Katherine drove ambulances in England and France and Marjorie did drafting for the Navy in Washington, D.C.

Many women, unable to best use their talents and skills for the benefit of their country during wartime, were diverted to quite ancillary and sometimes frivolous pursuits. In America, Bernetta Miller flew the first monoplane demonstration flight for U.S. government officials in 1912. Yet, in 1917, forbidden to fly at the front, she went instead as a canteen worker. She washed dishes and slung hash. Bernetta Miller—pilot and donut dolly! Helen Hodge learned to fly in 1916 and subsequently taught U.S. aviation cadets and did some exhibition flying as well. Alys McKey Bryant, first female to fly in Canada, after being rejected for combat flying in World War I worked for Goodyear building military dirigibles. Ruth

Law, the first woman to loop-the-loop and holder of the women's altitude record in 1916 was infuriated by her inability to fly in the First World War. In 1917 the American Secretary of War flatly rejected Law's appeal. "We don't want women in the Army." Law wrote a protest titled *Let Women Fly.* "It would seem that a woman's success in any particular line would prove her fitness for that work, without regard to theories to the contrary." Law spent the war years raising money for the Red Cross through exhibition flights.

It comes as no surprise that female flyers were subjected to intense sexual harassment and abuse, intimidation and discrimination in the few instances in which they did serve. Mostly they were kept in their place, on the ground. Whether women can fly as well as men, and certainly their fitness for combat missions, is still controversial. The statements of the first female pilot ever, Frenchwoman Raymonde de Laroche in 1910, are fighting words even today: "Flying does not rely so much on (physical) strength as on physical and mental coordination." Yet these few brave women blazed a trail in the sky for their sisters to follow. Amelia Earhart, Beryl Markham, and Sally Ride owe a debt to their greatly ridiculed, and courageous predecessors.

CHAPTER III

1915
Taking It to the Skies

In the machines I flew previously a speedy retreat was the best means of defence against enemy airmen. Things are going to be different now.
—Max Immelmann, German ace

As the new year dawned France led the air campaign, both conceptually and organizationally, with differentiation and clearly defined uses for their air arsenal. French leaders recognized the need to maintain continued aerial reconnaissance, to deny the enemy their eyes in the sky, and to use bombing as an offensive weapon. Their lead was challenged as the campaign on the technological front shifted, and the see-sawing balance of power that typified the First World War in the air began. New fronts also opened up for aerial operations in 1915. Warplanes made their appearance in the skies above Italy, Turkey, and eastern battlefields. New strategic bombing efforts began in 1915, and the much feared Zeppelin assaults finally got underway.

But the first course of business was to serve the immediate needs of the ground forces with reconnaissance and artillery spotting. Both sides set to this task with equal vigor. The trench lines needed to be plotted in detail and objectives clearly investigated if the "Poor Bloody Infantry" would have any hope of advancing past the desolate strip of ground now known as "No Man's Land." Visual observation and drawing of maps gave way to aerial photography. New cameras were developed

Maurice Farman M.F.11 "Shorthorn" replaced the "Longhorn"in the French reconnaissance role.

and carried aloft as standard equipment. A photograph provided a clearer map of the enemy's positions than could be
drawn. Cameras magnified the image and brought the viewer
closer to a target of interest, and the photograph could be
viewed in comfort on the ground, as opposed to what an
observer in the air had to contend with, struggling with binoculars against the wind and vibration of the plane. The aerial
cameras used individual photographic plates that the observer
changed between each picture. There were very few automatic
serial cameras in use like the one developed by the Italian
visionary Giulio Douhet. Such cameras took a sequence of
pictures at timed intervals by automatically changing the plates.

France's new Maurice Farman M.F.11 "shorthorns" replaced
the older M.F.7 "longhorns" in the reconnaissance escadrilles.
The shorthorns did away with the large stabilizer mounted in
front of the pusher nacelle that obstructed the observer's view.
They instead mounted a camera of 1.2 meters focal length on a
bracket at the nose of the nacelle to take photos either obliquely
or directly downward. The German "B" class two-seater aircraft
though, like the British B.E.2, were less suitable to mounting the
cameras because the observer sat in front of the pilot, behind the
engine, and above the lower wing of the biplane. Such a seating
arrangement was not only restrictive for using photographic

equipment but was especially impractical for carrying weapons to defend themselves.

In 1915 aircraft carrying radio transmitters performed artillery cooperation work. Before radios were in general use, the planes fired flares, dropped written notes, or landed at the artillery battery to communicate. Radios only transmitted in Morse code from the plane to the artillery battery receiver. To receive communication from the ground, the plane flew back to its own lines periodically to observe messages laid out in ground panels or smoke bombs. Two-way radios did not appear until the end of the war and were never commonly used. The French artillery-attached escadrilles used the tractor engined Caudron G III because it could carry the weight of the transmitter and allow the antenna to drag freely behind the cockpit nacelle. The more powerful twin-engine Caudron G IV came on line during 1915 as the G III's replacement. One escadrille of Caudrons was attached to each corps along the front for its artillery cooperation needs. Even though the first radio carried into the air over the western front was a German Telefunken in December 1914, the Germans did not form specially designated artillery cooperation squadrons until late in 1915 when fourteen "Flieger Abteilungen (A)" were created.

Fixed position kite balloons provided anther type of observation from the sky. These kite balloons were hydrogen filled gas bags tethered to a ground winch by a 3,000 foot long steel cable. The Germans led the way with Major August von Parseval's very stable "Drachenballon" design whose shape prompted the Allies to dub them "sausages." The Allies at first tried to use their old spherical balloons for observation purposes, but they were too unwieldy in strong winds. The Allies then copied the Drachenballon design and later improved on it with the successful Caquot balloon. French Captain Albert Caquot placed three inflated stabilizing tail fins on his balloons and designed faster more powerful winches. One or two observers suspended in the small wicker basket hanging below the balloon could communicate directly to the ground by telephone. Artillery could be directed and observations reported continuously from dawn to dusk while the balloon was aloft. With high powered binoculars, the balloon observers could see nearly fifteen miles, so stable was the balloon basket compared to a plane's vibrating cockpit. One disadvantage of the balloon observation was that they could not search for interesting targets deep behind enemy lines or provide deep counter battery sighting like aeroplanes could. The balloons were stationed several miles behind the front line to avoid being used for target practice by the enemy artillery.

HEADS-UP

With trench lines blocking penetration into enemy territory, aerial bombing was the only way to extend the war behind enemy lines. Both sides experimented with tactical and strategic bombing. The Allies pursued an ultimately more effective course in strategic bombing. The French specifically grouped all their Voisin LA5 equipped squadrons together as strategic bombardment groups. The first Group de Bombardement, GB1, was made up of the Voisin bombing Escadrilles VB101 (previously named V14), VB102, VB103, and VB104. The group was joined at mid-year by groups GB2, GB3, and GB4 creating a sixteen squadron force nearly one hundred planes strong. The modified Voisin planes boasted rudimentary bomb sights and bomb racks to carry larger bombs. On May 27 sixteen bombers of GB1 took off from their base at Malzéville near Nancy, flew three hours to Ludwigshafen and bombed the Badische Aniline plant that was a major supplier of explosives and the recently unleashed poison gas weapons. Formations of up to 62 aircraft bombed other industrial towns including Karlsruhe, Dillingen, Trier and Saarbrücken. The French accepted that mass attacks were required to achieve reasonable success on an industrial target. By July, Voisins with the larger 140 hp engines capable of carrying 130 pounds of bombs at speeds of 90 mph joined the escadrilles.

French and British reconnaissance squadrons carried out more tactical bombing. Captain Maurice Happe of Escadrille MF25 bombed targets behind the enemy trenches. His Farman shorthorns at first had two nails hammered into the nacelle to help aim as the observer threw the artillery shells with fins over the side. Earlier in January, Captain Happe scored the first aerial victory over an observation balloon by dropping a small bomb right onto the hydrogen gas bag. Happe, with his black beard and piercing gaze, thus gained a reputation as the "pirate of the air." The Germans even put a price on his head after he took his escadrille on strategic attacks augmenting GB1. After a particularly costly attack on the gunpowder factories at Rottweil, Happe threw down a note challenging the enemy to come after his own plane to spare his men. He painted the underside of his wings red so that the Germans could find him. Happe also developed the "V" formation to provide mutual defensive support for his escadrille.

The RFC and RNAS pursued bombing as well. The first two aerial Victoria Crosses (V.C.), Britain's highest military honor, were awarded for bombing actions. The RFC attacked the railway system behind the enemy front, disrupting supply and reinforcement efforts. On April 26, Lt. W. B. Rhodes-Moorhouse of No. 2 Squadron flew his B.E.2c biplane over the Courtrai rail yards in support of the Neuve Chapelle offensive. He buzzed in at 300 feet through sprays of machine gun and rifle fire to drop one 100 pound bomb. He hit the target, but at great cost. Lt. Rhodes-Moorhouse returned to his squadron so severely wounded that he did not live to see his medal.

The RNAS had dual obligations: protect England from the Zeppelin threat and the sea lanes from the U-boat menace. Aircraft based at Dunkirk bombed the enemy submarine pens at Ostend and the Zeppelin sheds in Belgium. Bombing at that time was also the only way to knock a Zeppelin out of the air. On the night of June 6, No. 1 Wing (the RNAS called their squadrons wings) attempted to intercept three Zeppelins returning to Belgium after a raid on the English coast. Four RNAS planes took off into the darkness. Two of them found the German Army Zeppelin shed at Evere and bombed it, destroying the *LZ 38* within. Another flown by Flight Sub-lieutenant R.A.J. Warneford ran across the *LZ 37* in flight. Warneford stalked the airship until he could get above it with his little Morane-Saulnier Type L monoplane. From directly above, he dropped all six of his 20 lb Hale bombs on the Zeppelin, igniting the hydrogen gas in a ball of fire that singed Warneford's plane. All the German airmen perished, but for one who fell through the roof of a

French Ace Roland Garros used the Morane-Saulnier Type L parasol monoplane as test bed for his machine gun exploits; above, an escadrille of Morane Type L two-seaters for reconnaissance and pursuit.

convent, landing in a nun's bed. Miraculously he survived with minor injuries. Warneford returned home a hero. As the first airman to shoot down a Zeppelin, Warneford received the Victoria Cross. Like Rhodes-Moorhouse, he didn't live long enough to enjoy it, dying in a freak air crash in Paris days after receiving the award.

German bombing aircraft were a disappointment. The planes of the reconnaissance abteilungen infrequently performed tactical bombing. The hazards of meeting armed Allied planes prevented them from attacking targets deep behind the Allied lines. The *Ostend Carrier Pigeons*, Germany's strategic bombing group, contained the best flyers in the Air Service, but its aircraft were no different from the standard type B two-seaters. Only one plane reached the white cliffs of Dover in the first year, and the rest did not noticeably disrupt British troop or supply movements at Dunkirk. The new leader of the German Air Service, Colonel Hermann von der Lieth-Thomsen, chose a defensive aerial posture in the West, and he shipped the *Ostend*

Carrier Pigeons off to the eastern front where a general offensive was underway.

The Zeppelin was Germany's choice for strategic bombing in 1915, and the English homeland was its target. Both the German Army and Navy turned to their airship divisions as the only way to strike at England. Corvette Captain Peter Strasser, commander of the naval airship division, emphatically believed that he could subdue England by an effective strategic air offensive. His campaign began January 19 when naval Zeppelins *L 3* and *L 4* bombed Yarmouth and Norfolk on the English coast. Four British subjects were killed and sixteen injured. Newspapers on both sides sensationalized the event. Germans heard about the heroic voyage across the North Sea; the rest of the world heard about the "common murderers" wielding their "blind barbarian vengeance."

The German Army airships wanted to be the first to bomb London itself. After replacing their losses of the previous year, the army made several attempts to strike toward the capital. High winds and bad weather kept them on the continent until the spring, but they did good work bombing Calais and Paris in the meantime. The army achieved this using the Goerz sub-cloud car. The Goerz car was a streamlined basket for an observer and a telephone, suspended on a cable 1,000 meters below the Zeppelin. By dropping the Goerz car down through the clouds, the observer could guide the airship to its target while the airship remained hidden by clouds.

A new class of larger Zeppelins containing a one million cubic foot hydrogen gas capacity came on line in the spring. Captain Erich Linnarz led his new Army airships *LZ 38* and *LZ 39* across the channel and successfully bombed England. On one mission three English planes severely damaged these airships, spurring the infuriated Linnarz to toss down a note saying, "You English! We have come, and we will come again to kill or cure!" True to his word, Linnarz returned May 31 and bombed London for the first time with three thousand pounds of explosives, killing seven and causing £18,000 in damage to the city. The stunned British government prevented newspapers from publishing the extent of the damage. Linnarz boasted of his glorious success at beating his rival Strasser to London. The RNAS assigned to

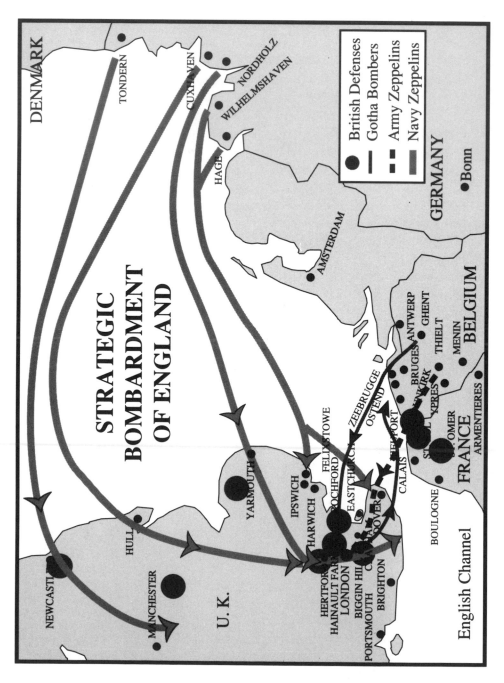

protect the British Isles spent the next weeks avenging Linnarz' attacks by destroying his new airships and his Belgian bases. The German Army pulled their airships out of Belgium and redeployed them to the Russian Front.

During the summer the Naval Airship division built up their fleet with the large million cubic foot Zeppelins. In early September the most experienced airship commander Captain Heinrich Mathy with Zeppelin *L 9* bombed the British capital. He caused the most serious material damage to London of the entire war. The Kaiser himself summoned Mathy for a debriefing, not only to congratulate Mathy but also to ask if any royal, religious, or historical buildings were inadvertently damaged. Kaiser Wilhelm placed restrictions on what targets in London could and could not be bombed. For example, Windsor Castle, his cousin's home, was off-limits. The month after Mathy's success, a full squadron of five Zeppelins raided English counties around London causing 71 deaths and 128 injuries. The bloodiest raid of the war was also the last of the 1915 raiding season; oppressive weather stopped further operations more effectively than anything the British defenses could send up.

INVENTION OF THE FIGHTER

While many aircraft were now carrying carbines or machine guns aboard to harass enemies encountered during their mission, successful victories were still few and far between. Two-seat pusher aircraft with forward mounted guns like the Vickers F.B.5 "Gunbus" were too slow to pursue an enemy. The two-seat tractor aircraft had the observer's field of fire limited by the propeller, wings, struts, and the backseat pilot's head.

Airmen experimented to gain control of the air. Lt. Louis Strange of No. 1 Squadron RFC was at it again, this time mounting a Lewis machine gun on the top wing of his single seat Martinsyde S.1 Scout so that it fired over the top of the spinning propeller. The only problem with that idea was changing the gun's ammo drum each time 47 rounds were fired. To change the drum, Strange had to stand up in his cockpit and reach up to the gun while holding the stick between his knees. Once, while trying to change drums in the middle of a fight, Strange's plane

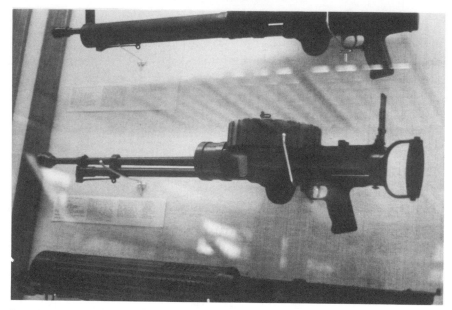

Lewis gun, as carried on the S.E.5a and other British aircraft. The infantry version had an outer cooling barrel and shoulder stock. **(Author photo)**

rolled upside down. Hanging from the Lewis drum with his feet dangling in the wind, Strange kicked desperately to get back into the cockpit and eventually righted the plane. Another innovator, Harry Hawker of No. 6 Squadron RFC, mounted a Lewis gun to his single seat Bristol Scout C to fire obliquely to the side, thus missing the propeller. A remarkable marksman, Hawker downed two German two-seaters with his Bristol on July 25, winning the Victoria Cross. He became the first British ace by shooting down his fifth victory in August.

Organizationally and technically, the French air force was the most advanced. They used their fast sporty Morane-Saulnier equipped squadrons for pursuit and destruction of enemy machines. Prewar aviation pioneer Roland Garros joined Escadrille MS 23 and worked with Raymond Saulnier at the Morane-Saulnier plant on machine gun synchronization. He returned to the front with a fast maneuverable Morane Type N "Bullet" monoplane equipped with one Hotchkiss machine gun mounted to fire directly forward. The machine gun was unsynchronized, but special armored deflector wedges affixed to the propeller blades prevented it from being broken by the stream of bullets. The system worked well in tests with only one in ten bullets actually hitting the armored propeller wedges. When the plane was wrecked in transfer to Escadrille MS 26 at Dunkirk, Garros switched the gun and armored propeller to a standard Morane Type L parasol monoplane and took off into air war history. On April 1 he flew towards Ostend, zoomed up behind a lone German two-seater and riddled it with bullets, killing both occupants. He then shot down two more on the 11th and captured the attention of all France. The gun and plane combination was a success! All his squadron mates wanted the same system. And, all of France wanted to see Garros the "ace." Parisians used the term "ace" for anything outstanding or on top of the deck, and Garros and his plane were certainly the rage. The term soon came to be applied to anyone who achieved five aerial victories, and through most of 1915 there were only four aces in France. On April 19, Garros was forced down behind enemy lines. The great Garros and his fighter plane were in enemy hands!

This gift was all that the German air service needed to get into the fight for control of the air. Anthony Fokker, the Dutchman who built monoplanes patterned after the Morane, examined Garros' device. He took the propeller from Garros' plane and a Parabellum machine gun, and in just twenty-four hours, he fashioned a mechanical synchronization device that prevented the machine gun from firing whenever the spinning blade passed before the barrel. Fokker demonstrated the device on his light Fokker E.I mid-wing monoplane, much like a Morane Type N. Although the German officers at the demonstration scattered when bullets ricocheted in all directions as Fokker drilled a target from the air, the officials wanted to see an actual victory at the front. Under duress, Fokker traveled to the front to prove the deadliness of his plane. Several days went by without enemy engagement. Then one day Fokker flew over the trench lines right up to a French Caudron. The Frenchmen were right in his sights but were apparently unconcerned. At that moment Fokker realized that he "had no stomach for this business, nor any wish to kill Frenchmen for Germans. Let them do their own

Mobile German anti-aircraft gun.

killing!" Fokker returned to the airfield and left for Schwerin. Knowing he held the key to win aerial supremacy in the skies, Fokker wrote, "I had not figured on the conservative military mind, which not only has to be shown, but then wishes to be shown all over again, after which it desires a little more time to think the matter over again once more." Eventually an order for the new Fokker E.I monoplane was placed, but it would be months before any production planes became active at the front.

During the summer of 1915 the Germans actually introduced *two* remarkable weapons that turned the air war in their favor. The first to reach the front was not the Fokker, but a new class of two-seat reconnaissance biplane named the "C" type. On the C the observer sat in the rear cockpit behind the pilot, opposite the earlier B type. A Parabellum machine gun was mounted on a swivel on the observer's cockpit. This arrangement provided an extensive field of fire to both sides, to the rear and above. The planes could protect themselves as they fled toward their own lines, unlike the Allied pushers, or maneuver and attack on occasion. An aggressive young flyer named Oswald Boelcke

Swooping down on the blind spot, a Fokker E.III closes for the kill.
(NASM)

took his new LVG C.I over the front lines on July 4 and attacked a Morane Parasol. While the observer in the Morane shot at Boelcke with a carbine, Boelcke's observer opened up with a machine gun and sent the Morane to the ground. It was the first victory for the new type, and the beginning of the change in aerial dominance.

The new Fokker E.I Eindekkers finally started arriving by mid-summer. The first few had a less than perfect synchronizer gear and shot their own propellers off, killing the pilots and officially grounding the type for several weeks. When this first flaw was corrected the pilots at the front eagerly greeted their anxiously awaited Fokker Eindekkers. Oswald Boelcke said of the type, "I have attained my ideal with this single-seater; now I can be pilot, observer and fighter all in one." He and Max Immelmann of *Feldfliegerabteilung 62* were the first flyers to receive a Fokker. On the first day of August, Immelmann scored his first victory over a British B.E.2c above the town of Douai. Boelcke scored the next victory, and soon both were racking up kills. By the end of October both had accumulated eight victories and received the Pour le Mérite award, also known as the coveted Blue Max, for valor. A number of other Fokker pilots

German Kagohl air units were geared for strategic mobility, which included ground transportation to new battle zones.

started scoring victories. So precious were the small number of Fokkers that none were allowed to cross the lines and risk falling into enemy hands. The high command had no intention of returning the gift that Roland Garros had brought them just months before. The Eindekkers protected planes in their own squadron and hunted for the enemy within their own territory. The small number of Fokkers, with just a couple parceled out to each observation squadron, were a devastating force.

The "Fokker Scourge" had begun. Germans gained four victories to every loss in aerial combats. The Allies were aghast at the vulnerability of their planes in the face of the Fokkers. The Allies lost their aerial dominance. The combination of the Fokker E.I monoplanes and the type C two-seater biplanes completed the formula for achieving German aerial supremacy. The offensive weapon, the multipurpose type C two-seater, conducted its missions with impunity because of the new sting in its tail. The defensive weapon, the single-seat Fokker, viciously attacked any enemy planes caught encroaching on German lines. The German air service received an organizational boost as well. Colonel Hermann von der Lieth-Thomsen was made Feldflugchef with Major Wilhelm Siegert, the founder of the Ostend bombing group, his second in command. Lieth-Thomsen acquired greater responsibility for all aviation at the front and worked closely with industry to procure better planes.

The Allied armies responded in panic to the grave situation at the front. Strategic bombing ground to a halt due to the growing losses and limited results. On one mission, Fokker Eindekkers and Aviatik C.I planes shot down six French bombers. Bombing was reduced and restricted to the immediate tactical front of the armies. New squadrons of machine gun equipped pursuit aircraft were created to counter the deadly Fokker Scourge. The British sent Number 11 Squadron equipped solely with the Vickers F.B.5 Gunbus to the front as the first true fighter squadron. The Vickers two-seat pusher design gave the gunner a free field of fire forward. The French formed Escadrille N 65 with the fast new Nieuport sesquiplanes: the Nieuport X and Nieuport XII two-seaters with a machine gun for the observer, and the tiny single seat Nieuport XI Bébé (baby) with its Lewis gun mounted above the top wing. The Nieuport Bébé escorted the bombers on short range sorties and patrolled for enemy aircraft.

CONCLUSION

Allied headquarters also went through a shakeup. The head of the British RFC was recalled to England in August to oversee development of aviation, leaving the newly promoted Brigadier-General Hugh "Boom" Trenchard in charge of all the RFC at the front. Trenchard was an aggressive and resourceful leader who would drive the RFC forward in the coming years. In France a senator named René Besnard took over the organization of aviation supply and industrial procurement. Instead of supplying Commandant Barès with the new bombers and specialized pursuit aircraft he needed at the front, Besnard promoted development of a single multi-purpose "omnibus" aircraft type, the three-seat Caudron R IV, to perform every mission. Besnard even attempted to undo Barès' concept of squadrons with specialized roles and equipment. He proposed eliminating pursuit escadrilles, reducing bombing and corps artillery escadrilles, and replacing all of these with omnibus-

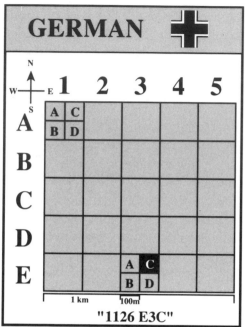

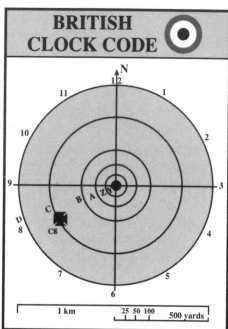

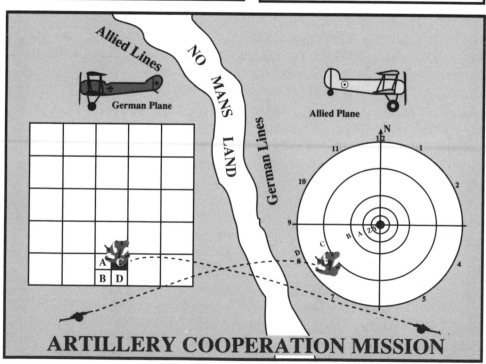

equipped all-purpose combat squadrons. This reversal of direction crippled French aviation.

In 1915 the belligerent air forces hit the ground running to correct the inadequacies of 1914. They soon learned another dimension of the modern war in the air—that technological breakthroughs radically and immediately upset the balance of air power. France began the year with a clear aerial superiority in leadership, purpose, strategy and material. Their bombing sorties went unhindered while their armed two-seaters inhibited the enemy from pursuing their missions. They invented the fighter concept, but then lost this edge to Germany. The German Air Service rose at mid-year with a newly appointed leader, with new models of Army cooperation aircraft, and with a refined and classic fighter weapon. Germany seized the means to defend its airspace, forced the Allied bombers into ineffective nighttime actions, and took control of the air above the trenches.

Artillery Spotting and the "Clock Code"

Artillery was the great killer of the First World War, and it was aimed by aircraft and balloons. Balloons handled most routine barrage adjustment and tracked changes occurring in the trenches. Observation aircraft took on targets deeper behind the lines and specialized in counter-battery fire, one of the primary roles of two-seater aircraft during the war. Observers in these planes were often from the artillery and were trained in aerial observation, Morse code, and Panneau signaling.

Artillery fire adjustment missions were generally solitary with one aircraft assigned for a day to a given artillery battery in that sector. Close escort was not generally performed for these missions because shuttling a whole flight back and forth between the front and the artillery post would tie up too many planes. General patrol and upper altitude escort planes kept watch over the "Art. Ops." or "Quirks" as they were sometimes called. An artillery observation plane would take off and climb to ten thousand feet to cross the lines and begin observation of its target. Aircraft were usually called to spot counter-battery fire on enemy artillery positions, to spot the bombardment of ammo dumps and new targets behind the lines, and to range the long range guns onto railroad spurs and troop concentrations. The plane flew into the wind in large oval patterns above the target.

The observer unwound his spool of antennae wire several yards, depending on the assigned radio frequency for the day, and contacted the artillery base by one-way wireless radio telegraphy using Morse code. When the shooting began, the observer gauged the results visually and reported the fall of each shell in relation to the target. After the target was successfully destroyed, the plane flew back to the artillery position. The ground crews communicated to the plane by Panneau signals, large white strips of cloth on the ground in certain patterns. Typical messages from the ground included: spot for the next target, adjust radio frequency, continue with another battery, or finish for the day and return to base.

After the battle of Neuve Chapelle in 1915, the British introduced to their allies a simple flexible targeting system called the "Clock Code." A circular celluloid disk, scaled to about one kilometer in diameter, was placed on a map with the designated target at the center. Concentric rings (labeled Y, Z, A, B, C, D, etc.) emanated from the target on a clock face whose twelve o'clock position was aligned with true north. Using this code, short concise messages could be radioed in Morse code from the plane to the artillery battery. For example: a message "C 8" meant that the last fall of shot was 200 yards away (zone C) and a bit southwest (eight o'clock) of the bullseye.

The Germans used a method in which their targets were plotted in squares of successively finer detail. Every square kilometer of the entire Western Front was mapped and given a sequential block number. Each numbered square kilometer block was divided into smaller squares of 100 meters, and each 100 meter block was divided into four subunits. A target could be designated as "km #1126, E 3 c" for map square 1126, row E, column 3, subunit c. These squares were often plotted from photographic maps made by special photography flights attached to the artillery squadron. Precise aiming based solely on map calculations was made for each artillery piece before the plane took off. Finer adjustment was then performed by radio.

Aircraft Class Designations
German Aircraft Category Designations

To keep track of the growing diversity of military aircraft types developed during the air war, the combatant nations designated specific categories of aircraft based on their structural design features or their intended purpose.

German aircraft were classified by the military according to their structural design. There were only two categories before the war, type A for monoplanes and type B for biplanes. This alphabetical classification trend expanded as the war continued and new types of aircraft evolved. Numbers after the category reflect the military designation for a given model. The Fokker D.VII for example is the seventh Doppledekker type single-seat fighter to be accepted by the military from the Fokker company.

GERMAN CATEGORY CODES

A Single-engined, unarmed monoplanes, prewar through 1915

B Single-engined, unarmed biplanes, prewar through 1916

C Single-engined, armed two-seaters, introduced mid-1915

CL Light single-engined, armed two-seaters, introduced 1917

D Doppledekkers: single-engined, armed single-seat biplanes, introduced mid-1916

E Eindekkers: single-engined armed single-seat monoplanes, introduced mid-1915

F Triplane fighters; replaced by the "Dr" designation after modification of the Fokker triplane

Dr Dreidekkers: single-engined, armed single-seat triplanes, introduced late 1917

G Grossflugzeug: twin-engined, armed multi-seat biplanes, introduced early 1916

J Infantry Airplane: armored and armed two-seat biplane, introduced 1917

N Night Bomber: types similar to G and R classes

R Riesenflugzeug: giant multi-engined, multi-seat long-range bombers, introduced 1917

S Ground Strafing: types similar to J class

W Wasserflugzeug: seaplanes and flying boats

Not all of the German aircraft strictly followed these designations. Many planes were designated according to the type of stable-mates they replaced in their units. The Fokker E.V of 1918 went to Jastas at the front containing other D-types, and was renamed the Fokker D.VIII after its wing was strengthened to avoid any negative prejudice against monoplane E-types.

French Aircraft Category Designations

The French grouped their aircraft according to the function they performed. French aircraft designations recorded the manufacturer's name, the model number accepted, the intended use of the type, and the number of crew members carried. For example, the "Caudron G III A 2" was the third design by Gaston Caudron for army cooperation with a crew of two. The "Sopwith B 1" was a single-seat bomber version of the famous "Strutter" and the only Sopwith design accepted by France at that time. The "SPAD XII Ca 1" is a single-seat cannon-armed fighter and the twelfth design allocated from the SPAD company.

FRENCH CATEGORY CODES

A Corps d'Armée: army cooperation, artillery spotting, and photo reconnaissance

Ap Long range, high speed photo-reconnaissance scouts

B Bombardement: bombing aircraft

Bn Bombardement Nuit: night bombing aircraft

C Chasse: pursuit and fighter aircraft

Ca Canon: aircraft whose main armament is a 37mm gun

E Écolle: Training aircraft

H Hydroavion: Float planes and flying boats

S Santé: Medical transport

British Aircraft Category Designations

Unlike the French and Germans, the British military did not uniformly classify their aircraft by codes. Manufacturers' designations were often used, or the military serial number sequence assigned to the first examples frequently became the common designation. The most official codification came with the planes produced at the Royal Aircraft Factory, Britain's government run aircraft design facility.

ROYAL AIRCRAFT FACTORY CATEGORY CODES

B.E. British Experimental: originally "Blériot Biplane Experimental," pre-war biplane designs

F.E. Fighter Experimental: pusher design fighters

R.E. Reconnaissance Experimental: two-seat corps cooperation aircraft

S.E. Scout Experimental: single-seat tractor design fighter aircraft

Machine Gun Synchronization

Allowing a machine gun to fire forward through the spinning propeller was key to aerial combat. Before the war, Raymond Saulnier developed the idea of mounting a rigidly "fixed" machine gun to fire straight ahead through the propeller arc. Firing bullets were "synchronized" with the spinning propeller so the blades would not be shot off. Several machine gun synchronization systems were designed as the war in the air heated up. All similarly used a cam plate that was fixed or geared to the propeller shaft. This cam was linked by a push-rod to the gun's trigger mechanism to fire the gun only when the propeller blade was clear. Firing was "interrupted" by releasing the trigger whenever the blade passed in front of the gun barrel. Synchronizing methods greatly reduced a machine gun's maximum rate of fire—the first Fokker design allowed only 100 rounds per minute. The Fokker Gestänge Steuerung push-rod system first appeared on the Fokker E.I. In 1916 this was modified to the Zentralsteuerung series for twin gun mountings and faster rates. The Allies first tried to synchronize a Lewis, but later focused only on the Vickers. The Vickers-Challenger design reached the front in March 1916 on Bristol Scouts and the Sopwith 1½ Strutter. The French Alkan-Hamy gear was used on Nieuport fighters starting mid–1916, and the Birkigt Gear first appeared with the SPAD VII. The Scarff-Dybovsky Gear, a joint Russian and RNAS design, was used on Sopwith Pups, and the Sopwith Kauper Gear came on board with the twin gun Camel. The ultimate design allowing the fastest rate of fire was the Constantinesco-Colley CC Gear which appeared in 1917. It replaced the push-rods with a hydraulic tube that could transmit pulsations from the cam at the speed of sound.

Peter Strasser

Peter Strasser (1876-1918) was an outstanding German naval leader during the First World War. Strasser was a career military officer, a gunnery specialist, embued with the spirit, energy, discipline, and dedication necessary to succeed. Dedicating his life to the Naval Airship Division, he never married. He was appointed Chief of the Naval Airship Division in 1911. Strasser built the Airship Division from 2 airships to 72 in 1918. Throughout the war he kept close contact with the Zeppelin company, having his ideas and specifications designed into each new airship class. By war's end naval airships had flown over 300 sorties against the enemy and participated in over 1000 aerial reconnaissance missions. Strasser became obsessed with the belief that the Zeppelin was the ultimate weapon to win the First World War. Strasser wrote, "England can be overcome by means of airships...through increasingly extensive destruction of cities, factory complexes, dockyards, harbor works with war and merchant ships lying therein, railroads, etc. The airships offer a certain means of victoriously ending the war." He broached no argument in his fanatic devotion to the Zeppelin. In a letter to his mother Strasser complained, "We who strike the enemy where his heart beats have been slandered as 'baby killers' and 'murderers of women.' What we do is... but necessary. Very necessary. Nowadays there is no such animal as a noncombatant. Modern warfare is total warfare. My men are brave... their cause is holy.... If what we do is frightful, then may frightfulness be Germany's salvation." Strasser was a tough boss, and demanded much from his men. "Your sacred obligation, the demolishment of London. Be prepared to make the supreme sacrifice for the Fatherland, which is the crowning glory for any loyal son of Germany." But Frigate Captain Strasser's fanatical devotion to the dream of conquering England by air power clouded his vision to the effectiveness and risks of the airship war. He refused to stop airship raids despite their dubious utility because it would leave "the British laughing at us behind our backs." Strasser received the "Blue Max" or "Pour le Merite," Germany's highest award for outstanding military service, on August 20, 1917. Strasser continued to work toward perfecting the Zeppelin for military service, building a new high performance, faster, higher climbing class of airship. After the *L 59* proved that an airship could travel non-stop 4,200 miles from Bulgaria to the Sudan and back unnoticed, he planned to "attack the United States by Zeppelins!" Strasser went to Admiral Reinhold Scheer to propose that the harbors of New York City be bombed by his newest class of airships. This, Strasser claimed, would strike fear in the populace, demonstrate the might of Germany, and impede the flood of doughboys sailing to Europe. Scheer nixed this idea, seeing the extremes of fanaticism that consumed his leader of the airship division.

Strasser longed to see London burn, so on August 5, 1918, he went aboard the *L 70* in another five-Zeppelin raid on England. It was the last. Breaking one of his own rules about radio silence, Strasser's mistake drew a flight of British planes toward him. A D.H.4 manned by Major Egbert Cadbury and Canadian Captain Robert Leckie, each of whom already had one victory over a Zeppelin under their belts, took off from Great Yarmouth naval air station and caught the airship armada in the twilight just off the coast of England. With explosive bullets they blazed away at the *L 70* which was leading the pack until a glow developed in its bowels. Moments later, Strasser, the crew of the *L 70*, and the heart and soul of the Imperial Naval Airship Division plunged to their deaths, "a roaring furnace from end to end."

CHAPTER IV

1916
Air of Battle

There can be no standing on the defensive.... Survival in three-dimensional warfare depends on maintaining the offensive, whatever the odds or cost.

— General Hugh "Boom" Trenchard, Commander of the Royal Flying Corps

While enjoying the fruits of the Fokker Scourge, the chief of the German air service Col. Lieth-Thomsen struggled throughout January and February of 1916 to develop the Fliegertruppe (German Army Air Service) organizationally and materially. For the air service to be a critical element in the next big offensive required new strategies. Lieth-Thomsen knew that his aerial forces were numerically inferior to the Allies: so to achieve any local superiority he must concentrate Flieger Abteilungen for the vital offensive. The individual army corps commanded their own field reconnaissance and artillery squadrons and would not release their control over them to the Feldflugchef. Instead Lieth-Thomsen reorganized select formations like the old Ostend and Metz Carrier Pigeons into combat (Kampf) groups responsible only to the German General Headquarters (OHL). Each Kagohl (Kampfgeschwader of the OHL) combat group included five to seven Kastas (Kampf Staffels) which were equipped with six type C armed two-seaters. Many of the Fokker Eindekkers, previously parceled out in pairs to every Feldflieger Abteilung, were also drawn away from direct army corps control and grouped into special single-seater fighter detachments called Kampfeinsitzer Kommando (KeK). With these two types of aircraft organizations Lieth-Thomsen attained greater tactical control of the air arm and a new level of independence from the old ground army command.

The cataclysmic attack on Verdun erupted on February 21. The Germans hoped the Battle of Verdun would be the great offensive that bled the French white and drove the Allies to beg for an end to the war. Lieth-Thomsen amassed 168 planes to take part in the great battle. Ten Feldflieger Abteilungen (Fl. Abt.) were on hand, four of which had extensively photographed the enemy trenches over which the German troops now advanced. Six Artillerie Flieger Abteilungen, the Fl. Abt. (A), directed the guns against the French artillery to suppress them. Fourteen observation balloon units also provided constant ranging information to bring the artillery down on the French defenders of Verdun. Infantry contact patrols by the new Flieger Abteilung-Infanterie squadrons kept the divisional commanders informed of the successes and needs of their men on the ground. Four army Zeppelins were even brought to the Verdun battle to provide deep reconnaissance and bombing. The enlarged combat groups *Kagohl I* and *Kagohl II* bombed the French rear areas to impair resistance and prevent counterattack. Over two tons of bombs were dropped in the first days on railway centers behind Verdun, on bridges, on supply routes, and even on French aerodromes. From the ground, German artillery units even took the new French Caquot observation balloons into account. Special pairs of artillery batteries slipped up to the front. On the opening day of battle, one gun of each pair shot directly at the French balloon while the other gun barraged the French winch operators to prevent them from hauling down the balloon before the Germans destroyed it.

The Fliegertruppe achieved all this without any French aerial interference. Aviatik C.I and L.V.G. C.I biplanes of the Fl. Abt. mounted large scale continuous barrage patrols called Luftsperre over the German lines to literally blockade the French from crossing. This aerial blockade tied up a tremendous number of aircraft on monotonous patrolling when they could have been used more effectively in other more important duties. Additionally, two new large three-seat twin-engine A.E.G. G.III

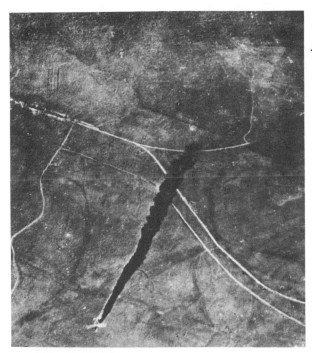

"One hostile aircraft flamed." A French Voisin falls victim to a German C-type.

Grossflugzeuge planes, attached to the Kagohl, flew as aerial gunnery platforms defending German airspace. Twenty-one Fokker Eindekkers, nearly half the Fokkers on the entire Western Front, also protected the Verdun sector. Organized into three Kampfeinsitzer Kommandos (KeK), these Fokker units, while still not proceeding beyond their own trench lines, formed a defensive net to catch any French aircraft that penetrated the Luftsperre.

Oswald Boelcke, one of the most aggressive Fokker Eindekker pilots, came to the Verdun sector and immediately continued his own Fokker Scourge. He took a small group of Fokkers to Sivry, just 11 km from the front, to establish a forward airfield closer to the trenches. He felt it mandatory to position fighters where they could best intercept enemy aircraft. He even set up a system for the forward artillery officer to telephone his small unit whenever a French aircraft crossed into his area. Boelcke brought his victory total to ten on March 12. The next day while flying his new 160 hp Fokker E.IV, he spotted a French pursuit plane attack a German reconnaissance plane over Fort Douaumont. Boelcke easily chased the Frenchman away towards his own lines. Then on his afternoon flight he saw a squadron of Voisin bombers flying over the embattled Mort Homme. Boelcke dove and machine-gunned a straggler of the group, and the Voisin banked away sharply with its control cables severed. Oddly the plane leveled off, and when Boelcke came in for the second attack he saw that the observer had climbed out on the wing to balance the plane in flight. Boelcke hesitated a moment, pondering the defenselessness of the Voisin, and then shot the pilot at close range sending the plane into No-Man's-Land. When the rest of the French escadrille turned to avenge their squadron mates, Boelcke sped back into German territory. He noted in his log that some of these aircraft were armed with 35mm cannon. His victories were written in the official communiqués. When Boelcke dined with Crown Prince Wilhelm, commander of the *5th German Army* at Verdun, he regaled him with tales of aerial high jinx.

Boelcke's plane was an E.IV, the latest of the Fokker monoplane line. It had two machine guns mounted to fire slightly upward at 15° above the line of flight, and a 160 hp engine. Boelcke found the plane faster but much less maneuverable than the earlier less powerful versions of the Eindekker. The engine was essentially two 80 hp rotary engines combined as a double bank of 14 cylinders. The great weight and torque of the spinning mass inhibited its climb and turning so much that it was dangerously inferior to the Nieuport Bébé. The guns caused problems with aiming on any attack angle except from below. Boelcke reported these deficiencies, recommended that a biplane fighter with guns mounted in line of flight be developed, and returned to flying his old 100 hp Fokker E.III monoplane with a single synchronized Spandau machine gun.

The French air force was completely overrun in the first days of the German aerial offensive at Verdun. The French escadrilles at Verdun were too weak to keep the Germans out of their territory, could not protect the French lines from bombing, and could not cross the barrage patrolled German lines to perform their own duties. Blinded by the suppression of their observation aircraft and balloons, the vitally important French artillery could not strike at the German artillery with counter-battery

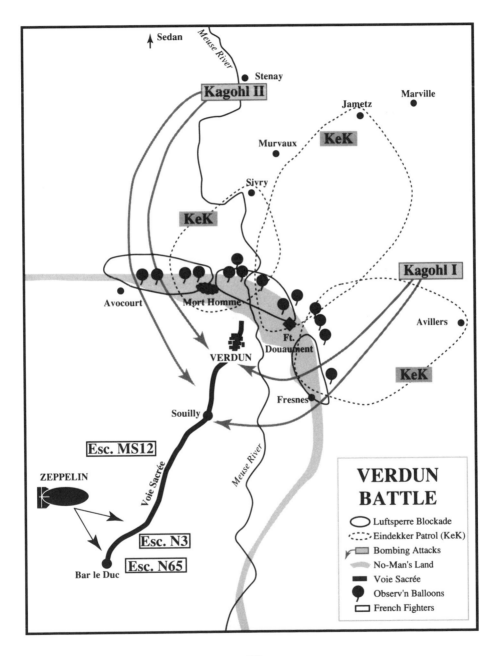

fire. Ground commanders could not receive information on the extent of enemy concentrations or approaching reinforcements.

Commander of the French air service Colonel Barès had to regain control of the air or Verdun would remain in peril. He concentrated French aerial forces into Verdun with the blessing of General Joffre, nearly doubling the number of planes in the sector to 261. Barès appointed Commandant Tricornot de Rose of Escadrille MS12 to lead this force and wrest aerial supremacy over Verdun. Commandant de Rose collected the Morane-Saulnier and Nieuport equipped pursuit escadrilles together with the best pilots and expanded the two fighter units at Verdun into fifteen elite fighter squadrons. He released the fighters from obligations to protect corps reconnaissance aircraft so that they could patrol and attack German planes. The corps reconnaissance aircraft themselves were sent into German territory in groups to drive down the German planes.

The Nieuport and Morane fighters patrolled the front in escadrille formations of up to six aircraft. The machine gun equipped Morane-Saulnier Model N "Bullets" used the Garros type steel wedge protectors on the propeller. The Nieuport XI "Bébé," with its unsynchronized machine gun mounted on the top wing to fire over the propeller blades, had superior performance over the Fokker Eindekkers. However, its gun was awkward to handle and difficult to reload. The first Nieuports carried a Hotchkiss with only a 25 round clip and later ones carried a Lewis with a 47 round drum. The German aircraft they encountered were seldom in groups larger than three, and the French tactical numerical advantage sent many German planes to the ground. Their larger numbers chased the Fokkers away from interfering with French reconnaissance planes. The French pursuit squadrons began to learn how to fly in groups, an unusual condition considering that nearly all of their previous victories were made by aces flying on lone patrols. Typical patrols included a group of four to five aircraft flying together with a more experienced pilot or ace covering from above and behind the others. The group patrols paid off.

The French employed new patrolling concepts to maintain their aerial control. De Rose assigned escadrilles to specific sectors to patrol continuously in order to be present in the air whenever a threat was encountered. Sections of each escadrille took turns patrolling throughout the day. Observation aircraft patrolled assigned sectors in shifts each day as well. By maintaining continuity of their observation missions, the observers grew intimately familiar with their own sector and could more easily note changes on the ground.

One of the squadrons formed during this period of expansion of the French fighter force was N124, also known as the Escadrille Americaine. This squadron of small Nieuport XI single seat pursuit aircraft was fully manned by American pilots and led by French officers. It was the brainchild of three Americans: Norman Prince, a skilled pilot from Massachusetts; William Thaw, a Pennsylvania native and member of the French Foreign Legion; and Dr. Edmund Gros of the American Ambulance Corps. After German protestations that neutral America had a fighter squadron at the front, N124's name was officially changed to the "Lafayette Escadrille."

By April, the Germans felt aerial supremacy slipping from their grasp. The Kampf Staffels of the Kagohl groups interrupted their bombing activities to provide much needed escort duty for the corps observation aircraft. This was a crucial turning point in the land campaign brought about by the aggressive French air arm. The key supply link supporting the French ground forces at Verdun was a single road called the Voie Sacrée. German artillery intensively bombarded this road near the front. Enemy aircraft bombed the Voie Sacrée farther from the front. Had the Germans spent more effort to continue intensive aerial bombardment of this slender route, they may have reduced the flow of French reinforcements and ammunition to the pinched Verdun pocket so that German ground troops could triumph. The actions of the French pursuit aircraft significantly blocked these German bombers from reaching the Voie Sacrée, ensuring the lifeline of Verdun.

Once the French had the German bombers and observation aircraft on the run, they next concentrated on the fixed observation balloons. These Drachen balloons were the Germans' most effective aerial observation platform for ranging the all-important artillery during the battles of Verdun. French plans to blind the Germans of their remaining "eyes in the sky" included

Nieuport XVI with LePrieur rockets for balloon busting.

arming their pursuit aircraft with Le Prieur incendiary rockets. These air-to-air missiles, up to eight per plane, were fired from tubes mounted on the struts of Nieuport XI fighters and several Farman shorthorns. An electrical wire to each of the tubes ignited the rockets that looked much like oversized Chinese fireworks. On May 22, 1916, the Le Prieur armed Nieuports attacked the German balloon line in complete coordination with the great French counter-attack on Fort Douaumont. The Nieuports immediately shot down five Drachens in flames, all but one that were up that day and a quarter of the German balloon force in the area. So shocked were the Germans by this novel attack that none of the German observers were able to make use of their new Paulus parachutes in time.

While the French battled at Verdun, the British RFC geared up to support their own great offensive on the Somme. During the first half of 1916, Major-General Hugh Trenchard expanded and reorganized the RFC into four brigades containing two wings each. One brigade was assigned to each army of the BEF. One

Flight Commander McClelland, RNAS, and a night-flying B.E.2c at Chingford, England, early in 1916. Leather flying coat of standard pattern for 1915-1917.

wing of each brigade was placed under the army headquarters command for strategic use, while the other wing comprised all the squadrons serving the corps commanders for tactical reconnaissance and artillery ranging. For special missions called for by RFC headquarters, Trenchard reserved an independent wing of two squadrons called the 9th (HQ) Wing. Trenchard also moved toward making each squadron more specialized in its purpose and equipment. He stripped the corps squadrons of their single-seat fighter types and pulled them together in new fighter squadrons. He called for new fighter types, improved designs, larger numbers, and better trained pilots. By the summer, Trenchard had expanded the RFC to over 420 aircraft in 27 squadrons at the front. A shortage of trained pilots at the front hindered greater expansion, forcing Trenchard to borrow over a dozen pilots from the RNAS while new training programs were established in Great Britain.

DeHavilland D.H.2 fighter—the RFC's pusher alternative that subdued the Fokker Scourge.

Supply of aircraft was also an issue, not only in quantity but also in quality. The British corps observation aircraft were clearly technologically inferior to the German aircraft. Trenchard complained of the over-reliance on unsophisticated aircraft designs coming out of the Royal Aircraft Factory at Farnborough, particularly the B.E.2c and the R.E.7, which continued to place the observer's seat ahead of the pilot, restricting defensive use of the machine gun. The only good fighting plane from this source was the F.E.2b, a two-seat pusher aircraft where placing the observer up front made sense. Single seat fighters from the growing aviation industry were still only parceled out in handfuls. Of these, the quicker tractor engined biplanes like the Bristol Scout and Martinsyde G.100 still had no synchronized machine gun for adequate combat. Only the D.H.2, a single seat pusher designed by Geoffrey de Havilland, could out fly as well as out fight the Fokker Eindekkers. The D.H.2 now equipped three squadrons including No. 24 squadron led by Britain's first ace Lanoe Hawker. With this collection of aircraft, Trenchard outfitted the RFC with 15 corps squadrons for artillery cooperation and photo reconnaissance, and 12 army squadrons for bombing and offensive actions deeper behind enemy lines.

The only Allied plane with a real synchronized machine gun

at this time was the Sopwith 1½ Strutter. In the spring of 1916 the innovative RNAS immediately snapped up the Sopwiths as day bombers and fighters for their first strategic bombing group, No. 3 Wing, RNAS. The RFC had to borrow Sopwiths from them, and could barely maintain two partially equipped Sopwith squadrons in France. The Strutter was a two-seat rotary engined biplane with the pilot seated correctly in front of the observer. The observer had an excellent field of fire with his ring mounted Lewis gun. The pilot's fixed Vickers machine gun of the Strutter became the experimental platform for all the new synchronizer devices suddenly in development in Britain: the Ross gear, the Vickers-Challenger, the Sopwith-Kauper, and the Scarff-Dibovsky gear. The best design at the time was the creation of Lt. Commander V.V. Dibovsky of the Imperial Russian Navy, who came to England and worked with Warrant Officer F.W. Scarff of the RNAS. Their gear became standard on all RNAS Sopwiths.

The great Battle of the Somme commenced on July 1, 1916, the bloodiest day in history with 60,000 British deaths and 100,000 British casualties on the ground. The RFC leapt to action as well on July 1, achieving greater aerial gains but suffering a high percentage of casualties. The 400 British and French aircraft Trenchard amassed along the Somme battlefront achieved a 3:1 advantage over the German air service in this sector, the traditional numerical advantage required to triumph over a defensive force. Trenchard focused on offensive actions, dropping 13,000 pounds of bombs on enemy headquarters and communication centers, updating the artillery by ranging new targets, and identifying the extent of any infantry advance. Trenchard called upon his French Allies to make Le Prieur rocket attacks on the German balloon line to blind them for the first day's assault. The French sent a combat group under Major Brocard with four escadrilles of Nieuport 17 fighters to Cachy. This group, which included the ace Georges Guynemer, represented one of the first inter-Allied cooperative efforts to achieve aerial supremacy. Trenchard's forces also crippled the German aircraft from performing their duties. While the German two-seaters were under orders not to initiate combat over enemy lines and leave fighting to the Fokkers, the British airmen

Lieutenant W.C. Cambray, MC, of No. 20 Squadron, RFC, demonstrates precarious method of firing to rear from forward Nacelle of F.E.26 Pusher.

attacked anything they met with anything they flew whenever they could. With greater numbers and a dynamic aerial tenacity, Trenchard achieved aerial supremacy over the Somme throughout the entire month of July and into August.

On the receiving side, General von Below of the *Second German Army* at the Somme placed even greater praise upon the RFC. "With the help of air spotting, the enemy neutralized our artillery, and was able to range his own guns with the utmost accuracy on our infantry trenches; the information for this was provided by uninterrupted front-line reconnaissance and photography. ... The enemy aircraft gave our own troops a feeling of helplessness, such was their mastery of the air."

However, this aggressive spirit cost plenty. While achieving remarkable control of the air above the Somme for much of the battle, Trenchard's force suffered four times as many losses in combat as in previous months, nearly 100 aircraft and crews in

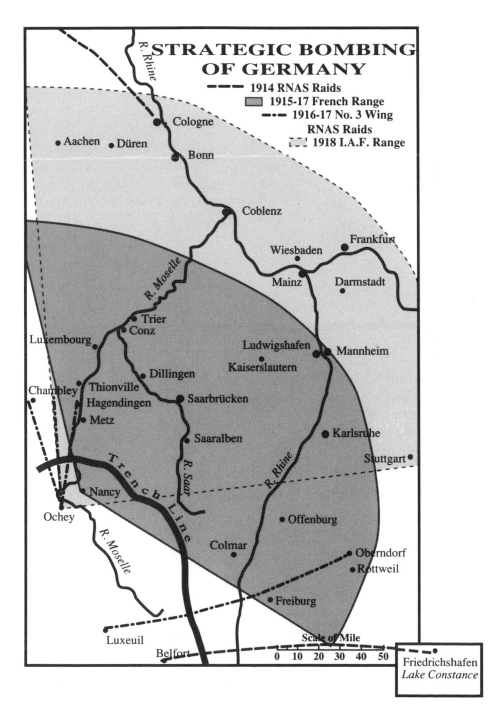

STRATEGIC BOMBING
OF GERMANY

- ---- 1914 RNAS Raids
- 1915-17 French Range
- -·-· 1916-17 No. 3 Wing RNAS Raids
- ⌐⌐⌐ 1918 I.A.F. Range

Aachen   Düren

Cologne

Bonn

Coblenz

R. Rhine

Frankfurt

Wiesbaden

Mainz   Darmstadt

R. Moselle

Trier
Conz

Luxembourg

Ludwigshafen

Kaiserslautern   Mannheim

Dillingen

Chambley

Thionville
Hagendingen

Metz

Saarbrücken

Saaralben

Karlsruhe

R. Saar

R. Rhine

Stuttgart

Trench Line

Nancy

Ochey

R. Moselle

Offenburg

Colmar

Oberndorf
Rottweil

Freiburg

Scale of Mile

| 0 | 10 | 20 | 30 | 40 | 50 |

Luxeuil

Belfort

Friedrichshafen
Lake Constance

July alone. As the offensive continued through the summer and into the fall, the RFC losses reached a morbid 100 per cent, losing and replacing as many air crews and planes as had existed in the entire RFC prior to the battle. The RFC planned that up to four hundred per cent casualties could be expected in the coming year, so greater training programs and supply of personnel and equipment were required. Trenchard held firm despite the losses and put this conviction in writing with his *Future Policy in the Air* on September 22. In this historic document Trenchard defines the purpose of the air offensive to directly and continuously support the actions on the ground. His Royal Flying Corps would push the air offensive continuously into German territory and remained undeterred regardless of the casualties. Clearing ones own lines of enemy aircraft was not enough; it was only by keeping the air war above German territory that aerial superiority could be achieved. "Carry the war into enemy territory and keep it there." War in the air must emphasize the offensive because, "the sky is too large to defend."

The coming of the autumn brought greater casualties to the RFC and Trenchard's aerial supremacy faded. One reason for these great losses was the ascendancy of the German fighter arm. Throughout the first half of 1916, the German KeK fighter units lacked an operationally aggressive doctrine and German fighter aircraft became technologically outclassed by the new British DeHavilland D.H.2 and the French Nieuport XI. But all this changed with the development of the Jagdstaffel in the fall of 1916. The Jagdstaffel, or hunting squadron, was a concept proposed nearly a year earlier by Oswald Boelcke. Boelcke felt that only an independent unit composed of specialized high performance fighting biplanes commissioned with the task of ridding the skies of enemy aircraft could truly make the skies safe for German observation aircraft. In the summer of 1916 he codified his thoughts during a vacation and information gathering trip through Turkey, Bulgaria, and the Russian Front. Actually the high command removed Boelcke from front line activity to protect Germany's most popular war hero after the demoralizing death of Max Immelmann, "The Eagle of Lille," in June. On August 11, however, Boelcke received a telegram from Lieth-Thomsen to return immediately from Kovel on the east front and form the first Jagdstaffel on the Somme front. On his way back, Boelcke selected several distinguished pilots to join his Jasta. One of these was a young pilot in the Kasta by the name of Manfred von Richthofen. Boelcke's new squadron, named *Jasta 2*, was equipped with Fokker D.III biplanes and the speedy new Albatros D.I biplane. He scored the unit's first victory and his own 20th on September 2, shooting down a British D.H.2 while flying his Fokker D.III biplane. Captain Boelcke led his squadron of fighters on purely fighter missions in group formations. Boelcke taught and experimented with group tactics, earning the title "Father of Air Fighting Tactics."

More British fell prey to these hunting units each day as the German Jastas grew stronger and more confident. This combative spirit exemplified the new Jastas, 24 of which were formed by the end of 1916. Each Jasta was equipped with 14 new fighter aircraft, mostly of the D-type. These D category planes carried two machine guns synchronized to fire through the spinning propeller. They were "doppledekker" biplanes, and were much stronger and more maneuverable than the old E-type monoplanes. The Albatros D.I's were sturdy biplanes with plywood formed fuselages much like the monocoque design, powered with inline 160 hp Mercedes engines, and could reach speeds of 108 mph and altitudes of 17,000 ft. This type of plane completely outclassed the D.H.2 pushers, the single-gun Nieuports, and all the slow two-seaters that the Allies flew. Prompted by Trenchard, General Haig pressed his concerns to the War Office in late September, "... the enemy has made extraordinary efforts to increase the number, and develop the speed and power of his fighting machines. He has unfortunately succeeded in doing so.... It is necessary to realize clearly, and at once, that we shall undoubtedly lose our superiority in the air if I am not provided at an early date with improved means of retaining it." As their numbers increased, the Jastas won back control of the air over the German lines. During September and October the Jastas shot down 211 enemy aircraft with the loss of only 39 of their own. Twenty-one of these victories were gained by the great Boelcke himself. Unfortunately, he was also one of the 39 losses. The next commander of Germany's air service, General von Hoeppner, proclaimed that German air power had bounced back from its defeat at the Somme "due in no slight measure to Boelcke and the Jagdstaffel he led."

The tide of aerial supremacy was clearly changing in Germany's favor as autumn progressed. The German air service had been licked earlier in the two greatest battles of the war so far, and something had to be done now to keep this rising tide of German supremacy from slipping away again. Col. Lieth-Thomsen had been pushing all year for a totally independent air force so that he could control and develop German air power. This didn't sit well with the traditional armed services represented in the War Ministry and the Navy, but things began to change when Hindenburg and Ludendorff took over supreme leadership of the German army in August, replacing General Falkenhayn after his failures at Verdun. Field Marshal Paul von Hindenburg had grand plans to reorganize and revamp the entire German war effort and was conducive to innovative ideas. His Quartermaster General Erich Ludendorff held an interest in aviation and knew Lieth-Thomsen from before the war. On October 8 the army high command procured an imperial order making all military aviation activities into a unified army air force called the *Luftstreitkräfte*. The *Luftstreitkräfte* was not an independent air force, but it was a respected division of the army and is more commonly called the Imperial German Air Service. The commanding general of the air force (Kogenluft) became Generalleutnant Ernst von Hoeppner who reported directly to Hindenburg at army general headquarters (OHL). Lieth-Thomsen became Hoeppner's Chief Staff Officer for Aviation, controlling all aerial activities at the front while Major Wilhelm Siegert oversaw aviation supply and industry as Inspectorate of Flying Troops (Idflieg). The aviation staff officers, Stofl, advising at corps level were promoted to commanding positions at the army level called Kofl, and a group leader, or Grufl, was appointed to each corps to coordinate its aerial contingent. No longer were planes tactically controlled directly by corps ground commanders, administered under the transportation division, and procured by the munitions department. All antiaircraft batteries (Flak), observation balloons, army airships, air raid defense and the *Flugmeldedienst* aerial warning system also fell under Kogenluft Hoeppner's command. Aviation supply and operational chain of command was unified at last.

A key to maintaining aerial dominance in the future, and one of the main causes of losing aerial supremacy earlier in the year, was supply related. Lieth-Thomsen could see that the Allies had a great number of planes and at times superior quality aircraft. More planes, new aircraft types and new unit organizations were needed. There were currently 1,544 aircraft in the *Luftstreitkräfte*, 885 of which were active on the western front, and by the following spring Lieth-Thomsen wanted another 800. He proposed tripling the number of D-type "doppledekker" single-seat biplane fighters to 630 which would increase the number of active Jagdstaffel (Jasta) to 36. The number of big G-type "grossflugzeug" three-seat twin-engine bombers like the A.E.G. G.IV would be quadrupled to 108 to outfit the Kagohl units, and a specification for a larger R-type "riesenflugzeug" giant long range bomber was put forth. Some of the C-type two-seater units, the old Kasta that had been forced primarily into escort service for the corps cooperation Flieger Abteilung, were redesignated Schutzstaffel (Schusta) for defensive work. Lieth-Thomsen also entered a specification for the CL-type, a fast new light weight two-seat fighter to join the schusta squadrons. His current force of C-type aircraft numbered 910. To these, Lieth-Thomsen requested another 200 with further specialization to equip the photographic Fl. Abt. with faster C-types and the artillery Fl. Abt.(A) with improved radio carrying types. It was up to Siegert as the Idflieg (inspector director for the Fliegertruppe) to stimulate the German industry and cut the strings to achieve these goals. Such a task involved managing industry, labor, government, and legal issues as well as communicating the technological needs of the front and the capabilities of the manufacturers.

The Allies reacted to the new German challenge in the closing months of 1916 by calling for more men and machines to fuel their air services, particularly more fighters. Major-General Trenchard of the RFC asked the RNAS again for a squadron of fighters from their small fleet of eighty planes stationed near Dunkirk to be sent to the Somme front. The RNAS assembled a new squadron, No.8 (Naval) Squadron, from flights of several other squadrons. This "Naval Eight" was the most elite squadron in Trenchard's stable, with one flight of six Nieuport scouts, one flight of six Sopwith 1½ Strutters, and one flight of six new sporty Sopwith Pups. Compared to the other fighter groups in the RFC that flew the D.H.2 and F.E.8 pushers at best, Naval Eight was the most capable of dealing with the new German Albatros and Halberstadt fighters.

The final curtain call for the outmoded pusher type fighters came on November 23. Major Lanoe Hawker, the great British ace and commander of No. 24, flew his D.H.2 along with two squadron mates on its second patrol of the day. Over Bapaume, Manfred von Richthofen and several members of *Jasta 2* jumped the three Britons and a large fight ensued. The D.H.2 flight drove off two Germans and sent one down out of control, as the dogfight broke down into individual combats splintering off from the flight. Hawker and Richthofen found themselves in a private duel, twisting and turning and circling around each other to gain advantage. "I was soon keenly aware that I wasn't dealing with a beginner," wrote von Richthofen, "for he did not even dream of breaking off the fight. To be sure, he had a very maneuverable crate, but mine climbed better and so I succeeded in getting above and behind the Englishman." Both planes had drifted far into German territory due to the winds and lost altitude in their maneuvering for almost half an hour, falling to 3,000 feet. Closing in with a good shot at one point, Richthofen's guns jammed. Low on fuel, Hawker turned for his own lines. At last Richthofen cleared one gun, and in the next opportunity riddled Hawker's plane from the rear. Major Lanoe Hawker, VC, DSO, nine victory ace, fell to the ground as the eleventh victory of Manfred von Richthofen. As a trophy, Richthofen mounted Hawker's machine gun above the door to his room. In the span of less than a month, Germany's 25 year old pioneering ace Oswald Boelcke died in an accidental collision during combat, and Britain's 25 year old pioneering ace died in combat against a superior machine flown by Boelcke's student and future ace of aces. Hawker's loss was keenly felt on the British side of the lines. General Haig again recounted the needs of his air corps, writing, "I desire to point out that the maintenance of mastery of the air, which is essential, entails a constant and liberal supply of the most up-to-date machines, without which even the most skillful pilots cannot succeed."

CONCLUSION

The year 1916 both opened and closed with Germany wielding tactical superiority while the middle months witnessed the greatest Allied aerial dominance of the war. Germany prepared a very detailed air strategy and successfully concentrated their forces for the Verdun offensive, but the ideas it was based upon turned out to be ill fitted to the requirements of an air campaign. The implementation of the Luftsperre demonstrated the failure of massed barrage patrols as a viable technique for control of air space. France rose from the Verdun assault with a superior fighter plane in the Nieuport, and superior use of these fighters in large amalgamated groups of squadrons in the Groupe de Combat. These concentrated fighter units proved to be the trick to gain local air superiority. The Allies battled back for control of the air and won mid-year during the conclusion of the Verdun bloodbath. At the beginning of the Somme the British used tactical tenacity to take back the skies, and as a result learned valuable lessons for the future. Trenchard noted that tenacious air offensive was the best way to both attack the enemy and defend one's own aircraft, and that inter-allied tactical cooperation worked well. German resurgence began in the fall, brought about by superior organizational and technological advances. Their D-type aircraft and Jasta fighter units remained a step ahead of the Allies. Lieth-Thomsen won his own battle for an air force and achieved the formation of the *Luftstreitkräfte* as a distinct unified entity responsible only to the supreme high command of the German Army.

Tactics of the air war changed and matured in 1916. The previous year's experiments in observation and bombing grew into standard operational procedures involved in all offensives. Greater inter-Allied cooperation developed in the strategic bombing campaign when GB 4 flew with No. 3 Wing, RNAS to bomb the Mauser Arms factory in Oberndorf 230 miles behind the lines from Luxeuil. It was truly an international raid, as the 34 French aircraft and 21 British Sopwith 1½ Strutters and

Mr. T.O.M. "Tommy"Sopwith, English designer and manufacturer of fighter aircraft.

Breguets were escorted by American flyers of the Lafayette Escadrille. This daylight raid on October 12 also demonstrated to the French how desperately inferior their Voisin pushers were for daylight operations when 9 of their planes never returned. Night bombing became the new standard procedure. The fighter plane gained its rightful place in 1916 with custom designs produced in larger numbers and supplied to specified fighter units. Fighters equipped specialized units like the German Jastas rather than being parceled out to defend in army cooperation squadrons. The French officially grouped their fighting escadrilles into a larger fighting arm as the Group de Combat. Lone patrols by single fighter planes diminished while technical formation flying by whole squadrons became the imperative standard procedure.

Supply for the campaign in the air also truly came up to speed in 1916. New prototypes of aircraft with specific purposes appeared, giving birth to the models that would fight in the coming years. German and French military and industrial organizations improved testing and production of planes. A greater level of inter-Allied cooperation regarding production capabilities and supply requirements grew between the French and British air services. The British realized that the French fighter designs were generally better than those currently available in Britain, so Trenchard ordered Nieuport scouts and SPAD VII's, which had just recently made their appearance at the front. Likewise, the French air service realized the superiority of Britain's Sopwith 1½ Strutter in the army cooperation category, and prepared to order and build under license both the two-seat observation version (called the Sopwith A2 by the French) and the single-seat bomber version (called the Sopwith B1). Ultimately, nearly four times as many Strutters were built in France during the war as in Britain. The French also decided to standardize their machine gun equipment with the British Vickers and Lewis guns. The French aero and auto industries excelled in engine design and mass production, so the British ordered large quantities of the Clerget and Le Rhone rotary engines and the fabulous new Hispano-Suiza 150 hp V-8 engine. But would this be enough to wrest back control of the air in the coming year?

Oswald Boelcke

Oswald Boelcke was a legend in his own time. A pioneer of combat aviation tactics, advocate of formation flying, and father of the German Air Service, Boelcke was born in 1891, the son of a schoolteacher. In school Oswald much preferred action to studies and enrolled in the Prussian Cadet Corps. Boelcke spent a few years as an officer in the Telegraphers Battalion before transferring to aviation in June 1914. From mobilization to February, 1915, Boelcke flew unarmed reconnaissance planes in *Feldflieger Abteilung 13* with his brother Wilhelm as his observer. Other officers complained and Wilhelm was transferred, much to Oswald's displeasure. Other than this sour note Boelcke's career was a story of never-ending success. A natural leader, as a young cadet Boelcke was already thinking ahead. He wrote, "You can win the men's confidence if you associate with them naturally and do not try and play the high and mighty superior."

Boelcke was no straightlaced Prussian prude. Even at the front, he knew a good time when he saw one. There was nothing finer on a sunny summer afternoon than to take a nurse up for a ride in his Fokker monoplane, a tight squeeze to be sure, with the girl's arms cuddled around his waist like riding that motorcycle he sported before the war. He also had a good sense of humor. Witness the following treatise on flying he wrote in 1915, early in his career, when the publicity was getting a bit much for his taste:

PLEASE!!!!

Do *not* ask me anything about flying.

You will find the usual questions answered below:

(1) Sometimes it is dangerous, sometimes it is not.

(2) Yes, the higher we fly, the colder it is.

(3) Yes, we notice the fact by freezing when it is colder.

(4) Flying height 2,000-2,500 meters.

(5) Yes, we can see things at that height, although not so well as at 100 meters.

(6) We cannot see well through the telescope because it waggles.

(7) Yes, we have dropped bombs.

(8) Yes, an old woman was supposed to have been injured, and we put the wind up some transport columns.

(9) The observer sits in front and can see a bit.

(10) We cannot talk to one another because the engine makes too much noise.

(11) We have not got a telephone in the machine, but we are provided with electric light.

(12) No, we do not live in caves.

His first air victory came while piloting an LVG C.I with *Flieger Abteilung 62*. Due to his aggressiveness in the air, Boelcke was one of two pilots picked to fly the squadron's new Fokker monoplanes; the other was friend and flying partner Max Immelmann. Boelcke's career accelerated through 1915 as the drum roll of his "kills" increased. In friendly competition with Immelmann, he scored his eighth victory and won the Pour le Mérite on the same day as his buddy Max.

But Boelcke's genius lay beyond mere flying. He was the first to push for the offensive use of aircraft as the Allies had been doing. Flying together with his partner Immelmann he discovered that to be fully effective fighter planes should be used in groups rather than singly, the origin of formation flying. It took awhile to convince the German General Staff (OHL) of this wisdom. But, finally, after the death of Max Immelmann in June 1916 and the debacle at Verdun, the top German generals were ready to listen and Boelcke's stock rose. After meeting with the Kaiser, Boelcke was assigned to fix the inadequacies of the German fighter command and reorganize the German fighter forces. Typically, Boelcke set to work with a vengeance. The new Chief of Staff for the German Army Air Service, Col. Lieth-Thomsen, wrote, "the reports on tactical, technical and organization questions ...which Boelcke continually gave me, formed a unique and valuable basis for the official battle orders drawn up by my staff." Boelcke quickly organized Jagdstaffels, hunting squadrons of single seaters, whose job was to protect the observation Fliegerabteilungen and to search and destroy enemy aircraft. Each "Jasta" had 6 planes originally, but later in the war it was up to 21. Then, in September 1916, Boelcke published the official doctrine of the German Air Service, the first codified rules for fighter pilots ever written.

BOELCKE'S DICTA

• Try to secure advantages before attacking. If possible keep the sun behind you.
• Always carry through an attack when you have started it.
• Fire only at close range and only when your opponent is properly in your sights.
• Always keep your eye on your opponent, and never let yourself be deceived by ruses.
• In any form of attack it is essential to assail your opponent from behind.
• If your opponent dives on you, do not try to evade his onslaught, but fly to meet it.
• When over the enemy's lines, never forget your own line of retreat.
• Attack on principle in groups of four or six. When the fight breaks up into a series of single combats, take care that several do not go for one opponent.

Simplistic today, state of the art, 1916.

Boelcke took command of *Jasta 2*, the first German squadron equipped solely with fighters, in the fall of 1916. He hand-picked his flyers, the most famous choice proving to be Manfred von Richthofen. Boelcke took to the skies again to teach his students a thing or two. Each dawn he mounted a lone patrol, scored a kill, and returned to teach his protégés a lesson over breakfast. Then the whole squadron would take off to apply its new knowledge. Within two months Boelcke scored 20 kills, doubling his total to 40.

But success did not come easy. A friend wrote of Boelcke, "My captain kept on growing thinner and more serious. The superhuman burden of seven take-offs a day for fights and the worries about his Staffel weighed him down.... a couple of days before his death he said 'I found an opponent who was a match for me today. There'll be hard fighting... but no bullet will ever hit me.'" Boelcke was right about that as well. Richthofen describes what happened on October 28, 1916, when Boelcke collided with Jastamate Erwin Bohme: "Suddenly I saw both machines moving unnaturally. 'Collision' flashed through my head. I had never seen a collision in midair and imagined it would be quite different. It was really no collision, but just a touch. But with the great speed at which such machines fly, a gentle touch is a terrific impact."

Boelcke's death convulsed Germany in sadness. His squadron was renamed *Jasta Boelcke* by Imperial Decree. "I will be a Boelcke" was the battle cry for a generation of young German youths. As Richthofen said of his mentor, "I am only a fighting airman, but Boelcke was a hero."

Training
Blériot Hop, Skip, and Jump Method

The technically advanced air services required a high level of training. Few people could drive a car before World War I, and even fewer had ever seen an airplane. Training new pilots increased at a steady rate until late 1916 when the combat losses of airmen reached catastrophic proportions. Training programs then switched into high gear, but their graduates reached the front with fewer than seventeen and a half hours experience in the air. Though the quantity of replacements reaching the front increased, the quality of these replacements dropped tremendously. Squadrons at the front complained that poorly trained rookies reduced squadron effectiveness. By September 1917 the RFC provided trained pilots with 48½ hours flight time. These pilots received basic, advanced, and aerobatic training courses as designed by Major R.R. Smith Barry of the Training Division.

French flying schools were the largest in the world, doubling their output of pilots each year of the war and graduating 18,000 pilots by the armistice. Basic level flight schools like the one at Tours used the Blériot method of training. In this method, students flew alone immediately after ground instruction, and advanced from various types of clipped wing single seaters to actual planes. Eugene Bullard, an American Lafayette Flying Corpsman undergoing French training, described the typical course of the French training program: He first flew, or rather drove along the ground, in a 25 hp Blériot with clipped wings called a "Penguin." After a few days practice, he learned how to control it in a straight line and advanced to the "Roleur." The Roleur was an old Blériot with standard wings, but students were not to take off with it either, only to get the feel of the plane for three weeks. Then Bullard advanced to the "Décolleur" which he could take off the ground some three feet. A special depression in the middle of the runway allowed the Décolleur to become airborne for short stints. Bullard eventually took this plane to 500 feet above the airfield. The last step before receiving a pilot license or "brêvet" was real flying, again all solo. This time Bullard's mount was one of the old Caudron trainers held together by wires and glue known as "chicken coops," or as the French called them, "cages a poules." With the Caudron G III he successfully mastered serpentines, spirals from 2,000 feet, and two forty mile cross country flights to distant airfields. After their brêvet, pilots like Bullard were "granted six days leave in Paris." Then, before being posted to the front, pilots in the later years of the war went to "écoles de perfectionnement" schools at Chateauroux or Avord for reconnaissance training, Cazaux for aerial gunnery and shooting at moving targets on the lake, or Pau for aerobatic experience on actual Nieuport and SPAD fighters. The whole program took six months, on average.

Most other nations used the standard dual control training method begun by the Wrights. The classic trainer was the Curtiss JN-4

Jenny. Many British, Canadian, and American pilots learned to fly exclusively on Jennies in the U.S. and Canada. Germans similarly used two-seat Taubes and old B-types. The dual control method was generally safer for the new student but more hazardous and time consuming for the experienced instructors. Casualties were high in the training schools, accounting for a large percentage of the deaths in the air services. Casualties at the front due to combat and accidents also related to the time spent in training. Around Bloody April, RFC pilots were coming to the front with less than 48 hours flying time—often as little as 25 hours in the air. By the end of 1917 the hours of air time doubled and advanced training in formation flying and aerobatic skills were conducted at Honslou in Scotland. Fighters with camera guns mounted on the fuselage helped flyers improve their shooting. Skilled aces periodically returned from the front to offer pointers and bring the schools up to date. These practices helped the new pilots keep pace with the new perils found at the front.

In the Cockpit

Aircraft of the First World War were open cockpit craft, meaning that the airmen were not covered or enclosed in any type of canopy or cabin. Their only protection against the 150 mph winds blowing back from the propeller and the sub-zero cold at high altitude was their personal flying suit. Fleece lined leather jumpsuits called "teddy bears" or

canvas combination suits lined with dog hair called "monkey-suits" became standard issue later in the war, but earlier airmen had to improvise with fur lined overalls and black leather jackets. Ted Parsons of the Lafayette Escadrille said he wore a crash helmet donated by a British airman, suitably decorated, usually topped off with his college campus mackinaw jacket. Fur lined hip boots protected the feet while fur lined mittens warmed the hands—two fingers of which could slip open to operate the gun triggers. Leather flying helmets topped off the whole affair. The French and German bomber flyers wore a hard protective helmet while French ace Jean Navarre wore a silk stocking on his head. A decent pair of motorcycle goggles usually had to be purchased in Paris or Geissen because those issued by the army were no good. Scarves were a necessity for warmth and to wipe the castor oil spraying from the rotary engine off goggles. A woman's silk stocking was the best thing to wrap around the neck to relieve the chafing from continually twisting and turning to scan the skies for the "Hun in the sun." Beneath all this were mascots, uniform, and lucky charms. Ernst Udet wore his best dress uniform to impress the girls of Paris should he get captured, while Manfred von Richthofen wore his pajamas underneath on occasion.

The pilot's cockpit contained all the controls and gauges for flying the plane. In reach was the joystick (often a wheel and rocker arm on large bombers and flying boats) and rudder pedals for maneuvering, machine gun trigger buttons on the joystick, the "blip switch" cutting ignition to reduce speed on rotary engines, throttles and carburetor valves to adjust engine speed and altitude requirements, magneto "contact" switch, the valve to switch to the emergency fuel tank, a hand pump to pressurize the gas tanks with air, a map board, and little else. Between the pilot's knees was the box holding the ammunition

belts and directly overhead were the butts of the machine guns, padded to protect his face in a rough landing. Two types of gunsights were commonly mounted above them. Eddie Rickenbacker always carried a copperheaded hammer on a leather thong fastened to his right wrist, "A sharp blow with it cleared many a (gun) jam."

Flying instruments ranged from primitive to nonexistent, the most important being a good clock, commonly referred to as "my fuel gauge." An aneroid altimeter (completely susceptible to barometric pressure changes) and a compass (which spun wildly when most needed) fixed general location. Air speed could be measured from a pitot tube or a sprung vane on the interplane struts. Engine rpm and radiator temperature gauges were used. Flyers rotated the faces of the gauges so that the optimal setting was displayed when the needle pointed straight up. This let the pilot check his status at a glance. Illuminated gauges for night flying did not appear until 1917. Bombers like the Liberty DH-4 carried a Sperry gyroscopic banking indicator, a clinometer, and sometimes a Clark stall indicator—but most of the time flyers just tied a cloth string on their strut and flew by the seat of their pants. As America's first ace Doug Campbell put it, "by guess and by God" was the order of the day.

All the tools of the trade were located in the observer's "office" as his cockpit was called. There were ammunition racks for the flexible mounted machine gun, flares and a Very pistol for air-to-air and air-to-ground communication, stick grenades for another kind of ground communication, message bags and streamers, a map board, mountings for the camera and extra photo plates when on reconnaissance, brackets for the radio and Morse key when on artillery ranging missions, and sights and bomb release levers when bombing. Bombsights superseded the aiming nails driven into the side of the plane, and became necessary when antiaircraft fire drove the bombers to higher altitudes. Bombsights carried included the British C.F.S.4, the equal-distance sight, the German Görz or Zeiss bombsight, the American Sperry, and the French Dorand and Lafay sight.

Noticeably lacking were parachutes. While observers in balloons had them, no other aviators were authorized to use parachutes except German pilots, and not until the last year of the war. German observers and Allied flyers were denied parachutes because many of the upper echelon desk officers believed that flyers might be tempted to abandon their planes if they had a chute. Future organizer of the Luftwaffe Ernst Udet survived leaping from his flaming Fokker D.VII in June 1918 due to his Heinecke Parachute. He went on to become Germany's highest ranking ace to survive the war. When the same circumstances befell Raoul Lufbery in May 1918, America's leading ace leapt from his burning Nieuport 28 inferno to his death. Like all Allied flyers, he had no parachute to save him.

The Eye in the Sky
Development of Aerial Cameras and Aerial Mapping

The first war in the air was the first military action to fully and significantly utilize photography for aerial mapping. Aircraft began carrying cameras as soon as the opening campaigns stagnated into the deadlock of the Western Front. The details of the trench fortifications were too complex to record by hand on maps. With the advent of cameras, seemingly insignificant features could be studied in depth by more than one pair of eyes after the mission was over. At first commercial cameras were held by hand over the side of the aircraft by the observers, but soon new models were specifically designed for the aeroplane.

Second Lieutenant J.T.C. Moore-Brabazon and Lt. C.D.M. Campbell developed the first standard aviation camera for the RFC in 1914. The Model A camera consisted of a 9⅞ inch Zeiss-Tessar lens housed in a tapering wooden box. It exposed 4" by 5" plates. The Model C and later Model E with metal housing introduced a magazine to hold a dozen photographic plates fed by gravity. These and the British Mark I became standard for the RFC for much of the war. Cameras advanced from being hand-held to types mountable on brackets over the side of the aircraft fuselage. Observers had to brave the cold gales of the propwash to operate the camera. Later in the war, cameras were mounted inside the observer's cockpit over an opening in the floor.

German motion picture pioneer Oskar Messter introduced a roll film camera in 1915 to replace photographic plates. The 100 feet of film could take 250 four inch square negatives. A single crank motion by the observer advanced the film and cocked the shutter of the camera. This freed the observer from manipulating the camera to change plates and allowed more photos to be taken in less time over the target. Messter later developed a fully automatic camera, run off a wind driven propeller, for mapping 37 miles at a stretch. The camera used by the high altitude "Rubild" aircraft of 1918 had a complex multiple lens configuration that the Allies tried desperately to capture.

The French advanced strategic mapping of the entire German rear areas to track daily changes. They developed cameras with focal lengths from 50 cm to 2.1 meters. In 1918 a special group of two Breguet 14 escadrilles under Captain Paul Louis Weiller mapped the enemy lines to a depth of 100 km each day. Large blanket maps were printed from these photos and used in place of traditional maps. Subtle changes and enemy construction and movements yielded valuable and accurate predictions of enemy offensives before they occurred. So important was this technique that General Foch asked Weiller to keep his methods secret even after the war, and then appointed him to the Legion of Honor.

Aerial photo-reconnaissance was typically performed at a height of 10,000 feet. At this height a camera with 8" focal length lens can photograph onto a 4" by 5" photographic plate one square mile of land. The preferred altitude increased each year of the war as anti-aircraft fire became more dangerous. As the plane flew at about 65 mph, the observer took a picture every fifteen seconds, overlapping each image by up to 75%. This overlapping of the pictures not only gave multiple shots of the same targets from slightly different angles, but also provided the ability to view a target stereoscopically. After the photographs were developed, specialists viewed them in pairs through the popular hand-held entertainment device of that period called a "stereoscope." When viewed in this way, three-dimensional objects would stand out against the background terrain in an exaggerated manner. This "hyperstereoscopy" spotted everything from hidden gun emplacements to enemy observation posts. Shadows were also used to track three-dimensional objects, and their sizes could be determined by recording the day and hour that the photo was taken.

In the last year of the war, the British took and developed 6.5 million photographs, the French took 675,000, and in the last five months the U.S. Air Service took 1.3 million. The aerial photograph provided the only means of mapping enemy held territory and yielded strategic intelligence for predicting enemy actions. Aerial photographs supplied up to date and vital information to ground commanders and formed the foundation of future aerial reconnaissance techniques.

The Designers
The Men Behind the Technology of Flight

ANTHONY FOKKER

A Dutchman born in Java and raised in Haarlem, Holland, Anthony Fokker became Germany's most famous and respected aircraft designer of the First World War. He was inventive, rebellious, and self motivated as a boy and became fascinated with the mechanisms of flight as a young man. With financial support from his father, he built his first aircraft at a German flying school. A daring man, Fokker was the first to loop-the-loop in Germany. Unfortunately, he also was responsible for one of the first air fatalities in Germany when a passenger of his died in a crash landing.

Although creative, Anthony Fokker's best attribute was his keen eye for a good design. He spotted the new and important qualities in the aircraft of other designers and then capitalized on them. Often called a copycat, he never the less produced some of the most remarkable designs in aviation history. His pre-war mid-wing monoplane, the Fokker M.5K (military name "Fok. A.III") was commonly considered a mere copy of the successful pre-war Morane-Saulnier monoplanes. But this reputation for copying good ideas is what most likely brought the German General Staff to the 24 year old Dutchman when they captured Roland Garros' machine gun equipped Morane-Saulnier. With passing knowledge of the early Schneider gun-synchronization attempts, Fokker devised an even better synchronization method and put it on his plane, giving birth to the Fokker E.I which led to the "Fokker Scourge." His next great success, the Fokker Triplane design, was initiated immediately after Manfred von Richthofen showed a captured Sopwith Triplane to him and asked for a similar plane. Fokker again took the best of this style fighter, added internal cantilever structured wings and steel tubing framework, and returned a superior aircraft. With his main designer, Reinhold Platz, he developed the most famous plane of the war and the only plane specified for surrender in the Treaty of Versailles, the Fokker D.VII. Later in the war, when the ultimate fighter design seemed to be the modernistic Morane-Saulnier A1, Fokker put out his own high-wing monoplane design, the Fokker D.VIII, which proved to be the fastest plane of its type and the design of the future.

GLENN CURTISS

Glenn Curtiss was an American pioneer who built and raced motorcycles before putting his ideas into flight. He briefly collaborated with Alexander Graham Bell and his colleagues in Canada, but later split off to pursue his own novel designs. His June Bug caused a vicious patent dispute with the Wright brothers over wing-warping lateral control, so Curtiss produced the Gold Bug with interplane maneuvering panels—the first true ailerons. Curtiss also pursued seaplane design, and put together several successful seaplane and flying boat designs. His flying boats H.4 and H.12 became the mainstay of the RNAS North Sea patrols during World War I. In fact, it was a Curtiss H.12 "Large America" that became the first American built aircraft to shoot down an enemy aircraft in combat, when an Canadian flyer in a RNAS H.12 shot down a Zeppelin over the North Sea in 1917. These "America Boats" were later upgraded by the Royal Navy's Comdr. John Porte to become the Felixstowe F.2A. Other Curtiss seaplanes like the HS-2L and H-16 flying boats and the N-9 floatplane were grabbed up by the U.S. Navy for anti-submarine duties all around the Atlantic. The most famous Curtiss plane of all time, however, remains the JN-4D "Jenny." The Jenny served across the United States and Canada as a trainer for large numbers of RFC, RNAS, and USAS pilots. The Jenny continued its long distinguished career after the war in barnstorming and air mail.

LOUIS BÉCHEREAU

Louis Béchereau started in the French aviation industry working for the pioneer flyer Armand Deperdussin. He succeeded in designing fast racing planes for the Deperdussin company. Using streamlined fuselages and wing configurations, his Deperdussins repeatedly won the Gordon Bennett and Schneider trophies, one breaking the speed record at over 200 km/h, (124.6 mph). When the Société pour les Appareils Deperdussin collapsed with the arrest of its owner, the new owner, Louis Blériot, kept Béchereau on as chief engineer. Now called the Société pour l'Aviation et ses Dérivés

(SPAD), the company produced planes for the French war effort. Béchereau sought extra engine power for his designs, and found the water-cooled Hispano-Suiza V-eight engine. A young Swiss engineer working in Spain named Mark Birkigt designed this engine with overhead cams, an aluminum "mono-bloc," screwed-in piston sleeves, dual ignition, and many other modern features. Mark Birkigt also had a machine gun synchronization mechanism integral to the engine layout. With these components, Béchereau turned out the finest line of fighters of the war, the SPAD VII through XVII. The SPAD VII C1 started in late 1916 with a 150 hp "Hisso" and later upgraded to the 180 hp engine. The SPAD XII had a 37mm cannon for a weapon, and the type XIII C1 had twin Vickers guns with a 200 hp engine. The geared Hisso was later upgraded in the field to 220 hp and eventually 230 hp. Not as maneuverable as the rotary engined planes, the SPAD was the fastest of fighters and the favorite mount of top French and American aces. The SPAD XIII became the most manufactured plane of the war with 7,300 of the type being built for France and all of her allies.

T.O.M. SOPWITH

Tommy Sopwith was a wealthy young cosmopolitan who became hooked on aviation at the outset. Competition was his interest, and he won a £4,000 prize in 1910 for making the longest all-British flight across the English Channel. After starting the Sopwith Aviation Company, he continued to design and race his own sporty little biplanes.

By 1913 he won a military contract with both the RFC and RNAS when his chief engineering associate Harry Hawker demonstrated the fast and clean looking Sopwith Tabloid biplane at Hendon. Tommy's next newsworthy stunt was to slip off to Monte Carlo and win the Schneider Trophy with a sleek seaplane version of the Tabloid. The Great War drew greatly upon Sopwith's artistic skill designing good clean planes, and design them he did. He writes, "Development was so fast! We literally thought of and designed and flew the airplanes in a space of about six or eight weeks. Everything was built entirely by eye. Flying in those days was empirical. We really weren't structural engineers at all. It was a constant gamble, in a way. We just flew by the light of nature. Some of us were lucky and some of us weren't." As luck would have it, the Sopwith Camel became one of the most produced designs of the war with some 5,500 being built, and the most successful, accounting for some 1,500 enemy aircraft.

Tommy Sopwith produced the most memorably named aircraft of the war. His first success, the "Sopwith Tabloid," certainly got Sopwith's name in all the newspaper headlines. The "Schneider" was the slick racing seaplane that won the Schneider Trophy Cup in 1914, and its offspring the "Sopwith Baby" was an improved military version. Sopwith's two-seat armed fighting-reconnaissance plane originally had the drab designation of "Type 9400"

until flyers gave it a more descriptive nickname as the "1 and½ Strutter" due to its long and short pairs of interplane struts. The "Pup" was a single-seat fighter whose faithful qualities were its easy going handling and playful aerobatics. The "Tripehound" was of course the stockier triplane fighter of 1917. Sopwith's supreme air fighter was called the "Camel" because of the hump which enclosed the machine gun breeches between the pilot and engine cowling. The Camel, like its namesake, also had a nasty tendency to spin around and throw inexperienced pilots to the ground. Next came the "Dolphin" with its smooth round gray nose and a hole in the top of its backstaggered upper wing for the pilot's head to stick out, affording an excellent if chilling view. The high climbing and swift diving "Snipe" was a top of the line fighter which appeared in the closing months of the war. Sopwith also produced a number of special purpose aircraft. The "Salamander" was a development of the "T.F.1", an armored Trench Fighter which was expected to muddy itself supporting the troops on the ground. Another of the Sopwith family of aircraft was expected to take off an aircraft carrier deck with a 1,000 pound torpedo slung under its belly, fly across the sea to the enemy fleet's harbor, dive straight towards a 600 foot dreadnought battleship, release the torpedo while being shot at by dozens of cannon, and sink the ship. For some reason, this plane was called the "Cuckoo."

Hugh Montague "Boom" Trenchard

"Boom" Trenchard (1873-1956) was the daring, innovative, and strong-willed father of the Royal Air Force, the first independent aerial arm in history. Born in 1873 in Taunton, England, the third of six children, he preferred sports and games of strategy over academics. He sought to serve in the Royal Navy like his grandfather, but failed the entrance exam. With difficulty, he was able to pass the army requirements and became a Second Lieutenant. Trenchard's first post was India, where he sought self-education through avid reading. During the Boer War of 1899-1902 he went to South Africa as a captain. He created a "flying column" of mounted infantry with Australian volunteers that successfully pursued Boer raiding parties. In one engagement he received a shot in the lung that sent him back to England for several months. He returned to South Africa commanding the 12th Mounted Infantry. He later served in Nigeria for seven years overseeing expeditions and building the infrastructure of this emerging colony in the British Empire. His reputation for personal initiative, adventure, leadership, and for encouraging élan among irregular units was developed through his career in Africa.

Approaching retirement from the military at the age of 39, Trenchard was encouraged by a close friend to take up flying. While on leave, he paid for his own lessons at the Sopwith school. With barely an hour's flying time, he returned to become instructor and assistant commandant of the army's Central Flying School at Upavon—such was the state of the infant Royal Flying Corps. He organized novel training methodology and standards while advancing his own flying skills. His compelling and overpowering voice earned this old man of the air the nickname "Boom" with his young pupils. When war erupted in 1914, Trenchard took the role of reorganizing the expansion of the RFC from Farnborough as commander of the Military Wing.

Trenchard's service in France began on November 18, 1914, as commander of No. 1 Wing with the First Corps of the British Expeditionary Force (BEF). He struggled for better radio and camera equipment for his units and experimented with tactical bombing. A year later in August 1915 he took charge of the RFC at the front when Sir David Henderson was recalled to England. Trenchard received the temporary rank of Brigadier-General and reported directly to Sir Douglas Haig, the leader of the BEF. He drove his force constantly and encouraged increased aggressiveness to attain the aerial supremacy that he deemed vital to success on the ground. He encouraged new methods of air warfare and struggled to gain improved aircraft, better trained pilots, and larger forces. Trenchard developed the fundamental air doctrine that only by persistent attack can air mastery be obtained. In comparing the capabilities and implementation of British and German air power doctrine he pointed out, "The Germans still think of the airplane as a defensive weapon. That is why the work they have actually accomplished on the British front is about four per cent of what we have done. The one exception is their night bombing. They have inflicted thousands of casualties on our troops in bivouac by a new twin-engined aircraft called a Gotha. We must learn this."

Although Trenchard was convinced of the validity of creating a separate air force, he felt that such major changes would induce dissension between the Army and Navy during wartime. However, the politicians on the Air Board were driving Parliament to create an Air Ministry for themselves to head with a separate new military arm. Trenchard disliked Lord Rothermere of the Air Board upon hearing of his intention to use the popular press to discredit Sir Douglas Haig for his supposed misuse of air power. When Rothermere became the Air Minister directly over Trenchard at the creation of the Royal Air Force (RAF) on April 1, 1918, the man of action resigned rather than serve the man of political intrigue. Only after Rothermere also stepped down under pressure from Trenchard's supporters did Trenchard return to the RAF in May to lead a separate strategic unit called the Independent Force of the RAF.

Through the summer of 1918 Major-General Trenchard led this strategic bombing force on day and night raids against targets as far as the Rhine. On October 26 Trenchard's group became a multinational organization called the Inter-Allied Independent Air Force (IAF) responsible to Marshal Ferdinand Foch the Supreme Commander of Allied forces. Trenchard was aware of

the less than ideal effectiveness of strategic bombing with the materials available in 1918, but he foresaw great possibilities of such power in the future.

After the war Winston Churchill invited Trenchard to carry on the development of the Royal Air Force in peacetime. After consulting at Versailles, he developed a world cost saving strategy to maintain peace in the Middle East using a few airplanes and armored cars. He spent government money on an air force military college rather than maintaining more front-line squadrons. While criticized for this at the time, such a strong foundation for the RAF proved more vital in the next world war than extra obsolescent planes. The air marshal retired at the ripe age of 56, but went on to revamp the police force with new investigation and forensic colleges at Hendon (near his beloved airplanes). In World War II he came back to the RAF as a roving ambassador of the Air Council to inspire a new generation of flyers and report on conditions.

All the world's air forces owe credit for their existence to Boom Trenchard, the father of Britain's RAF. He not only stimulated the world's first completely independent national air force, but followed up that act by leading the first multinational strategic air command. Boom Trenchard epitomized the commander of action, and his doctrines and principles of air power remain the ideals and objectives of all the world's air forces to the present day.

CHAPTER V

1917
Prepare to Die

Like dueling, air fighting required a set steely courage, drained of all emotion, fined down to a tense and deadly effort of will. The Angel of Death is less callous, aloof, and implacable than a fighting pilot when he dives.
—Cecil Lewis, British pilot

Unlike the first two winters of the Great War, which provided brief respites for the aerial combatants as bad weather shut down aerial operations, the winter of 1917 brought with it a continually rising death toll for the Allies. The RFC suffered at the hands of the new German Jagdstaffeln. Trenchard needed to revamp his force both numerically and technologically before the spring offensives. The supply of trained pilots and crew became particularly critical with the upcoming expansion and growing losses at the front, so training programs at home were increased. The RFC received permission to expand to 106 front-line squadrons and 97 reserve squadrons in the coming year, only half of which were expected to be available by the spring. Trenchard planned to reconstruct the whole character of the RFC by placing critical emphasis on the fighter plane; there would be two fighter squadrons for every corps observation squadron. Furthermore, individual squadrons would be homogeneously composed of a single aircraft type, similar to the French aviation organization. In September 1916, the commander of the BEF, Field Marshal Sir Douglas Haig had called for new fighter designs capable of dealing with the new German

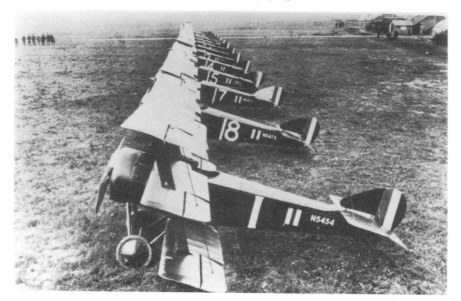

Full lineup of the Sopwith Triplanes of No. 1 Squadron, RNAS. Note unit insignia (twin bars), personal identification (Numbers 1 to 18), and individual purchase serial numbers of planes (N5454, etc.).

single seaters. He pointed out to the government that only the Nieuport, the F.E.2b, and the Sopwith Pup could stand up to the new German fighters, while "all other fighting machines at my disposal are decidedly inferior." He desperately needed newer types and more of them or the RFC would lose its battle for the air by spring.

Britain's aircraft industry had finally geared up and was producing new aircraft to meet the needs of the front. For Christmas 1916, the RFC received a new squadron of Sopwith Pups, No. 54 Squadron, with another Pup squadron arriving in March, No. 66. The purchase of French designs also bore fruit—No.1 Squadron had its obsolescent equipment completely replaced with the Nieuport 17 at Christmas, and No. 19 Squadron was receiving more SPAD VII's to replace its aging B.E.12's. The RNAS continued to support the RFC at the front. It provided Naval 3 Squadron with Pups, Naval 6 with Nieuport 17's, and two squadrons just re-equipped with the latest British design, the Sopwith Triplane, in Naval 1 and Naval 8. The

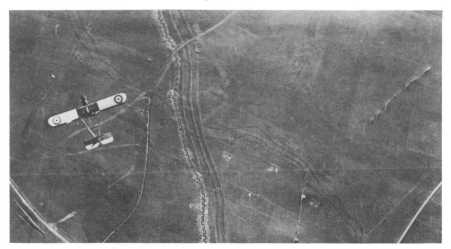

British F.E.2 photographs German reserve trenches.

remaining fighter squadrons of the RFC still flew the obsolete
D.H.2 and F.E.8 pushers.

The corps reconnaissance aircraft were in a worse predica-
ment. Two squadrons still flew the old Nieuport 12 and Morane
Parasol. The vast majority, fifteen squadrons, were still flying
the B.E.2c, a design that hadn't changed much since the war
began. The Royal Aircraft Factory sent their latest development,
the R.E.8, to five squadrons at the front, but it was a poor
performer and obsolescent the day it arrived. The F.E.2d pushers
with their superior Rolls Royce in-line engine replaced most of
the F.E.2b models with their low powered rotary engine, but the
"Fees" still could not hold their own against a German Jasta.

There were a few bright points for the British two-seater
squadrons. A new squadron (No. 35) of Armstrong-Whitworth
F.K.8's was attached to Third Army headquarters and a squadron of new Bristol F2A two-seat fighters (No. 48 Squadron) was
part of the 13th Army Wing also serving the British Third Army
at Arras. Three other two-seater squadrons in the RFC were
Sopwith 1½ Strutters. The Ninth Wing received the first squadron of D.H.4 two-seater bombers, No. 55 Squadron, which was
directly under the control of RFC headquarters as part of the
Ninth Wing. With this force, Trenchard pushed forward offensive sorties in an effort to regain aerial supremacy over the
battlefields in 1917.

His counterparts in the German air force continued their staunch defense. While the Germans could not claim aerial dominance over the British lines, they certainly prevented Trenchard from dominating German territory. This defensive posture of the *Luftstreitkräfte* was part of Hindenburg's overall plan for 1917. The German Army remained on the strategic defensive on the Western Front for all of 1917. Hindenburg actually retreated his armies to achieve a superior defensive position. During the second half of March, the Germans withdrew from their exposed positions at Bapaume, Roye and Noyon and took up residence on the high ground before Cambrai and St. Quentin. The new trench system was a previously constructed fortified zone called the Hindenburg Line.

To cover their withdrawal from the preying eyes of the British airmen, German Jagdstaffels flew constantly overhead. They attacked the enemy planes with increasing impudence, shooting down 120 RFC and RNAS planes in March. German Jastas destroyed large numbers of British planes with few losses of their own. Along the German *Second Army* front, the total victories for February and March came to 60 with the loss of only seven German fighters. In one two day period at the end of March, British airmen experienced 48 casualties. The flying units also exhibited exceptional mobility, shifting their air bases several times in as many days when the withdrawal to the Hindenburg Line progressed. They barely had time to settle down from this action when the British spring offensives erupted in April.

On April 4, Trenchard opened a general aerial offensive along the entire British front. In the immediate area of Arras, his numerically superior force of 365 aircraft in 25 squadrons tried to suppress the 195 aircraft of the opposing German *Luftstreitkräfte*. But while only a third of the British force was composed of fighters, the German force on this front was half fighters, and these fighters were significantly superior to any on the British side. For five days RFC and RNAS planes struck at the German reconnaissance aircraft and attacked German fighters. Trenchard planned to draw the Jastas away from his bombers that were preparing the way for the ground offensive along the actual axis of attack coming from Arras on the ninth. Enemy supply centers and troop concentrations were the bombers' chief targets. This air assault failed miserably compared to its predecessor the year before over the Somme. British flyers fell left and right at the hands of the new German fighter units.

German Jastas had grown to 36 by the time of the Arras offensive. Many of these Jastas were just replacing their state-of-the-art Albatros D.II and Halberstadt D.II fighters with the even better Albatros D.III fighter. The D.III was a more maneuverable Albatros design and adopted the "V-strutter" configuration. In previous months only the plucky French Nieuport 17 with its V-strut sesquiplane wings was a match for the German D-types, so German designers copied the V-strut in the Albatros D.III. This plane became the preferred mount of German aces like Manfred von Richthofen, once the weaknesses in its lower wing were characterized and corrected. It carried synchronized twin Spandau guns like other D-types. Meanwhile, the Allied planes carried only a single gun.

The German tactics had also greatly improved since 1916. The Germans abandoned their Luftsperre blockade flights of 1916 and capitalized on their improved communication system. Observation posts at the airfields and forward air defense Luftschutz officers at the front augmented the Flugmeldedienst aerial warning system. Any British planes observed crossing the lines were reported by telephone to the corps group leader for aviation, or Grufl, who determined which Jasta should take off to meet the intruders. A kette, or flight of four fighters, rose in formation when the orders came from the Grufl. The entire Jasta often patrolled in formation, but only seven aircraft were generally available in the Jastas of this period instead of the sixteen planes planned for on paper. Emboldened by each success above their own lines, the Jastas began extending their patrols over British territory.

One up and coming ace, Manfred von Richthofen, led the most deadly of these fighter units. His *Jasta 11* was stationed with several other squadrons at Douai, immediately opposite Arras. On April 5, the second day of the British air assault, von Richthofen led five Albatros D.III scouts against six of a new type of British two-seaters that came over the lines in tight formation. It was No. 48 Squadron with the first operational

Germany's main weapon during Bloody April was the streamlined, twin-gunned Albatros D.III.

Bristol F2A Fighters under the command of Capt. William Leefe Robinson. After winning the Victoria Cross, Leefe Robinson was promoted and entrusted with command of this new unit of inexperienced flyers as reward for his 1916 victory over the *SL 11*, the first airship to be shot down over London. He received erroneous advice that the Bristol Fighter had weak wings and should be handled gently like a delicate reconnaissance plane. Richthofen and his flight pounced upon the Bristols as they cautiously flew their reconnaissance sortie toward Douai. Richthofen shot down the two rearmost aircraft in quick succession, bringing his personal score to 36 victories. His squadron mates picked off another two in the ensuing dogfights that splintered off from the initial attacks. Only two Bristols escaped. A bullet in his engine forced Leefe Robinson down. Taken prisoner, severe treatment during his internment by a relative of the late commander of the *SL 11* led to Leefe Robinson's death in 1918. Manfred von Richthofen went on to score a total of 21 victories during the month of April, becoming the new German ace of aces with a total of 52, one dozen more than the great ace Oswald Boelcke. Taking on the same qualities of his mentor

A Schutte-Lanz airship under construction showing framework around the hydrogen gas cells.

Boelcke by teaching as well as leading his squadron, Richthofen's *Jasta 11* accounted for 89 enemy aircraft for the month.

Bloody April

The first five days of Trenchard's air offensive cost 75 British aircraft downed in battle. Another 56 were so damaged they had to be written off. When the ground actions at Arras started on April 9, it only got worse. The British Third and First Armies attacked into the German Sixth and Seventeenth Armies. Trenchard pushed his fighter patrols deeper into the German lines to occupy the Jastas while pressing close low level infantry support and artillery cooperation near the front. After completing their artillery or photographic missions, aircraft strafed the trenches with machine guns and attempted infantry contact missions using Klaxon horns to respond to strips of cloth on the ground.

On April 16 the French launched their spring offensive in the Chemin des Dames, later known as the disastrous Nivelle Offensive. French air action there did little to relieve pressure on the RFC to the north. On the contrary, it may have given the

Rare aerial shot of a No. 41 Squadron F.E.8. Layout of typical pusher craft is clearly shown. Though pushers beat the Fokker Scourge, they were obsolete by Bloody April.

Germans ideas for further massing their fighting forces. Commandant Du Peuty, the new French chief of aviation at the front, drew together 150 pursuit planes of combat groups GC11, GC12, and GC13 into an army group reserve (GAR) for conducting fighter sweeps of twenty aircraft at a time. This left only a single pursuit squadron with each army for observation plane escorting. The German fighters, informed by their Flugmeldedienst system, avoided these grand fighter sweeps and only came out to protect their own balloon line. To deal with the large British fighter sweeps north of Douai, the Germans grouped *Jastas 3, 4, 11,* and *33* into a temporary Jagdgruppe.

Bloody April clearly marked the high point of German Jagdstaffel superiority and the low point for Allied aviation. It was the worst casualty rate in British aviation history. The British lost 50% of their force in casualties during the month, including 316 killed in action, equivalent to a yearly loss rate of

German aviators prepare to take off for an observation mission.

600 per cent. Some squadrons had lost 100 per cent of their original crews and aircraft. The average life expectancy of a British flyer at the front fell to a mere 93 hours of flight time, just 21 days of active service. The French lost 130 combat casualties and even more in accidents. On the other hand, German losses were extremely low. For example, German fighter units within the *Sixth Army* opposite Arras reported 176 British planes shot down while their own losses were twenty-one killed, four missing, and fifteen wounded. Together, German flyers claimed 368 enemy planes, the majority by the Jagdstaffel pilots, with Flieger Abteilung and Schutzstaffels shooting down 17, and 52 more were brought down by antiaircraft and ground fire. Though they began the campaign with a 2:3 numerical inferiority, they finished with a victory tally of 5:1. The Germans achieved these successes due to the technological superiority of their equipment, the experience and training of their pilots, and the straightforward structure of their organization. Increasing experience and ability to retain a high number of well-trained airmen resulted less from the growth of the German flying

The sleek S.E.5a's of No. 85 Squadron, RAF, at St. Omer, France. Squadron alumni include Canadian top ace Billy Bishop, American ace Elliott White Springs, and British top ace Mick Mannock.

schools as from the significantly longer survivability rate of the German airmen at this juncture of the war. To the contrary, the Allies lost so many airmen in so short a time that pilots were drawn into combat squadrons with less than seventeen hours flight time under their belts. But while the superior quality of men and machines provided the German air force with complete dominance of the air, they could not claim aerial supremacy over the battlefield itself. They did not have the superiority in numbers to carry the air war very far into enemy teitory and had not dominated both sides of the front lines. Only with superior numbers as well as superior quality could such dominance lead to complete control over the battlefield in future offensives.

Field Marshal Sir Douglas Haig, commander of the BEF in France, reasserted the need for new fighter designs to the War Office in May. He praised the RFC for providing information

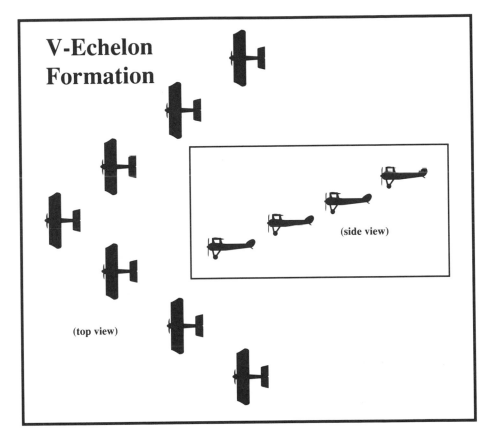

vital to the success of the artillery and infantry, and again emphasized the importance of superior fighters to check the appalling losses of corps aircraft and to destroy enemy planes. The first of this new generation of fighters had already reached the front in late April with No. 56 Squadron. Britain's premier ace, Albert Ball, was a flight leader in this new S.E.5 equipped unit. The S.E.5 was Britain's first twin gunned fighter, with one Vickers machine gun synchronized to fire through the propeller and one Lewis gun on a Foster mounting above the top wing to fire over the prop. The Lewis gun had less ammunition but a higher rate of fire than the Vickers, and could be slid back on its Foster mounting to fire up at the belly of enemy planes. The sliding Foster design also allowed for easy reloading of the 97 round Lewis ammunition drums. Albert Ball began racking up kills at the rate of two a day with his new plane, until the night of May 7 when he met Lothar von Richthofen, Manfred's younger brother, in the air. It was another of Ball's famous lone patrols at dusk after his day's work was through. An eyewitness described Ball's final battle:

> I thought that they wanted to stop the fight because of the darkness, but then both turned and rushed at each other as if they intended to ram. Lothar dipped under the other and then both turned and rushed at each other, only a few shots being fired. At the third frontal attack, Lothar came from the south and his opponent from the north. I waited. The machine guns peppered again. This time Lothar's opponent did not give way sideways, but dived down to the ground. I had wanted to see where the aircraft crashed.... I became anxious because Lothar also went down in a rather steep turn and disappeared in the mist.

Lothar's plane was damaged, but he made a successful forced landing within his own lines. Ball's plane was seen leaving the area, but then was spotted falling through the clouds in a spin. Britain's top ace with 44 victories died of injuries sustained in the crash. No one has ever determined the reason for Ball's losing control of his aircraft, but Lothar took credit for what he thought had been an enemy "triplane." The passing of Britain's greatest ace of that time represented the end of the "lone hunter" era in air fighting. Though some aces continued to periodically take on lone patrols, the great aces now had to become great flight leaders. Formation flying was not just the preferred tactic, but an imperative tactic for successful air fighting. The equipment which Ball brought to the front signaled the future return of British air might. The new S.E.5 and its more refined version, the S.E.5a, which followed immediately, brought British fighter technology closer to the state-of-the-art reached by the German Jastas.

The German High Command had other problems to worry about. On April 6, 1917, the United States declared war on Germany, joining the Allies in the Great War. American troops, resources, and industrial strength threatened to swell the Allied air effort and win the war. The Germans must grow their air force quickly enough to deal a blow that would finish off the Allies before America geared up to speed. On June 18, Kogenluft prepared the Amerikaprogramm detailing the requirements of the *Luftstreitkräfte*. The Amerikaprogramm called for: a dou-

Number of German Aircraft In Service by Class

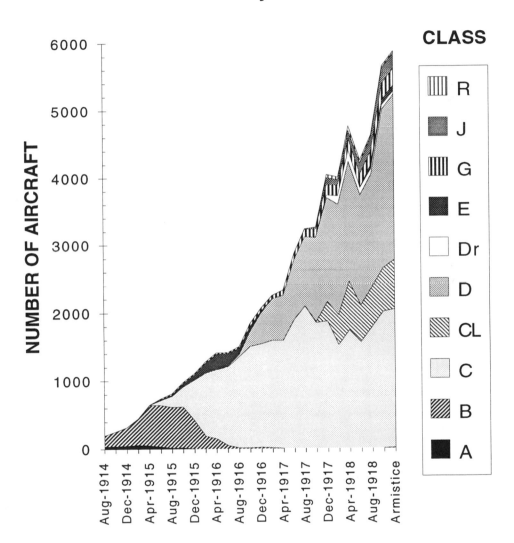

bling of fighters with 40 more Jagdstaffels, greater emphasis on artillery cooperation with an additional 17 Flieger Abteilungen (A), more flying schools and a special school for fighter formation experience, a doubling of the Hindenburgprogramm goals for industrial output to 2,000 aircraft per month and 2,500 aero-engines per month (four times the current German production rate), the release of skilled workers from the army to achieve these goals, and increased machine gun, fuel, and oil production. The German High Command also encouraged industry to continually develop new designs to keep abreast of the changing technology of military aviation.

The existing force reorganized as well. On June 23 von Hoeppner and Lieth-Thomsen created a new fighter formation, the Jagdgeschwader, by permanently grouping four Jastas together under the command of their newest national hero, Manfred von Richthofen. Richthofen's *JG I* (*Jagdgeschwader I*) included *Jastas 4, 6, 10*, and his own unit *Jasta 11*. The Jagdgeschwader provided a highly mobile fighter force that could be spirited into a threatened area as reinforcements to retrieve control of the air. The Jagdgeschwader, with tents for temporary aircraft hangars, with railroad cars for rapid overnight movement, and with bright flamboyantly colored airplanes, could draw no more appropriate a title than the "flying circus." The reorganization also eliminated the Army airships, and Zeppelins *LZ 88*, *LZ 113*, and *LZ 120* transferred to the Navy Airship Division. Strategic bombing of England, therefore, fell to the Gotha aircraft of *Kagohl 3* and later to the giant Zeppelin Staaken R.VI planes of *Riesenflugzeug Abteilung 501*.

General Hugh Trenchard marshaled his airmen again during the summer of 1917 to support the British army's attacks around Ypres. Opening each battle, he again sent his fighters in to drive back German aircraft behind their own balloon line. Meanwhile, the corps squadrons serviced the British infantry and artillery. Pairs of fighters now escorted the corps observation planes more closely than in the spring, and one or more flights of fighters provided top cover, thus reducing losses. Direct ground attack by aircraft took on a much greater role in the summer of 1917. Beginning on May 11, the RFC introduced better coordination between the planes and ground forces. Waves of aircraft performed repetitive low level attacks on German infantry timed to remain just beyond the forward edge of the artillery barrage. As the barrage lifted and the infantry came "over-the-top" the planes returned to harass enemy strong points. The tighter plans and distinct roles for each wave prevented the many losses from friendly incoming artillery fire that plagued ground sorties in the past.

Weeks of continuous photographic observation by RFC corps planes preceded the June 7 assault south of Ypres on Messines Ridge. Five fighter squadrons were brought in to support the three normally assigned to the British Second Army conducting the assault, with peripheral support from RFC units in adjacent armies. Aircraft also flew above the lines in the days before the battle to mask the noise from the heavy Mark IV tanks moving up to their start lines. Then just three hours into June 7, over one million pounds of explosive mines detonated beneath the German front-line trenches, obliterating the face of the Messines Ridge. The British troops next advanced with the support of ground attack planes under cover of an RFC air superiority of 4:1. Trenchard focused on controlling the immediate battle area by providing ground support to the troops and keeping German planes out of the way. Fourteen aircraft crossed the lines at low altitude. Their mission: to strafe enemy airfields to suppress the Jasta, and interdict enemy troop movements and transport. One S.E.5a of No. 56 Squadron flew at 200 feet in the pre-dawn light and strafed the hangars and sheds of one German aerodrome, shot up a railroad engine and strafed its freight cars, scattered troops in the town of Wevelgem, and flew down the Menin road to strafe another German airfield. The other fighter squadrons protected their own corps planes and destroyed German artillery planes. For example, Raymond Collishaw and his Black Flight of Sopwith Triplanes from Naval 10 fought a 35 minute battle above Polygon Wood. Collishaw shot down three Albatros D.III's escorting a two-seater while his flight brought down the rest of the six plane formation. Collishaw claimed a further three sent down out of control, becoming the first pilot to claim six victories in one day. Such exceptional British actions kept the loss of British corps aircraft at the hands of the feared Jastas to

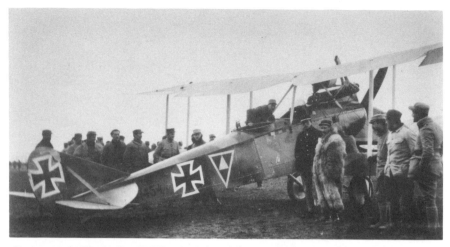

Germany's Rumpler C.IV, used for deep strategic reconnaissance. This one came down too far behind enemy lines. (NASM)

only three in the first week of fighting. Bloody April would not be repeated.

The Germans responded to Trenchard's activity in the battle-zone by calling in their own ground support aircraft: the Infanterieflieger and the Schustas. The Infanterieflieger were C-type aircraft, a flight of which was assigned to each infantry division since 1916, and were used to track the location of the front-line. They struggled to determine the extent of the Allied breakthrough and finally identified the new lines by nightfall. Signaling to the ground troops with colored pennants and reading the cloth strips laid out in return by the infantry, these planes kept the rear areas informed of action at the front by shuttling back and forth and dropping reports in message bags. The Allied advance was so rapid compared to earlier advances that Captain Wilberg, the Kofl for the German *4th Army*, introduced wireless to his Infanterieflieger units to maintain constant one-way radio communication with the rear. The Schustas, flights of C-type planes assigned to escort other C-type observation and artillery cooperation craft, were now coming down with the Infanterieflieger to strafe the British troops on the ground with machine guns and hand grenades. Losses mounted due to this dangerous tactic, indicating the

Sopwith Pup preserved at the Champlin Museum in Mesa, Arizona, carrying the white stripe of No. 66 Squadron, RFC. (**Author photo**)

need for specialized armored planes, but the effect on the ground troops was telling.

The RFC achieved complete aerial supremacy for the first weeks, but Trenchard's force soon became overtaxed. He called on unit commanders to conserve their flyers for the main offensive to follow. But the game just got tougher. First, Richthofen's *JG I* appeared on the scene. Then, two of his best squadrons were withdrawn to England following the sudden new German attacks on London by Gotha bombers. On June 13, Kommandeur Hauptmann Erich Brandenburg crossed the English Channel and attacked London with his formation of 17 twin-engined Gotha G.IV bombers of *Kagohl 3*. More raids followed, and the bombs and resulting fires killed 162 civilians and wounded another 432. The British populace was in an uproar, now that enemy aircraft as well as Zeppelins were bombing their capital. The well-known Pups of No. 66 Squadron and the S.E.5a's of No. 56 Squadron were specified to supplement the Home Defense as much because of their abilities as for their popular reputation which would calm hysterical British officials and citizens.

Both sides drew reinforcements for the next Ypres offensive. The British amassed over 800 planes and the Germans 600. Trenchard also received new aircraft types in the field, two squadrons receiving SPAD VII's, three with various Nieuports from the Nieuport 17 to the 27, three getting the De Havilland D.H.5 with its backward staggered wings, and all the Naval squadrons converting to the new Sopwith Camels armed with twin Vickers machine guns. The Germans at this time were re-equipping with a lighter faster Albatros called the D.V. And, planes were meeting in the skies in greater numbers. One battle involving 60 planes occurred on July 12 that lasted over an hour, and on the evening of July 26 the number of aircraft fighting above Polygon Wood reached 94. Patrolling by individual flights passed on to great patrols with several flights of aircraft tiered in different altitude bands.

The next phase of the British Ypres Offensive was scheduled for the end of July. Trenchard started his aerial campaign on July 11 with nightly bombing raids by the F.E.2d's of No. 100 Squadron. They bombed supply centers, railyards, and the aerodromes of von Richthofen's *JG I*. The ground action for the Third Battle of Ypres began July 31, but rain and dreary weather severely inhibited effective support by British aircraft. With clouds as low as 500 feet, the corps aircraft were unable to spot for their artillery units. After the skies started to clear the planes were too involved in ground attack duties. This left the artillery blind and unable to support the infantry. While the RFC fighters and corps observation planes conducted over a hundred strafing and light bombing sorties on the German troops beyond the front trenches, they misread the buildup of reserves and allowed the Germans to counterattack unexpectedly. Haig had to call off the offensive for a day to consolidate the ground gained and re-establish the artillery support. On August 9, the first clear day of the month, the D.H.5's of No. 41 Squadron made exceptional low level attacks along the 3rd Army front. They strafed the first German trench just before the infantry went over the top. Minutes later, F.E.2b's supported the attacking "Tommies" with infantry contact and ground attack work. The D.H.5 was well

The unusual back-staggered wings of the DeHavilland D.H.5 offered the pilot a good forward view and was used by four squadrons at Cambrai, France. The one shown was donated by the women of New South Wales for the Australian No. 68 Squadron.

suited to this assault support work, with excellent forward view and agile contour flying ability. It was less successful in aerial dogfights at higher altitudes, however, but held its own down near the trenches. In the next assault a week later, pairs of D.H.5's led the assault on each divisional front while a flight of D.H.5's stood watch above. In this way they cleared the way for their own ground cooperation aircraft and chased away German low level aircraft.

The air campaign continued through summer and into fall as the British forces drove toward Passchendaele. The number and intensity of battles in the air steadily increased as well as the complexity of ground support operations. The Allies had finally retrieved aerial supremacy with new equipment, tactics, and especially with the improvement in Allied pilot training. Allied losses had dropped each month since July while Allied victories increased. Even the great Manfred von Richthofen was shot down and wounded on July 6. While recovering in the hospital, and between photo-opportunities for the German press, von

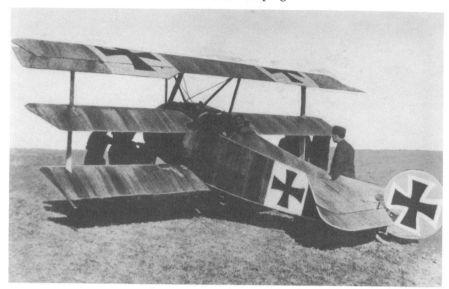

Fokker Dr. I. Triplane, favorite mount of German aces. **(NASM)**

Richthofen submitted a report lamenting the loss of Germany's technical edge, calling for another advance in aircraft design for the future. He pointed to the Sopwith Triplanes and Camels, the new SPAD XIII fighters, and the Bristol F2B two-seaters as superior to German aircraft of similar type. When he left the hospital, he was greeted by the plane of his dreams—one that would carry him to his destiny in the coming year—the Fokker Dr.I triplane.

By the fall of 1917, the German *Luftstreitkräfte* received its first examples of the next generation aircraft in several categories. For the fighters there were the Fokker Dr.I triplanes, one each given to the top aces Manfred von Richthofen and Werner Voss. Voss, leader of *Jasta 10* in Richthofen's circus and the second highest ranking ace at the time with 48 victories, who immediatedly took his new Fokker out to supplement his score. After much success with it, he discovered the limit of its wondrous maneuverability on September 23. On that day he single-handedly took on a flight of S.E.5a's from No. 56 Squadron, Britain's own squadron of aces. For ten minutes he looped and spun like a wildcat, damaging each of his opponent's aircraft with nearly no damage to his own plane. An Albatros D.V briefly came to his aid in an attempt to extract him from the fur ball, but was driven down out of control after a fierce melee. Britain's up and coming top ace James McCudden could not outfight Voss, and the rest of the S.E.5a's could not touch him, but his time was running out. Voss had almost made his get-away when, coming out of a cloud, he was pounced on by Arthur Rhys-Davids, who blasted the triplane with both his guns. Twenty year old Werner Voss, the most aerobatically skilled German flyer of the war, fell into a roll down to the ground. He was the nineteenth victory for 19-year-old ace Rhys-Davids, who himself would not live a month beyond his twentieth birthday.

German army cooperation Abteilungen also received a new generation of aircraft designs. While the Allies focused on how to improve the escorting of reconnaissance aircraft, the Germans were conceptually moving away from this by releasing the Schustas for other duties and trying a new approach based on the "Rubild" high altitude observation plane. Borrowing the "safety in height" theme generated by the Zeppelin campaign over London, as well as the engine that achieved this high altitude capability, the Rumpler C.VI and C.VII entered service. The Rumpler C.VI used the Maybach MB4a high-compression high-altitude engine. It had a special carburetor to accommodate the thin air of upper altitudes and a half sized radiator for the cold temperatures and to conserve weight. To attain the greatest heights, pilots left behind all weapons and ammunition and even the observer. With a ceiling of 23,944 feet the Rubild planes could photograph anything they could see without fear of Allied fighters reaching them.

For ground attack the German air service received two new classes of planes: the armored J-type two-seaters like the A.E.G. J.I and Junkers J.I to equip the Infanterieflieger unit, and the spry CL-types like the Halberstadt CL.II and the Hannover CL.II for the Schustas. The Junkers J.I was the first operational all-metal plane with a boxy metal tube framework and corrugated duraluminum skins covering the wings and tail surfaces. It flew low and slow, earning the name "the furniture van," but was well protected from ground fire by its 1/5 inch armor plate covering engine and crew compartments. It gave solace to the German infantry it flew over, and was a major frustration to

Allied fighters who often unsuccessfully tried to shoot it down. The Halberstadt and Hannover CL two-seaters went to the specialized Schutzstaffels (Schustas) and to those defense flights directly integrated within Flieger Abteilung (A). The Schustas were becoming so adept at ground attack themselves, however, that many of the thirty Schustas became reorganized into a new battle flight called the Schlachtstaffel. The Schustas and Schlachtstas had a great affinity for supporting the infantry as closely as possible since many of the fliers in these squadrons were enlisted men who had previously served in the trenches.

The Battle of Cambrai that opened on November 20 proved to be a remarkable foretaste of the great battles to come both in terms of aviation and ground actions. Intended by the British to be a limited offensive, it soon developed into a surprisingly fluid combat of advances and reversals. British tanks attacked in mass coordinated actions cooperating closely with the infantry. None of the standard preliminary artillery bombardment was used in order to provide an additional element of surprise. Using bombs and machine guns, aircraft performed the counter battery suppression that the artillery normally performed. The D.H.5's of the newly arrived No. 64 Squadron attacked the German gun emplacements in Flesquieres at dawn, causing the total disruption of these batteries. Nine Sopwith Camels from squadrons No. 3 and No. 46 similarly strafed two other artillery batteries, while three other Camels shot up the Albatros D.V scouts on the ground at the *Jasta 5* aerodrome. The four squadrons assigned to these low level attacks flew repeated missions into the battle zone throughout the day, dropping 25 lb. Cooper bombs and strafing infantry. The losses were high for the single-seater squadrons, averaging 35% casualties per day over the first three days. As the tanks advanced and the RFC strafed, the German Kogenluft sent in *JG 1* and numerous Schlachtstas. On November 30, the German Stosstruppen divisions counterattacked using their latest infiltration techniques and combined arms support. The Schlachtstas dove into the enemy front lines at 50 feet, strafing the British troops directly ahead of the advancing Stosstruppen. Their machine gunning and dropping of stick grenades totally demoralized British troops while encouraging the German infantry. With unrelenting aggressive counterattacks by the "sturmtruppen" on the ground and the "sturmflieger" in the air, the first great tank battle was totally reversed. Cambrai remained securely in German hands. With new lessons learned and the air war cooling down into its routine winter activities, both sides prepared for the great conflicts expected with the spring thaw.

CONCLUSION

The year of 1917 opened with the balance of power in the air tilted strongly to the German *Luftstreitkräfte*. Though they were behind the Allies in total number of aircraft available, they were materially ahead with their technology, their pool of trained pilots, and the implementation of these advantages through organizational structure. The German air service excelled in the application of aerial tactics developed by masters of their trade. Their numerical inferiority was more than masked by their ability to concentrate forces in critical areas. The development of massed fighter groups achieved localized aerial superiority when needed. In general, however, the German army was on the defensive during 1917, conserving its strength for the great drive to finish the war in the spring of 1918. The *Luftstreitkräfte* initiated the Amerikaprogramm and prepared the way to support their army.

The French air arm similarly took a non-aggressive stance after the disastrous Nivelle Offensive and the resulting mutinies. It undertook no major advances in the air campaign during 1917. The French used the year to prepare for the coming actions of 1918 by searching for the best equipment and struggling to get their force in order. The pusher planes of the past were withdrawn in preference for the newer army cooperation designs. Continued reorganizations inhibited the growth somewhat, but improvements were made in training and concentration of fighter groups. Again like the Germans, France stimulated its aircraft industry to rethink its preference for certain models and to increase production of the most militarily promising planes.

Above all, 1917 was the year of ascendancy for the British RFC. The RFC started 1917 with 717 aircraft in 39 squadrons and

Squadron Commander E.H. Dunning, RNAS, lands Sopwith Pup on HMS **Furious** *on August 2, 1917.*

closed the year with 997 planes in 54 squadrons. After experiencing its worst month of the war in April, British air power grew both in number and quality of its aircraft and crews to become the leader among the major combatants. Its horrific shortage of trained manpower was rectified by the time of the summer offensives around Ypres. Britain also introduced superior new aircraft designs like the Bristol F2B, D.H.4, S.E.5a, and the Sopwith Camel that propelled the RFC to aerial domination in the coming year. Trenchard's unrelenting drive to attack regardless of losses carried the RFC to the forefront, but at a terrible human cost.

Organizational Terminology of Air Services

Number of Planes	British	American	French	German
6 or less	Flight	Flight		Kette
6 to 18	Squadron	Squadron	Escadrille	Staffel & Abteilung
20 to 80		Group	Groupe	Geschwader
90 to 300	Wing	Wing	Escadre	Stofl
200 to 400	Brigade		Groupement	Kofl
650			Division Aérienne	
1000 to 4000	RAF	USAS	Aéronautique Militaire	Luftstreitkräfte

Fixed Synchronized Machine Guns

Vickers Mk. I*

Made in Britain   Caliber: 0.303in   Rate of Fire: 500rds/min
Ammo Supply: belt feed   Date Introduced: 1915   WeightL 28.5lb air-cooled

The Vickers gun, originally designed by American Hiram Maxim in 1884, was the standard infantry machine gun of the British Army through two World Wars. The water cooling jacket of the 1912 model was replaced by a louvered air cooled jacket to lighten it for aerial use in 1915. First used unsynchronized on some pusher planes like the D.H.2 and F.E.8, it was soon synchronized in late March 1916 for tractor aircraft. In this form, the Mk. I* became the standard fixed weapon of all Allied air services. French and British synchronizing gears were successfully employed on the Vickers, but all slowed the rate of fire markedly until the Constantiesco gear came on line. Lt. Cdr. George Hazelton's "muzzle-booster" sped the Vickers rate of fire from its standard 500 rds/min to a rate of 850 rds/min. Colt manufactured Vickers gun models in America for 0.30in ammunition, for 11mm anti-balloon ammunition, and some with a breech spring that sped the fire rate to 1,000 rds/min.

Spandau LMG 08/15

Made in Germany   Caliber: 7.92mm   Rate of Fire: 450rds/min
Ammo Supply: belt feed   Date Introduced: 1915   Weight: 13kg

The standard German army machine gun was the water cooled MG 08 designed by American inventor Hiram Maxim. The MG 08 was used without water with the first synchronizing gear in 1915 and 1916. A further lightened air cooled version, the LMG 08/15, manufactured by Königlich Gewehr und Munitionsfabrik in the Berlin suburb of Spandau, was introduced with the Albatros D.I in September 1916. This Spandau LMG 08/15 with the Fokker Zentralsteuerung synchronizer became the standard fixed weapon of German aircraft. It was usually mounted in pairs on fighter aircraft and singly for forward fire on observation craft.

Schwarzlose M 7/12 MG

Made in Austria-Hungary	Caliber: 8mm	Rate of Fire: 420rds/min
Ammo Supp;u: belt feed	Date Introduced: 1915	Weight: 13.2kg

The Schwarzlose Modell 7/12 used a "retarded blowback" sprung bolt recoil system. It had a shorter barrel and therefore shorter range than other fixed weapons. The water cooling jacket was emptied for aerial use, and eventually removed completely with the model M 16. In 1917 the M 16A with a spring and blow-back enhancer was sped up to 590 rounds per minute and later up to 890 rds/min, but Austrian synchronizing systems kept the rates of these guns while flying at 380 rds/min and 500 rds/min respectively. The Schwarzlose was the primary weapon for both fixed and flexible use on Austro-Hungarian aircraft.

Marlin Model 1917/18

Made in USA	Caliber: 0.30in	Rate of Fire: 650rds/min
Ammo Supply: belt feed	Date Introduced: 1917	Weight: 10kg

Produced by the Marlin-Rockwell Corporation (previously Marlin Firearms Company) in Connecticut, this was a gas actuated modification of the Colt model 1895. It was developed to alleviate America's dependence on foreign manufactured aerial guns. Marlin guns using the Constantinesco synchronizing gear were generally twin mounted on the U.S.-built DH-4 and the American flown SPAD XIII, SPAD XVI A2, Salmson 2A2, and Breguet 14B2. Twenty-two squadrons of the USAS were supplied with Marlin machine guns.

FLEXIBLE MOUNTED UNSYNCHRONIZED WEAPONS

Machine guns mounted on an aircraft where their firing arcs came nowhere near the spinning propeller didn't need to be synchronized. They could be moved freely on a "flexible" mounting to aim in any direction. They were usually a lighter weight type than the forward firing synchronized weapons and often used a magazine to hold ammunition rather than a long belt. They were first mounted in the observer's cockpit on pylons from which they could swivel. Ring mountings that revolved around the cockpit to give better fields of fire were developed by Schneider in Germany and by Étévé in France, but the ultimate ring mounting was the British designed Scarff mounting. The Scarff allowed one or two Lewis guns to easily be elevated, swiveled, and rotated around the gunner's cockpit. Unsynchronized guns were also mounted above the top wing of biplanes to fire forward over the top of a spinning propeller as on the Nieuport XI, Hansa-Brandenburg D.I, and S.E.5. Clever systems like the Foster mounting were needed to slide the gun down to the pilot for reloading these overhead guns.

FLEXIBLE MOUNTED MACHINE GUNS

Lewis Mk. I

Made in Britain & Belgium	Caliber: 0.303in	Rate of Fire: 550rds/min
Ammo Supply: 47 round magazine	Date Introduced: 1915	Weight: 25.25lb

The Lewis, a gas recoil operated gun, was designed by American Lt. Isaac Lewis in 1911. It was made in Belgium and England as their standard light machine gun. The supreme unsynchronized aerial weapon of the war, it was used by all Allied air services and was even sought after by German scavengers. It was mounted over the top wing on fighters from the Nieuport 11 to the S.E.5a, and as single and later double yoked Scarff ring mountings for observers. In mid-1916 the 97 round magazine was introduced. Some synchronized Lewis guns were briefly used on the Sopwith Baby seaplane.

Parabellum IMG 14

Made in Germany	Caliber: 7.92mm	Rate of Fire: 700rds/min
Ammo Supply: belt in 250rd drum	Date Introduced: 1915	Weight: 9.5kg

Developed in Berlin by the Deutsche Waffen und Munitionsfabrik from Hiram Maxim's model 1908, the Parabellum became Germany's standard flexible weapon. It was air cooled and lightened for use on airships and aircraft. Some were synchronized for a time on the Fokker EI. The 250 round "trommel" drum to hold the belt more conveniently was introduced in 1916. A clumsy twin mounting arrangement was introduced in late 1918 to compete with the twin mounted Lewis guns.

Hotchkiss Modèle 1909

Made in France	Caliber: 8mm	Rate of Fire: 600rds/min
Ammo Supply: 25 round strip	Date Introduced: 1914	Weight: 12.25kg

Another gas operated light machine gun was produced by a French company founded by the American inventor Benjamin

Hotchkiss. It was developed from an Austrian concept by American engineer Laurence Benet in 1895. The French Army soon adopted it as their standard infantry automatic weapon. It used small strip clips which held up to 30 rounds, but a cumbersome 75 round "bobine" drum was later developed. Used by French observers through 1916 until better weapons became available, the Hotchkiss was the first machine gun to bring down an enemy plane and the first to be mounted fixed on a fighter aircraft.

Revelli Modello 1914

Made in Italy   Caliber: 6.5mm   Rate of Fire: 450rds/min
Ammo Supply: 50 cartridge box   Date Introduced: 1915   Weight: 17kg

Italy's own standard aircraft weapon was known as the Fiat-Revelli. It was air cooled with no water jacket. Its inventor Maggiore Abiel Betel Revelli later designed a special twin barreled sub-machine gun whose combined rate of fire was 2,400 rds/min! This gun was frequently carried by aircraft late in the war despite its low range and small ammunition capacity.

Colt-Browning 1895-1914

Made in USA   Caliber: 0.30in   Rate of Fire: 450rds/min
Ammo Supply: boxed or spooled belt Date Introduced: 1914   Weight: 15.87kg

The Colt-Browning, produced in Connecticut and New York before and during the war, was used extensively by the Russian Air Service. Although it vibrated severely and needed a bulky ammunition box and shell retrieval bag, it filled the gap when Russia needed to arm its aircraft. Russia also mounted their version of the Maxim model 1910 machine gun and the exceptional Danish designed Madsen model 1902 light machine gun on their planes.

Madsen 1902

Made in Russia Caliber: 7.62mm   Rate of Fire: 425rds/min
Ammo Supply: 25 or 40 rd magazine Date Introduced: 1915   Weight: 9.07kg

The Madsen was an exceptional light machine gun developed in Denmark and used extensively by the Russian air service during the Great War. One of the lightest automatic weapons, it used a curved magazine mounted on top of the gun. Although they frequently jammed, the Madsens were used on many Russian aircraft.

Around the World in 123 ...Kills

Godwin Brumowski (1889-1936) was Austria-Hungary's ace of aces with 35 victories. Six feet tall, with blond hair and blue eyes, always monocled, Brumowski was a striking sight. Born in Wadowice, Poland, son of a military man, Brumowski attended a military academy near Vienna and graduated in 1910. He was already a 1st Lieutenant with the artillery at the outbreak of World War I. In 1915 he transferred to *Flik 1* as an observer on the Russian Front. Brumowski's first victory came bombing a Russian military review, literally "raining bombs" on Tsar Nicholas II's parade! Brumowski became a pilot in the summer of 1916 and transferred to the Italian Front. Soon enough Brumowski was charged with commanding *Flik 41J* (April 1917). In August of 1917 Brumowski scored 12 confirmed victories in 19 days in conjunction with the 11th Battle of the Isonzo, mostly flying in a Hansa-Brandenburg D.I "star-strutter." His first victory in an Albatros D.III didn't come until August 19, 1917. In February of 1918 Brumowski barely survived a fierce dogfight with eight enemy aircraft, and managed to land his blazing craft safely. Shortly thereafter, in June 1918, Brumowski went on leave. His victory total stood at 35 confirmed victories. In October 1918 Brumowski was named commander of all fighter squadrons of the Austro-Hungarian Army of the Isonzo.

While a brave soldier and successful pilot, Brumowski had a difficult personality. Several flyers, including fellow ace Julius Arigi, transferred from his Flik because of clashes with him. When advised to apply for the Knight's Cross of the Military Order of Maria Theresa, Brumowski replied, "If I have earned this award by my service, then it should be cause enough for the Commander-in-chief to present it to me. It is not my duty to ask or

demand it." That was one award Brumowski never received. After the defeat of the Austro-Hungarian Empire and the end of the war, Brumowski retired to manage the family estate in Transylvania. Unhappy, bored with the routine, Brumowski left his wife and daughter and returned to Vienna and opened a flying school. Brumowski died in 1936 in a plane crash. His daughter said of her father: "He died ... young.... I can still remember him saying 'I will never become an old idiot.' ... he despised weaknesses, imperfections, stupidity.... He was ... either very much loved, or hated, and even considered crazy...."

Francesco Baracca (1888-1918) was Italy's ace of aces with 34 victories. Schooled in Florence, Baracca joined the military in 1907 and served in a cavalry regiment for 5 years. In 1912 Baracca entered flight training, flying Nieuports and Hanriots. In 1915, when Italy entered the war on the Allied side, Baracca was posted to the frontier (Udine), flying Nieuport 10's. By 1916 Baracca was flying a Nieuport Type 11 fighter, but still had no kills due to gun jams. With this new plane Baracca achieved his first kill in April 1916, taking down an Austrian Aviatik. A year later in April 1917 Baracca received the Cross of the Officer of the Military Order of Savoia, and even better, a new and improved plane, the SPAD VII. Assuming command of the 91a Squadriglia at the front at Istrana, Baracca stepped up his pace of victories even as Italy suffered through the disastrous defeat at Caporetto in late 1917. In March 1918 Baracca received Italy's highest honor, the Medaglia d'Oro al Valore Militare.

Baracca continued to fly his single gun SPAD VII through 1918 even when his Squadriglia had the new twin gun SPAD XIII. He felt his light and familiar mount could climb and turn better with one gun than the heavier new SPADs with their extra firepower.

Baracca was a bit of a dandy, and fit the stereotype of the Italian flyer painted by an anonymous Red Cross worker: "...most daring bastards in the world...crazy for the girls, the vino...grand in their uniforms, and scented like a Kansas City whore." Baracca painted an idyllic picture of life: "...they are transferring us from this beautiful place...we live in a very fine villa, just three kilometers from our airfield, where we are taken by car in the morning and back here at noon for lunch...I have my own horse and began riding with great pleasure...." Typically, Baracca chose the griffin, a lion with a hawk's head, the symbol of boldness and ferocity, as his unit's insignia.

Baracca took off on his last mission on June 18, 1918. A search party eventually located Baracca's burnt SPAD, Baracca's body nearby, one bullet hole through the head. Baracca's last flight remains shrouded in mystery. Undoubtedly, Baracca's motto was proved true once again: "Provided you are a good fighter, a single gun is just enough."

A.A. Kazakov (1891-1919) was Russia's ace of aces with 17 victories. A tall, balding man with a quiet and humble manner, Kazakov was not an average fighter pilot. Kazakov began the war in the cavalry and remained an avid horseman, taking his horse with him to every post throughout the war. In 1915 Kazakov designed and employed a grappling hook at the end of a long steel cable to bring down enemy aircraft. He rammed an Albatros with his wheels and undercarriage for his first victory. By 1917 Kazakov was in command of the No. 1 Fighter Group (composed of 4 squadrons), flying Morane-Saulnier Type N and Nieuports. The squadron's planes were painted with skull and crossbones, and referred to as the "Death's Head" squadron. By the end of 1917 his unit dissolved due to the Russian Revolution. Kazakov joined up with the British in 1918, and commanded the No. 1 Squadron against the Soviet Red Army during the Russian Civil War, with the rank of Major in the RAF.

In August 1919, despondent over the British withdrawal from Russia, Kazakov committed suicide. According to an eyewitness account: "Kazakov's behavior was peculiar....The machine took off, and Kazakov made no attempt to gain height then, suddenly, he pulled her up in a sharp climb ... and then dived vertically into the center of the aerodrome." Kazakov was killed instantly.

Willy Coppens (1892-present) was Belgium's ace of aces with 37 victories. A short, colorless fellow, Coppens served with the 3rd Battalion before joining the air arm in September 1915. He then went to Britain for two months of flight training, paid for out of his own pocket. Coppens also trained for several months on Maurice Farman F13's and F14's. He joined the 6th Escadrille of the Belgian Aviation Service in July 1916, flying B.E.2c and Farman reconnaissance missions.

Following "Bloody April" he flew the squadron's new Sopwith 1½ Strutter into a gallant air battle with four enemy fighters and got his first mention in dispatches. Having shown the initiative to be a "Chase Pilot" Coppens joined Fighter Escadrille No. 1 at the front in July 1917 flying Nieuports and later the nimble Hanriot HD 1. He painted his single gunned Hanriot pale blue and flew three-plane patrols with his squadron mates. Finally in April 1918 Coppens brought down his first confirmed kill, a German fighter. In May 1918 Coppens devised a strategy to take down German observation balloons with incendiary bullets. He flew through the hurricane of antiaircraft fire to within 150 feet of the target and unleashed four incendiary bullets, setting the balloon ablaze. He skillfully conserved these precious incendiaries because the Belgium Air Service received only a handful from their French suppliers. Coppens himself was allocated a mere 20 rounds of the "magic bullets" each month. His squadron also received one 11mm Vickers gun for balloon busting, and Coppens proudly used the Hanriot equipped with this gun as his own second plane. On one mission, he flew in close to the balloon, made a diving attack, and turned back for another pass. The balloon's ground crew was rapidly hauling it downward, and when Coppens came in for another pass he miscalculated the balloon's rate of descent. Coppens plane hit the top of the balloon, his wheels pressing into the leaking gas bag. For a moment it appeared that Coppens landed on the balloon, but luckily he was able to coax his plane to drop off the sausage with-

out becoming entangled in its cables. In only five months Coppens took down 28 balloons, becoming the world's most famous balloon buster.

The Germans so detested the brash Belgian that they set a trap for him with a balloon manned only by explosives. Coppens foiled their plan by sneaking up and flaming the balloon before it had even risen to its full height! Destroying German kite-balloons was like putting on a performance for the troops in the trenches, and Coppens often closed his act with a loop just above No-Man's-Land. He judged his successes not by his official commendations but by the number of Belgian helmets tossed into the air by cheering Belgian infantrymen.

On October 14, 1918, Coppens hunted his last kill. Coppens' plane was hit by anti-aircraft fire, and a piece of shrapnel tore through his leg. He managed to crash land and survived, barely. Coppens' leg was amputated, and he suffered through months of agony in the hospital and at home. After the war he traveled throughout the world promoting the advancement of air power and commemorating the first great flyers. Never much admiring the brass hats that ran the military, Coppens bitterly regretted the actions of the Belgian Air Force in the Second World War. He criticized the policy makers for allowing such complete capitulation at the start of the Second World War in place of the tenacious struggles that exemplified the First World War. Willy de Houthulst Coppens remains one of the longest living heroes of the Great War.

Formation Flying

Formation flying was a key component of aerial fighting in the Great War in the air, but its development did not come until the second year of battle. Through 1914 and most of 1915, planes flew mostly individual missions. Only the bombers found it important to fly in groups since they were only effective in large massive attacks. These bombing groups still did not maintain any planned flying formation; the only requirement was that each plane arrive at the same target at about the same time.

The first organized formation flying developed as a defensive measure against the Fokker Scourge in the fall of 1915. Maurice Farman pushers of Escadrille MF25 under Captain Maurice Happe began flying in a V pattern to provide mutual machine gun fire support against attacking Germans. Known as the "Vee" or "Vic" formation, it became the most popular flying pattern. By 1916, escorting of the working two-seater by an armed aircraft became standard doctrine. Boelcke began grouping fighters in larger formations of about six planes and Richthofen used the "V-echelon" formation for his hunting patrols.

The V-echelon stepped the planes in three dimensions with the leader in the front and lowest position, followed by the others in two rows slanted upward, back, and outward. Rookies generally flew in the last position that was the highest and furthest to the rear. In this location the rookies could do the least damage if they could not hold formation well, and could have the best view to learn what the others were doing. It also was the most dangerous position, as enemy fighters tried to pick off the stragglers of a formation.

The group would fly at ¾ of their top speed so that a flight member could zoom up in front of the leader to bring attention to something he may have spotted that the leader did not. Formation flying was not an easy matter with the aircraft of the period. The throttle of First World War aircraft was not intended to control the speed of the plane as precisely as that of an automobile, so pilots pulled their control sticks to bounce their planes in short climbs and dives to modify their flight speed. Thus came the adage, "set the throttle for your altitude, use the stick to control your speed." The trickiness of the highly maneuverable Sopwith Camels and the Fokker triplanes required constant kicking of the rudder bar to twist the plane back into a relatively straight course. In this way the planes of the formation bounced and twisted along in their approximate assigned positions. It is a credit to all the flyers that there were so few collisions in the air with less than fifty yards between each plane of the formation.

Other formations served special purposes. A diamond formation of four planes was the best way to provide escort to a two-seater. Bombers often flew in single file line-astern to coordinate their bomb dropping attacks. Fighters sometimes flew in line-abreast or a single sloping echelon both to communicate better and to optimize their fields of fire in an attack. The British F.E.2d pushers, obsolete when facing a German 1917 era Jasta, adopted a unique defensive formation. When attacked, they rounded up the wagons into a circular pattern and fired at their attackers while rotating in merry-go-round fashion. This carousel of planes inched its way back to its lines while each plane covered its squadron mate's tail with mutually supporting fire.

Formations of five to seven planes became the optimum size for single flight formations. Any less was too small to defend and any more was too unwieldy to control. As the air fighting escalated later in the war, larger numbers of up to a hundred planes in combined formations often fought. In 1918 the RAF conducted multiple squadron fighter sweeps in a grand formation. An Army wing of the RAF typically included a couple of squadrons of Camels, S.E.5a's, and one Sopwith Dolphin squadron. These would rendezvous and patrol together with each squadron flying in tiers about 2,000 feet above and three miles behind its predecessor. Elliott White Springs described how this grand formation took advantage of the traits of each aircraft type. "The S.E.'s worked best at 15,000 feet, so they were to stay high up. The Camels were no good above 12,000. At 18,000 were the Dolphins.... That's where the Dolphins had the advantage. They were no good down low."

Lucky Charms

Pilots are a superstitious lot. Many believe in charms that safeguard them against bullets flying their way and other risks of flight. But a few brave souls ridicule such sentimental claptrap. Perhaps tempting fate, Max Immelmann wrote to his mother: "...So I am to always carry that leaf with me? If I did the same with every lucky flower, every bit of clover, etc. I should carry a small kitchen garden with me. And then, for the sake of fairness, I should have to take along all the rosaries, crucifixes and other talismans which have been sent to me ..." As it happened, that was Immelmann's last letter. He died three weeks later. Undoubtedly no charm could have saved him, but a mother is left to wonder.

THE FLYERS' GOOD LUCK PIECES

A. A. Kazakov: icon of St. Nicholas

Werner Voss: best tunic and a colored silk shirt to impress the girls in Paris if ever shot down!

Tab Pflaum: stuffed baby kangaroo, "Joey"

Eugene Bullard: pet monkey named Jimmy

Elliot White Springs: a bottle of gin & a bottle of milk of magnesia

Albert Ball: slice of Mom's plum cake

Jean Navarre: a woman's silk stocking

Eddie Rickenbacker: crucifix inside leather case, worn over heart

John MacGavock Grider: a piece of his first crash a stocking to tie over face

a Columbian half dollar
and that last sixpence

Most popular charms: horseshoes, cloth dolls, teddy bears

Ultimate lucky charm: garter from left leg of a virgin

As well, all good teams have their mascots—a focal point to cluster around, a pet to share what can't be spoken to another, and a symbol of the commaraderie of the whole group. Many men in flying squadrons cherished their mascots because they reminded them of home while their everyday lives were otherwise transformed by the realities of war. Other mascots were of the more exotic type. The Lafayette Escadrille kept two lion cubs dubbed Whiskey & Soda, Germany's *Jasta 2* sported a stork named Adolar and the RFC's 60 Squadron doted on a pet pig.

Letters Home

The letter home is a timeless classic of literature. During wartime it takes on a greater urgency, a deeper poignancy. While the "Dear John" letter is infamous, it is the everyday letters from sons to their mothers waiting at home that speak of the quiet heroism in the soul of a soldier. Not one of these letter writers survived the war.

From Oswald Boelcke's letters:

November 2, 1915: *...you need not imagine it is all much worse in reality. As long as one keeps one's head and judgment, my fast, nimble Fokker makes a fight in the air hardly more dangerous than a motor trip. So don't worry about me! Promise me that.*

October 19, 1916, last letter home: *...By the way, mother need not paint such a ghastly picture of the circumstances and dangers in which I live. She only need think of the extra experience and routine with which I go into action, quite apart from all our technical advantages in flying and shooting gear. I hope to spend at least a couple of days with you at Christmas.*

Oswald Boelcke died on October 28, 1916.

Frank Luke's last letter, written September 21, 1918:

Dear Mother:
I have not written for some days now on account of being so busy, as no doubt you have already heard. This is only a line to let you know that I am o.k. Now, Mother, remember that I have passed the dangerous stage of being a new hand at the game, so don't worry, for I now know how to take care of myself.
Love to all,
Frank

Frank Luke died on September 29, 1918.

From Mick Mannock's letters:

July 1917: *The journey to the trenches was rather nauseating— dead men's legs sticking through the sides with puttees and boots still on—bits of bones and skulls with the hair pulling off, and tons of equipment and clothing ly-*

ing about. *This sort of thing, together with the strong graveyard stench and the dead and mangled body of the pilot combined to upset me for days.*

June 16, 1918, last letter home:

Things are getting a bit intense just lately and I don't quite know how long my nerves will last out. I am rather old now, as airmen go, for fighting. Still, one hopes for the best. I hope Mother and Nora are getting along okay. These things are so horrible that occasionally I feel that life is not worth hanging on to myself, but "hope springs eternal in the human breast." I had thoughts of getting married, but...? I am supposed to be going on leave on the 19th of this month (if I live long enough) Cherrio...

Mick Mannock died on July 26, 1918.

Franz Pernet was the stepson of General Erich von Ludendorff, commander of the German Army. Ludendorff and his wife lost two sons, both flyers, in the First World War. Margarethe Ludendorff later recollected that "one of my favorite dreams (was) to see Ludendorff and my boys sitting around our table as officers. How differently everything turned out." From one of Franz's last letters:

Mother, you can't imagine what a heavenly feeling it is when all the day's fighting is successfully over, to lie in bed and say to oneself before going to sleep, "Thank God! you have another 12 hours to live.

Franz Pernet died on September 5, 1917, shot down over the English Channel.

From an undated letter of American ace David Putnam:

Mother, there is no question about the hereafter of men who give themselves in such a cause. If I am called upon to make it, I shall go with a grin of satisfaction and a smile.

Putnam died on September 12, 1918. He was 19 years old.

Manfred von Richthofen

Manfred von Richthofen (1892-1918) was a natural born killer. A skilled hunter, his mother wrote of him: "He wanted to conquer anew every day, at the risk of his own life. That was his nature.... He had the phenomenal eye and steady hand of my husband... when Manfred was just a boy.... the word 'hunt' fascinated him..." As a child, Richthofen hunted everything...from tame ducks to wild boar. But before long

Richthofen's favorite activity was bagging English machines.

Richthofen was the son of a military officer, and graduated cadet school (1909) and the War Academy in Danzig (1912). An excellent equestrian, he was promoted to lieutenant of cavalry in 1912 as well. At the outbreak of the First World War in 1914, Richthofen led his reconnaissance squad of Uhlan cavalry to the Silesian frontier to look for advancing Russians. He was surprised and outflanked by Cossacks, but managed to get his men back to their own lines. Richthofen's regiment then transferred to support the campaign in France. His mounted Uhlans served the reconnaissance function for von Below's *9th Infanterie Division* on the Western Front, but when the front solidified he found himself dismounted, stuck in the trenches with the *Fifth Army* near Verdun. The war looked bleak, hunkered down in a dugout, fighting boredom, and "promoted" to supply officer. Frustrated with his duties, Richthofen indignantly wrote in his bid to join the Flying Corps, "I didn't join the war to collect eggs and cheese." Whatever he wrote, it worked. In June 1915 Richthofen transferred to flying school in Saxony, in training to become an observer. Assigned to a bombing squadron in Poland, part of the old *Brieftauben-Abteilung Ostende (BAO)* that had been transferred to the Eastern front, Richthofen was happy to be involved with mobile warfare again. He crossed the changing front daily in an Albatros B.II and C.I. War spirited him and the *BAO* again to the Western Front where he flew in twin engined A.E.G. G.II bombers and saw his first Fokker Eindekker. Off on a patrol in an Aviatik C.I, Richthofen swung his Parabellum machine gun around on a French Farman and to his own surprise shot it down after 100 rounds. He never received credit for it, but this and a chance meeting with Oswald Boelcke stimulated his desire to fight the campaign in the air. As autumn leaves fell in 1915, von Richthofen obtained permission for pilot training. This experience with

all forms of aircraft missions and types proved valuable in the next phase of his flying career.

After a short course at Döberitz and three tries at the final examination, Richthofen received his pilot's certificate. Always close to his brother, Manfred urged Lothar von Richthofen at this time to follow him into the Fliegertruppe. While Lothar went off to train, Manfred arrived at the front in March 1916 in the midst of the Verdun offensive. Being posted to *Kasta 8* of *Kagohl II*, he piloted C-types and occasionally the unit's Fokker Eindekker. Like many an ambitious two-seater pilot, he fixed a jury-rigged machine gun above the top wing of his Albatros C.III and shot down a Nieuport scout (again unconfirmed). When Russia launched its Brusilov offensive in July, Manfred and the *KG II* were thrown into that fray. Luckily for Richthofen, this was exactly where Oswald Boelcke toured to collect flyers for his new Jagdstaffel. He again met his future mentor Oswald Boelcke on the front one day, and was soon called to join him at the Somme as a founding member of *Jasta 2*. Later, Richthofen commented, "All I became, I owe to Boelcke's schooling." Finally, in September 1916, Richthofen began his combat career on the Western Front, as a true fighter pilot in *Jasta Boelcke*, flying an Albatros D.I single-seat biplane. Richthofen painted sections of his fuselage red for identification in flight, and this color soon became his trademark. In January 1917, after his 16th confirmed victory, Richthofen was awarded the coveted Pour le Mérite, the "Blue Max," and given command of his own unit, *Jasta 11*. He immediately took on the attributes of his mentor by leading *Jasta 11* as a teacher of aerial tactics and promoter of aerial strategies. Richthofen was recognized for the advancement of formation and group tactics and his opinions received the acknowledgment of the high command as Boelcke's had. Richthofen considered "flying tricks while fighting" as "just reckless and useless." He taught that "Surprises can be avoided only when flying in close order. No machine should be allowed either to advance or keep back." Richthofen's fame and success climaxed during Bloody April 1917 when he scored 21 kills in the month and was promoted to Rittmeister. Airmen and ground troops on both sides of the trenches recognized his red Albatros D.III and Halberstadt D.II scouts. From this point on his name became known worldwide and his reputation struck fear in anyone who glimpsed his scarlet plane diving upon them.

The first Jagdgeschwader, *JG I*, formed under the command of von Richthofen in mid 1917 much the same way the first Jasta had formed under Boelcke one year earlier. Richthofen continued scoring victories wildly and passing along his new-found wisdom to all Jastas. He not only wrote detailed technical notes that were circulated through the military, but also published his memoirs in *Der rote Kampfflieger* which was an instant best-seller among civilians and flyers alike. His popularity and fame was used by the press and government to lift morale. Once Richthofen was shot down, a bullet grazed his scalp, and he nearly died in the crash. Unable to tolerate convalescence, Richthofen slipped away from the photo opportunities, returned to the front and flew with bandaged head. Said to be worth a whole division by the Kaiser, von Richthofen received the best equipment. He flew the first Fokker triplane at the front and tested the first Fokker D.VII before it was put into mass production based on his suggestion.

Richthofen and his group became known as the flying circus because it traveled by train to perform wherever its talents were needed and because each of the four Jastas took on a different bright color pattern for recognition in the air. The flying circus worked as interceptors and hunters of enemy planes by Richthofen's precepts and were never assigned to escort duty. Von Richthofen's Jastas scored the most victories and generated more aces than any unit in the German Air Service. From June, 1917 until November, 1918, the *Richthofen Flying Circus (JG I)* scored 644 victories with the loss of only 52 planes, an astonishing 12:1 ratio.

During the war von Richthofen scored 80 confirmed victories, more than any flyer of any nation in World War I. Whenever he shot down a victim he scavenged a piece of it as proof and kept a collection of all these trophies. Von Richthofen also awarded himself a silver goblet for each victory as a momento. Richthofen was proud of achieving the greatest number of victories, but sometimes downplayed his role, saying, "the decisive factor in victory is simple personal courage." Air war was a brutal contest, and even for the great Richthofen the thrill of the kill faded. "When I read my book, I smile at the insolence of it, I now no longer possess such an insolent spirit. It is not because I am afraid, though one day death may be hard on my heels; no, it's not that reason although I think enough about it.... I am in wretched spirits after every aerial battle.... When I set foot on the ground again at my airfield after a flight, I go to my quarters and do not want to see anyone or hear anything. I think of this war as it really is, not as people at home imagine, with a Hoorah! and a roar. It is very serious, very grim...." Just weeks later, on April 21, 1918, death caught up to the Red Combat Flyer.

CHAPTER VI

America Gears Up

He kept us out of war!
—Woodrow Wilson's 1916 Campaign Slogan

One of the actors that finally made their appearance in the air campaign in 1917 was the United States. The U.S. spent 1917 building its aviation forces and hoping to approach the state-of-the-art attained by the European powers. When they entered the war back on April 6, 1917, the U.S. Army Signal Corps Aviation Section fielded a mere seven squadrons scattered between the Philippines, the Panama Canal, and across the states. Its 142 planes were completely obsolete for the type of combat occurring in Europe. Congress appropriated a record $640 million funding for developing an aviation program that was expected to produce 22,625 aircraft and 44,000 aero-engines by mid 1918 to supply an estimated Aviation Section of 263 squadrons. These ambitious goals were never met, as corruption and waste eroded much of the effort. However, it did demonstrate a powerful acknowledgment of the vital necessity of air power in modern warfare.

The United States air services sorely needed modern aircraft, engines, and flyers. A mission to Europe led by Army Major Raynal Bolling including Colonel Billy Mitchell provided recommendations for what aircraft to build. This mission designated the French SPAD XIII, the British Bristol Fighter and the D.H.4, the Italian Caproni bomber, and the British Handley Page O/400 as the best combat aircraft in service. The Navy already selected American built Curtiss seaplanes that performed exceptionally well in British service. American aviation planners believed that production focusing first on trainers for American pilots and next on bombers would be the most advantageous to the Allied war effort. However, production difficulties ranging from improper blueprints to license disagreements, hampered the start of all these projects. The large bombers were slow to get moving at all, and General Pershing ordered that the fighters be bought directly from the Allies. The DH-4 was the only combat type to see notable manufacturing success. Production began in October 1917, at the Dayton-Wright Airplane Company in Ohio. It took six months before the first American DH-4 arrived in France at the Romorantin air depot, and another four months before a large enough quantity of planes of adequate quality could outfit squadrons at the front in July 1918. As a day bomber this design was excellent for 1917 and was conducive to multi-purpose army cooperation applications, but its airframe fell into obsolescence in 1918. Crew members were separated by a large pressurized fuel tank that engulfed the craft in flames when hit, engendering the nickname "Flaming Coffins." Had a greater level of foresight been instituted in the manufacturing of the American "D.H.4" it may have been easier to accommodate the rapidly changing qualities required for action on the Western Front.

American manufacturing did much better supplying the American air services and all of their Allies with a superior engine. A group of engineers, most notably Jesse Vincent of Packard Motor Co. and Elbert Hall of Hall-Scott Motor Co., sequestered themselves in the Willard Hotel in Washington, D.C., for 48 hours in May. They emerged with a complete design incorporating the best components from each of America's automobile and aero-engine manufacturers. Its modular layout allowed it to be built in various sizes from a V-four to V-twelve, but the twelve-cylinder version became the most desired. Called the "Liberty Engine," it generated 330 hp and was later boosted to 400 hp. It was light in weight relative to its performance, but contained duplication of many components like the ignition system. In this way, several wires, plugs, or even a magneto could be shot away in battle without seriously crippling the

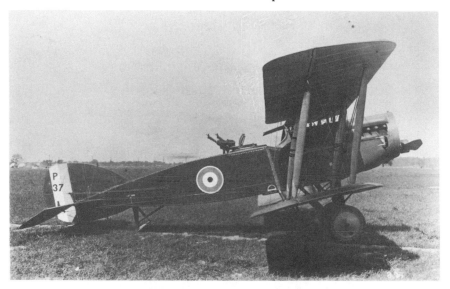

Prototype of a Liberty-8 powered Bristol Fighter. It did not meet U.S. Signal Corps expectations and was not put into production. **(NASM)**

plane. By August 1918 the sound of the 400 hp Liberty 12 could be heard over the Western Front in squadrons of American DH-4 and British D.H.9A.

The training of Americans for all these expected squadrons began immediately. With only three military flying schools in the States, America sought the help of all her new Allies in training her flyers while new schools were built and curriculums modernized at home. America rapidly made arrangements with Canada to share the training burden by establishing new schools in Texas and enlarging existing schools in Ontario for both nations' flight cadets. By placing emphasis on Ontario during the summer months and on Texas in the winter months the Allies achieved year round training facilities available nowhere else. After basic air training in the States, many cadets continued advanced training in England and Scotland. A group of over 300 young cadets trained in Italy under the tutelage of New York Congressman Major Fiorello La Guardia. La Guardia not only established a school in central Italy that provided flyers for both the Western and Italian fronts, but negotiated for both the American and Italian air services to obtain raw materials for

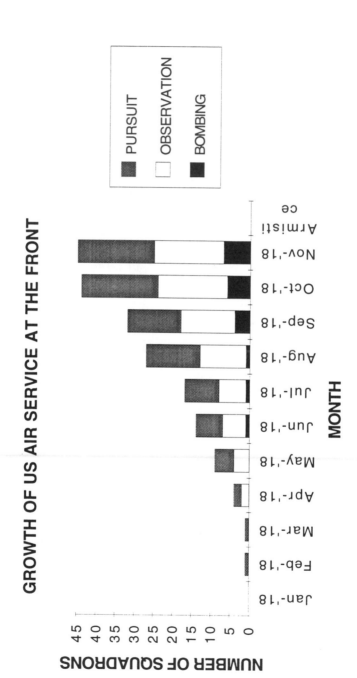

GROWTH OF US AIR SERVICE AT THE FRONT

better planes. The major sites for training American flyers were in France. Fifteen hundred American aviation cadets flooded into France starting in July of 1917, but there was not enough room in existing French schools to accept more than a few of them. They had to first build their own aviation centers. Cadets were stunned to find themselves digging ditches and sawing boards when they had signed up to fly. General Pershing, inspecting the Third Aviation Instruction Center at Issoudun, France, shared the same shock upon seeing his air cadets swinging pick-axes and shovels. Inquiring as to the purpose of this training camp, Pershing asked, "You mean INstruction, don't you, not CONstruction?" In November the Americans took over the Second Aviation Instruction Center at Tours for preliminary training from the French, but many French instructors remained until enough American instructors became available to replace them. The first center was a small administration in Paris, the third a large 1,500 plane school at Issoudun for fighter training. The Fourth Aviation Instruction Center for advanced training was at Avord; a school near the Michelin factory at Clermont-Ferrand was for bombing; and a half dozen other schools were built or expanded from French facilities for gunnery practice, observation, artillery, and balloon work. Air mechanics attended schools in France as well as England and were assigned to British and French squadrons pending the creation of American squadrons at the front.

Though American volunteer flyers came from all walks of life, the military felt that college students would be good candidates for a branch of service involving such complex modern technology as the airplane. The military began recruiting at colleges, starting with the Ivy League, with excellent results. The Navy had already established a reserve unit earlier in 1917 at Yale University where a seaplane club had existed since the pioneering era of flight. These young aviators were trained and shipped overseas to naval bases in Great Britain, France, and Italy for further training and service. Princeton University students formed an early detachment for the Army's air service. Most of the Princeton group sailed to England and was set up at Oxford University for basic flight training. Most of them, like Elliott White Springs and George Vaughn, continued to France as part

Whiskey and Soda, lion cub mascots of Escadrille Lafayette, N124.
(NASM)

of British squadrons upon completion of their training. Springs went to France in late spring 1918, with No. 85 Squadron flying S.E.5a's under the great Canadian ace Billy Bishop. Vaughn went to No. 84 Squadron commanded by Major William Sholto-Douglas, Canada's future Air Marshal in World War II. Both these young Americans, after learning from the best, became leaders of the American 148th and 17th Aero Squadrons and two of America's top aces (Springs had 16 victories and Vaughn 13 victories).

While young cadets trained in the new schools, a ready made pool of experienced American veterans already existed in the service of France as the Lafayette Flying Corps (LFC). This corps included three hundred Americans scattered throughout various French squadrons, one of which was the original Lafayette Escadrille. During the fall of 1917 each of these Lafayette Flying Corps members received physical examinations by American doctors. Some tension erupted when it was discovered that many of the most famous and most skilled members of this group failed their physicals. Apparently many of the long term Lafayette Escadrille veterans had rather debilitating conditions such as bad eyes, horrible hearing, and general poor physical profiles. Ultimately, General Pershing had to give special dispensations to allow them to join the American forces. As a result, the U.S. Air Service received a flood of qualified squadron commanders, flight leaders, and experienced aces. During the process of transferring the men from French service into the service of their homeland, all LFC members were temporarily drawn together in the old N124 "Escadrille Lafayette." Most of them eventually shipped out to fly in the air services of the U.S. Army or U.S. Navy. In February, the Lafayette Escadrille officially became the 103rd Aero Squadron of the USAS. The Lafayette pilots put their SPAD VII and SPAD XIII equipment to immediate use and began shooting down enemy planes again on March 11. Paul Baer scored that victory and collected another eight before he got shot down and captured in May.

While the Army's Aviation Section of the Signal Corps was building up, the U.S. Navy urged on its meager aviation force and put it to work. The U.S. Navy had 54 aircraft and even fewer pilots to fly them when America declared war on Germany, but immediately jumped into a rapid expansion program. The very first American aviation unit to arrive in Europe was the Navy's First Aeronautic Detachment, which landed in France on June 5, 1917, three months before any Army aviation units. The seven officers and 122 men came without any planes, but went right to work training, obtaining French seaplanes, and building bases at Dunkirk, Moutchic, and Le Croisic. The first operational sortie by an American squadron in France was by U.S. Naval personnel on November 18, 1917. Naval aviators with French-built Tellier T-3 flying boats began coastal patrols from Le Croisic on the Bay of Biscay near St. Nazaire. They scouted for German U-boats and escorted the vital convoys of American troop ships on the last leg of their trip across the Atlantic. The Marine Corps joined in by January 9, 1918, when the First Marine Aeronautic Company shipped out from Philadelphia to the Azores. Here they patrolled for and bombed submarines using Curtiss N-9 and Curtiss R-6 floatplanes.

American naval aviators were also attached to the British RNAS bases patrolling the North Sea in American built Curtiss H-12's. Ensign Stephen Potter was one of the flyers assigned to the RNAS base at Felixstowe for operational training on the North Sea. He is credited with the first aerial victory by a U.S.

The American built Curtiss H.12 flying boat used by the RNAS to hunt U-boats and Zeppelins.

naval aviator. On March 19, 1918, he copiloted a flying boat under the command of the Canadian flight leader Lt. Norman Magor. Potter's plane was towed across the North Sea on "lighters" to within range to reconnoiter the German High Seas Fleet anchorage. They took off from the sea and progressed across Heligoland Bight into Germany. Friedrichshafen two-seater floatplanes of the Imperial German Naval Air Service rose from Borkum Island and elsewhere to drive off the intruders. A fight erupted, and Ensign Potter crawled forward in his flying boat to operate the Lewis gun in the bow. In a running battle between the two seaplanes, Potter managed to critically hit the German and shoot him out of the sky. Potter scored the first victory by a U.S. naval aviator. Sadly, he was also one of the first naval air casualties just a month later. Potter's plane was shot down off the coast of Holland on April 25 when seven new Hansa-Brandenburg W.29 floatplanes under German ace Frie-drich Christiansen (21 victories) attacked his flight of five British Curtiss H.12 and Felixstowe F2A flying boats.

In organizing the business end of the U.S. Army's Air Service, General Pershing chose General Benjamin D. Foulois to be the Chief of the Air Service in November 1917. Foulois flew aboard the first reconnaissance mission for Pershing over the Mexican

Eugene Jacques Bullard (1894-1961), the first African-American fighter pilot. (Museum of Aviation, Robins AFB)

border back in 1916. Foulois divided his command between the Zone of the Interior to oversee training, supply, and technical duties, and the Zone of Advance that handled military operations. Colonel Bolling continued as part of the Joint Army and Navy Aircraft Committee to tour the front and learn how the Royal Flying Corps fought their war. Unfortunately he got too close to the action and his car was overrun after a shootout during the German March offensive at Amiens. Colonel Billy Mitchell was the aviation officer on Pershing's staff and became the Air Commander, Zone of Advance. As the newcomers on the block, the pickings for equipment were not good. The old combatants like France could only spare obsolete types and second string hand-me-downs. As trained crews graduated from the schools they were assigned to the front with these dangerously out-of-date aircraft. The 1st Aero Squadron was assigned to the front in April of 1918 flying the SPAD XI, a plane

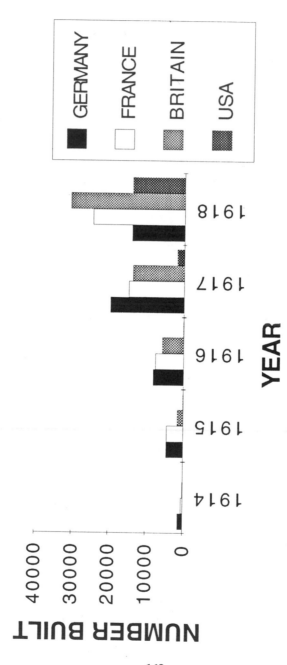

Aircraft Production

YEAR

(Includes Military, Seaplanes, and Trainers)

NUMBER BUILT

GERMANY
FRANCE
BRITAIN
USA

the French had retired from service. On April 7 the 1st Aero Squadron flew its first reconnaissance mission over enemy lines for the 26th U.S. "Yankee" Division. In May two more observation squadrons came into service: the 12th Aero Squadron flying antiquated A.R. II two-seaters and the 88th with its ancient Sopwith 1½ Strutters.

Of the fighter squadrons, the 94th Aero "Hat-in-the-Ring" Squadron and the 95th Aero "Kicking Mule" Squadron went to the front with the Nieuport 28. This Nieuport model was an acceptable fighter, but one that the French had rejected in favor of the superior SPAD XIII. The Nieuports of the 94th didn't even have any guns when they first reached the squadron in mid-March. Raoul Lufbery, past veteran of the Lafayette Escadrille and an ace with 17 confirmed victories, led the first patrol over enemy lines near Chalons-sur-Marne with fledgling flyers Eddie Rickenbacker and Doug Campbell in three unarmed Nieuports. Lufbery wanted to show his new flyers what to watch for at the front, and he apparently succeeded because both pilots became the first two new aces of the U.S. Air Service in the coming months. All the U.S. Air Service squadrons shifted to the quiet Toul front to replace French units that were drawn away to fight in the German spring offensive. There, the 94th borrowed enough machine guns from the 95th Aero Squadron to equip their planes with one gun each in place of the two they were designed for. Two planes of a Bavarian Jasta flew overhead to check out the new American arrivals on April 14. Doug Campbell and Alan Winslow lept to their Nieuport 28's and took off after them. In a brief battle above the aerodrome, each American shot down a plane, the first victories by American trained pilots of an American trained squadron.

CONCLUSION

America joined the war in 1917 with less of an air force than the European nations had in 1914. Both Americans and Europeans viewed American industry as the answer to the Allied supply problems. They set up grandiose plans and expected to fill the skies with American air power within a year and end the war in 1919. None of these plans could be achieved. In reality,

AIR SERVICE SECTORS

American air services had to accept what they could buy from their Allies and learn how to use their new air strength on-the-job. The DH-4 and the Liberty engine were the only finished products to come out of America's gearing up for war. At the front, squadrons had to put up with obsolescent craft for 2½ months before better equipment was purchased. The disappointed Air Service scaled down its expectations and worked side-by-side with its Allies in the air while it struggled to grow in size and experience.

Eugene Bullard
"All Blood Runs Red"

In early November 1917, Eugene Bullard (1894-1961) was 9,000 feet above the trenches of Verdun. Looking down he scanned the same ground he had fought and almost died for the year before. Now in his sky blue SPAD VII, Bullard rose to new heights. He had painted a bleeding heart and dagger on the side of his plane and above it his motto "All Blood Runs Red." His flying companion, a small rhesus monkey named Jimmy, stuffed in his flight suit was all that kept him warm from the frigid air. It had been a long patrol, and Bullard was alone in the sky, separated from his flight. Suddenly, tracer bullets sliced past his goggles. A Fokker triplane was hot on his tail. Bullard dove and sideslipped in the fight, unable to shake the triplane. Down several thousand feet he zoomed and got on the Fokker's tail. Finally a good shot splintered the struts and tore fabric off the tripe. The German pilot put his plane into a spin, belching smoke, and headed for his own lines. Bullard also pulled out of his power dive just above the German trenches, only to be riddled with machine gun fire from below. Dodging bullets at 75 feet, he managed to cross No-Man's-Land and make a rough landing near a French reserve trench. Eugene Bullard had triumphed over an enemy triplane, one of the first to appear at the front.

In the air Bullard controlled his own destiny. He became the first African American fighter pilot in spite of the racism of the era. However, Bullard's greatest struggles were not only with those who attempted to shoot him out of the sky, but with those whose prejudices tried to prevent him from ever rising into the sky.

The grandson of a slave, Eugene Jacques Bullard was born in Columbus, Georgia. He learned early the wretched intensity of prejudice when his father was chased from his home by a lynch mob. Bullard dreamed of a better life. His father told him that things might be different in a country called France. At the age of twelve Bullard crossed the Atlantic to find work in Great Britain. After numerous jobs as a laborer he joined a tour of professional boxers traveling to Paris. He found Paris to be everything he had imagined. "There never was any name-calling like 'Nigger' ... the French democracy influenced the minds of both white and black Americans there and helped us all to act like brothers.... It convinced me, too, that God really did create all men equal, and it was easy to live that way."

When the war broke out in 1914, Bullard volunteered for the French Foreign Legion on his twentieth birthday. Bullard fought gallantly with the Legion. His first action was at Frise in 1914, then trench warfare at Arras and the Somme in early 1915, hand to hand fighting in the Artois in May, and the Champagne Offensive in September 1915. Bullard believed in the ideal of the Foreign Legion—men of 54 nationalities from every race and religion working closely together for a common cause. His unit won the first fourragere, a coveted regimental award for group heroism of the Legion in battle.

Late in 1915, all Americans throughout the Foreign Legion transferred to a regiment of the regular French army. Bullard was then a machine gunner in the famous 170th Infantry, a group christened by the Germans as the "Swallows of Death." Bullard enjoyed referring to himself as the "Black Swallow of Death." The 170th was drawn into the hell of Verdun at its onset in February 1916. Defending the town of Vaux, Corporal Bullard saved the life of one panicked lieutenant and won the everlasting respect of his captain. Then at Fort Douaumont Bullard saved his squad when they were surrounded. Although he suffered a debilitating wound, Bullard was awarded the Medaille Militaire and Croix de Guerre, France's highest honors for bravery.

The crippling wound he received at Verdun exempted him from further service in the infantry, but Bullard would not let this hold him back. He wanted to fly as an aerial gunner, or maybe a pilot. After all, the great ace Charles Nungesser was just as crippled when he began to fly. Bullard transferred to the French Aviation Service in October 1916. When Bullard began aerial gunnery training he ran into his old Legionnaire friend Edmund Genet, now of the Lafayette Escadrille, who encouraged him to go for pilot training with other Americans through the Lafayette Flying Corps. This struck a chord in Gene Bullard, for not only would he learn to fly, but he would be the first black fighter pilot in history. He soon started training at the main French flying school at Avord. Being the highest ranking and most decorated of the American aviation students, he was in charge of the American aviators' barracks. His experience in war and knowledge of French proved valuable to all those who followed him. He earned his pilot's license in May of 1917.

Bullard did not get his flying assignment for several months due to the discrimination of Dr. Gros, the administrator in the Lafayette Flying Corps. However, Bullard's friends in the LFC pulled the right strings and he set off for the front carried on the shoulders of his cheering American comrades at the school. But racism continued to follow Bullard. Some fellow flyers named their pet dog, "Nigger." There were always the offhand, racist remarks—another flyer described Bullard saying, "The corporal is...as black as the ace of spades, but a mighty white fellow at that....men of old Southern families ...talk more like a darky than he does." Bullard's commanding officer welcomed Bullard and his pet monkey to the unit with the comment, "You are warmly welcomed to this group. And ...so is your son!"

In August of 1917, Bullard joined Escadrille N93 of Groupe de Combat 15 flying Nieuport XXIV's stationed near Verdun. After gaining experience in combat, Bullard transferred to Escadrille Spa85, another unit in GC 15 that was being re-equipped with the superior SPAD VII fighters. Bullard painted his personal motto "All Blood Runs Red" by the cockpit of his sky blue SPAD. He became a skilled flyer, attacked bombers, claimed victories over a triplane and a Pfalz D.III, and routinely patrolled with his group leader Victor Ménard and great aces like Armand Pinsard (27 victories).

When America started selecting LFC pilots for transfer to the new U.S. Air Service, Bullard anxiously awaited the call to serve his homeland, but it did not come. Instead, after a dispute with a French officer, Bullard was reassigned to demeaning supply duty with his old unit, the 170th Infantry. This rising fighter pilot and bemedalled hero, was thus prevented from being the first African American to fly for the U.S. Air Service.

After the war's end Bullard stayed in France, married, and fathered three children. He worked as a boxer, a musician, and eventually opened the successful Le Grand Duc nightclub. All the great writers, adventurers, and entertainers of the roaring 20's patronized his world famous Parisian night club. When Nazi infiltrators met in his club, he kept close tabs on them for French Intelligence. In 1940 when the Nazis rolled toward Paris, Bullard tried to join his old regiment, but was virtually ordered by hs old commander to head home for America. Arriving penniless in New York City, he lived in Harlem and worked at any job he could get—security guard, longshoreman, salesman, and elevator operator—not quite the jobs one might expect for a fighter pilot and honored hero, but the ony kind available to a black veteran. As unrecognized as he was in his own homeland, Bullard was greatly honored whenever French dignitaries came to New York. Bullard dined with General Charles de Gaulle, president of the French Republic, in New York in 1960 and was installed a Knight of the Legion of Honor of France. Bullard died of cancer just one year later. Thirty years later, in 1992, Bullard was finally honored as the first African American fighter pilot with a display in America's National Air and Space Museum. Back in 1961, Eugene Bullard, an American hero, was buried with the full military honors of France.

Billy Mitchell

Billy Mitchell (1879-1936) was born in France, the first of ten children born of the powerful and wealthy John Mitchell. On returning to their home in Wisconsin, John Mitchell was elected to the Senate. Billy, or "Willie" (his childhood nickname) grew up in Washington, D.C. In 1898, at age 18, in his third year of college, Mitchell bolted school to join the Army. He was promoted to 2nd Lieutenant within a week, the youngest officer in the service. He served in Cuba with the U.S. Signal Corps, then sailed to the Philippines, where he served under General Arthur MacArthur, Douglas' father. Then on to Alaska, where he scouted the territory for placing telegraph wires. In 1911 Mitchell, only 32 years old, was chosen for the General Staff. He wrote, "It is the most sought after position which a military man can aspire to.... It will be the greatest thing in my career so far...."

Mitchell soon showed what a superior politician he was. He made friends with Congressmen and Senators and wrote articles for newspapers promoting his views, including his air power theories. He saw the airplane as the instrument of future military strength and learned to fly in 1916. When promoted to a major, he took charge of the tiny aviation section of the Signal Corps and oversaw the creation of the 1st Aero Squadron.

As the fighting in Europe intensified, Mitchell kept a close eye on aerial developments. He set off for Europe to learn for himself the state-of-the-art in the air war, and supplemented the Bolling Commission in recommending how to overhaul the U.S. Air Service to meet the needs of modern war. He scoured the front lines to learn first hand what the air war was like. In May of 1917 he persuaded Major General Hugh Trenchard of the RFC to spend three days with him to show him every aspect of RFC operations. He learned Trenchard's handling of combat operations as well as the system of supply, the repair of equipment, and allotment of stores. Trenchard was impressed by Mitchell's intensity and strong mindedness saying, "He's a man after my own heart, ... If only he can break his habit of trying to convert opponents by killing them, he'll go far."

Colonel William Mitchell organized aviation in the Zone of Advance. He coordinated the squadrons that advanced from training for service at the front. In June Colonel Mitchell became Chief of Air Service for I Corps and moved his first pursuit and observation groups to the Chateau Thierry area. While his squadrons remained under operational directives of the French Army, Mitchell developed strategies for them that proved most valuable in future offensives. After the successes at Chateau Thierry, General Pershing promoted Mitchell to Brigadier General and made him Chief of Air Service for the First U.S. Army. Now it was Mitchell's turn to take overall command of aerial forces, and he orchestrated 1500 American, French, British, and Italian aircraft for the St. Mihiel offensive. Again in the great Meuse-Argonne offensive, Mitchell took interest in every aspect of the operation, introducing clever methods of concealment for the move, specifying the tactical makeup of patrols, supporting anti-balloon techniques, and pressing forward the use of tactical bombardment. As the air service grew under Mitchell's command, Pershing appointed him operational chief of the American Army Air Corps in October.

Billy Mitchell was famous for his lone patrols over the front to get a clearer picture and a better taste of the action. At Chateau Thierry he scouted the crossing of the Marne at night by German Stosstruppen. With his trusted assistant, the French Major Armengaud in the back seat of his SPAD XVI, he reconnoitered the St. Mihiel salient and detected information vital to the operation's success. In the Argonne offensive, Mitchell's personal observations averted a potential disaster, and his command of the squadrons ensured victory in the air as well as the ground.

After the Armistice, Mitchell continued to promote the importance of airpower. Serving as Assistant Chief of the Army Air Service, Mitchell struggled to prevent the dismantling of the Air Service that he built. He strongly urged the development of long range bombing units. To demonstrate the capabilities of aerial bombing, he obtained permission in 1921 to sink the battleship *Ostfriesland*, a German dreadnought that the U.S. received as reparations. After several waves of bombers attacked it, the unsinkable battleship capsized and sunk. American authorities denigrated and minimized the importance of this feat, but Japanese military observers present grasped the possibilities and took the lesson home with them.

Mitchell's popularity with the public and fellow airmen rose while his relationship with his superiors dwindled. He made political enemies by exposing the cartel of aircraft manufacturers that absorbed millions of dollars during the war to produce barely a handful of dangerous obsolescent flaming coffins for his flyers. He also envisioned the aerial revolution and crusaded for a separate Air Force, modern aircraft carriers, and better air defense of obscure places like Pearl Harbor. In 1925, Mitchell wrote, "A country should have the necessary air forces always ready at the outbreak of war, because this is the first of our arms that will enter into combat, and it is upon a favorable air decision that the whole fate of a war may depend." He also predicted that, "If a nation ambitious for universal conquest gets off to a flying start in a war of the future it may be able to control the whole world more easily than a nation has controlled a continent in the past." For civilian aviation he proposed commercial airline safety standards, and he fought for parachutes for military flyers.

Mitchell criticized the U.S. Navy for the handling of its airship fleet. After the airship *Shenandoah* crashed, killing 14 crewmen , he publicly accused the Navy of "incompetency, criminal negligence, and almost treasonable" failure to prevent the deaths of airship crewmen. In 1925 he was court-martialed and discharged from service. Numerous proponents of aviation, including Fiorello La Guardia and Eddie Rickenbacker, came to his defense and spoke in support of Mitchell's views, but to no avail. Mitchell died a decade later.

The Second World War began just a few years after Mitchell's death. Everything that Mitchell predicted—the rise of Japan, the vulnerability of Pearl Harbor, and the Battle of Britain—came to pass. A new generation of aviators recognized Mitchell's accomplishments, applied his lessons in combat, won the war, and fought to continue his dream with the establishment of an independent Air Force. These men strove to clear Mitchell's name and even sought the Congressional Medal of Honor for him. Though they were not completely successful, the United States Congress did award Colonel William Mitchell a "Special Medal" for honor as the Father of the U.S. Air Force.

Fiorello La Guardia

Fiorello La Guardia (1882-1947) was born in 1882 in New York City, but raised in the Territory of Arizona, son of an Army bandmaster. Before attending law school, La Guardia worked in the American consulate in Austria-Hungary and as an interpreter on Ellis Island. Always on the side of the underdog, La Guardia won his Manhattan district Congressional seat running on the Progressive/Republican ticket against the corrupt Democratic Tammany Hall political machine in 1916. The first Italian-American Congressman, La Guardia immediately signed up for the Air Service when America entered the First World War in 1917. La Guardia learned to fly before the war with aviation pioneer Guiseppe Bellanca, and dreamed of serving his nation as a bomber pilot. Despite his enthusiasm for the air war, La Guardia was realistic about its impact. He testified before a Congressional committee "...about this war being won with the airplane...this war will be won in a much more cruel and less spectacular fashion...." In October 1917 the short yet rotund "Flying Congressman" led 300 flying cadets across the ocean to Foggia, Italy, the town of his own father's birth, for training. As American aviator Josiah Rowe described it, "Foggia—the backyard of civilization... very, very old and very, very dirty and the people are very, very poor." Here Italian aces who couldn't speak English taught the American airmen how to fly. During training La Guardia crash landed, resulting in a lifelong spinal injury. La Guardia readied half of the American aviation cadets to join squadrons on the Western Front while the rest stayed with him in Italy to serve in Italian bombing squadrons. Never a great pilot, La Guardia nonetheless was determined to see duty flying bombers on the Italian Front. When ordered to serve as a staff officer, La Guardia complained, "I don't want to be a Brass Hat!" Soon enough La Guardia got his way, and the order was rescinded. He participated in several bombing raids over the Alps and across the Adriatic to Trieste, flying Caproni Ca3 and Ca5 bombers. He often came under intense enemy fire, returning after one night raid with 200 bullet holes in his plane. He named his bomber "The Congressional Limited" and his distinguished copilots included the Italian ace Federico Zapelloni and the parliamentary minister Cambiaso Negrotto. La Guardia's colleagues recalled, "He was never a really finished pilot—but, boy, how he loved to try! He flew by main strength and awkwardness ....The Italians loved him for his guts. He proved he had 'em from the very beginning." La Guardia admitted to trouble with takeoffs and landings, but otherwise "I can fly the son of a gun okay." Nevertheless, on August 5, 1918, La Guardia was promoted to Major, his favorite appellation for the rest of his life.

La Guardia always lobbied on the side of the underdog: for "big, well-balanced, American meals" for his men in Italy, condom distribution to those on leave, and always for better, more, and safer planes. On October 28, 1918, La Guardia, the soldier-congressman, sailed for home to fight for reelection. La

Guardia received the Italian Croce di Guerra and Commendatore military honors. La Guardia served in the United States Congress until 1933. He championed women's suffrage and public housing, and opposed Prohibition. He risked his political reputation to testify on behalf of Billy Mitchell at his sensational court-martial trial for insubordination. La Guardia was also instrumental in supporting the role of pilots, that they be treated as a captain of a ship rather than truck drivers or chauffeurs. La Guardia went on to serve as Mayor of New York City from 1933 through 1945. His crowning achievement as Mayor was the development of two of the world's biggest, and busiest, airports. Known as "Fiorello's Folly" until it opened, La Guardia Airport immediately became the world's busiest. So La Guardia started work on Idlewild (now known as JFK International). Fiorello La Guardia died in 1947, a year before Idlewild opened. America lost a tireless advocate for aviation, and the common man.

Sky Writers

William Faulkner thoroughly enjoyed his reputation as a World War I fighter pilot. He wrote: "I took up a rotary-motored Spad with a crock of Bourbon in the cockpit, gave diligent attention to both, and executed ... an Immelmann or two, and part of what could easily have turned out to be a nearly perfect loop." He also broke his nose "landing upside down" and suffered injuries from crashing his Camel through the top

of a hangar. Too bad none of it was true. This 5'1" writing master actually volunteered for the RFC and traveled to Canada for training. But he never even finished ground school before the armistice ended the war. It's doubtful that he ever was up in a plane at the time, much less piloted one. But that didn't stop Faulkner from pretending. And no doubt the experience of almost being a war hero inspired the author of *As I Lay Dying* and *The Sound and the Fury*. Even though the lifelong limp from war injuries and the British accent were fake!

Cole Porter was another famous writer guilty of impersonating an airman. The man who gave the world songs like *You're the Top* led the Yale Class of 1913 annual review to report that "Classmate Cole A. Porter has joined the American Aviation Forces in France." Nothing could be further from the truth. Porter sailed to Europe with a zither on his back and spent the war years living and partying at elegant homes in Paris. Despite Porter's tales to the contrary, he never served in the French Foreign Legion, the French Army, or the American Air Corps. He did write some great songs, though—*Night and Day, I Get a Kick Out of You*, and, of course, *Begin the Beguine!*

As for the true heroes of the sky, practically every well-known ace published a personal narrative (see Guide for the Interested Reader). Only a few flyers, however, went on to make writing their career after the war. Remarkably, some First World War sky heroes turned out to be even better sky writers.

Elliot White Springs was a 21 year old, hard-drinking heir to the Springmaid cotton mill fortune when he left Princeton University to be a fighter pilot. He joined the U.S. Air Service in 1917, trained under Billy Bishop in a British squadron, and finally commanded the U.S. 148th Aero Squadron. He returned to America with 16 kills and a dead friend's diary. Springs edited John Grider's words into the runaway bestseller *War Birds*, a heartrending and plainspoken account of the eve-

ryday life of a combat flyer. Inspired by this success, Springs later wrote other books about flying: *Above the Bright Blue Sky, Nocturne Militaire*, and *Contact*. He also wrote some trashy novels about flappers and the roaring 1920s: *Leave Me with a Smile, In the Cool of the Evening*. None approached the level of success or quality of *War Birds*.

Charles Nordhoff and **James Norman Hall** flew as *Falcons of France*. World adventurer Nordhoff advanced from driving ambulances to flying in the Lafayette Flying Corps. Hall flew in the Lafayette Escadrille and later transferred into the 94th "Hat in the Ring" squadron. Hall was shot down in 1918 and compiled his book *Flying with Chaucer* while a P.O.W. After the war, Nordhoff and Hall were reunited and wrote the enormous two volume official history of the Lafayette Flying Corps. Later they collaborated on the world acclaimed bestseller *Mutiny on the Bounty* and its sequels. After the team's successes, Hall continued to write novels while Nordhoff retired to a quiet island life writing children's books.

Arch Whitehouse, born in England and brought up in America, is one of the most prolific aviation writers from the Great War. He served in Bristol Fighters as a gunner-observer and later a pilot, scoring sixteen victories. After the war his writing career took him to Hollywood and the battlefields of World War II. His numerous histories on the First World War span the spectrum from *The Zeppelin Fighters* to *The Years of the Sky Kings, Legion of the Lafayette, Billy Mitchell*, and more.

Gabriele D'Annunzio, renowned Italian poet, promoted strategic uses of aviation and gained a position in the Italian military. While attached to Caproni bombing squadrons he organized grandiose raids against Trieste and the Austrian naval bases of Pola and Cattaro, dropping propaganda leaflets as well as tons of bombs. D'Annunzio's greatest feat was a 1,000 mile round trip to Vienna, dropping propaganda that symbolically initiated the defeat of the Austro-Hungarian empire. After the war he used his popularity to promote fascist attitudes. D'Annunzio died before the onset of World War II; his last years were plagued by mental instability.

The allure of the First World War in the air captivated many a man. Those who lived to tell the tale were few. As British ace Cecil Lewis wrote in the haunting *Sagittarius Rising*, "We lived supremely in the moment....Sometimes, jokingly, we would plan our lives 'after the War.' But it had no substantial significance. It was a dream, conjecturable as heaven....We were trained with one object—to kill. We had one hope—to live."

CHAPTER VII

1918
Year of Decision

It looked as though the war would keep up indefinitely until either the airplane brought an end to the war or the contending nations dropped from sheer exhaustion.
—Colonel Billy Mitchell, USAS

The year 1918 opened ominously. Each combatant nation looked forward to the most monstrous and complex struggles of the war. The Germans viewed 1918 as their last chance to win the war before the might of the United States could be felt at the battlefront. The Allies knew that they must not only prevent a German victory, but must clearly knock out the morale of German troops before the war-weariness of their own troops erupted again into outright mutiny. If the Allies could hold their troops together for another full year, and build their strength at the expense of the Germans, then a final offensive in 1919 should certainly bring peace.

Germany prepared for its great spring offensive, the Kaiserschlacht, in meticulous detail. However, insufficient materiel presented problems. The size of the German *Luftstreitkräfte* never reached the expected number of squadrons requested in the Amerikaprogramm, nor did industrial production reach the consistent level of output required to deliver the expected crushing blows.

The only alternative to insufficient numbers was to single out a superior aircraft design that could tilt the balance of air supremacy the way technological breakthroughs in previous years had done. The *Luftstreitkräfte* held a competition for single-seat fighters at Aldershof in January 1918. Top aces including von Richthofen were brought in from the field to evaluate the entries. All the major aircraft manufacturers that entered the competition wined and dined these aces hoping to gain points with them, but to little avail. On the other hand, Anthony Fokker closely watched every comment, especially von Richthofen's, made during the first round of competition on January 18. He decided that his V-11 prototype was too unstable. Fokker and his main designer Reinhold Platz worked 24 hours a day to redesign the plane before the competition reconvened. When they rolled their new plane with its lengthened fuselage out of the hangar it became the overwhelming hit of the contest. The new Fokker had thick airfoil section wings that both created increased lift while providing internal cantilever support instead of drag producing wire bracing. The new 160 hp Mercedes six-cylinder engine fitted with an automobile style radiator provided the power to climb 16,400 feet in a remarkable 31 minutes. The plane was highly maneuverable yet easy to fly and forgiving of poor handling by novice pilots, a valuable feature with the high attrition rate of flyers. Its welded aluminum framework made the Fokker durable and applicable to mass production. Kogenluft von Hoeppner awarded Fokker a contract on the spot for ten million marks. The Fokker D.VII was ordered into production immediately with optimistic hopes for another "Fokker Scourge" in the upcoming months.

Back at the front, von Hoeppner sought to capitalize on the quality of his fighter units to offset their small numbers. Realizing that local concentration of forces continued to be prerequisite in their air strategies, Kogenluft created two more rapid deployment fighter groups along the lines of the Richthofen circus. In February, *Jastas 12, 13, 15,* and *19* came together as *Jagdgeschwader JG II* under the command of Hauptmann Adolph von Tutschek. *Jagdgeschwader JG III* led by Hauptmann Bruno Loerzer consisted of *Jasta Boelcke,* and *Jastas 26, 27,* and *36.* For the Kaiserschlacht opening in March 21, *JG I* supported the German *II Army* in the center of the sector, *JG II* supported the *XVIII Army* on the left flank, and *JG III* went to the *XVII Army* on the right.

The Fokker D.VII, Germany's best fighter plane in the last year of the war. **(NASM)**

Like the ground forces, the *Luftstreitkräfte* concentrated the majority of its new special attack units just north of the Somme for the spring offensive. Three-quarters of the *Luftstreitkräfte's* 38 Schlasta on the Western Front stood ready to provide close support of the infantry assaults. One-half of the 81 Jastas including all three Jagdgeschwaders were called into the great battle to seize local air superiority. Four of the seven Bogohls along the front bombed British airfields and supply centers in the rear. One-third of the 153 Flieger Abteilungen focused on cooperating with the artillery and providing information about the advance. All told the Germans amassed 730 front line aircraft which outnumbered the 579 British planes along the Somme by 25 per cent.

While the Allies knew a German offensive was imminent, the time and place remained unclear. Special preparations kept this as secret as possible. The Germans did not build new aerodromes in the battle zone, specifically to prevent British reconnaissance from gleaning the exact date or location of the great attack. Instead, aircraft of the striking forces entered the point of

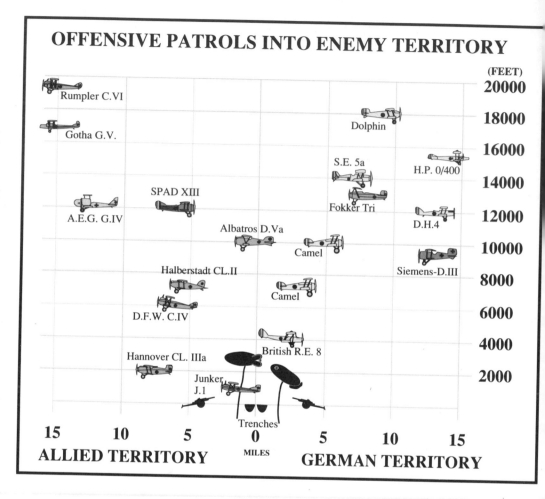

OFFENSIVE PATROLS INTO ENEMY TERRITORY

(FEET)

20000 — Rumpler C.VI

18000 — Dolphin

16000 — H.P. 0/400

S.E. 5a

14000

12000 — Fokker Tri / D.H.4

A.E.G. G.IV / SPAD XIII

Albatros D.Va

10000 — Camel / Siemens-D.III

Halberstadt CL.II

8000 — Camel

D.F.W. C.IV

6000

Gotha G.V.

British R.E. 8

4000

Hannover CL. IIIa

2000 — Junker J.1

Trenches

15   10   5   0   5   10   15
ALLIED TERRITORY   MILES   GERMAN TERRITORY

attack at night and were unassembled and stored under camouflage to avoid observation. They were assembled and tested only two days before zero-hour.

Operation Michael, the opening assault of the Kaiserschlacht, began on March 21. The initial attack from St. Quentin fell upon the southernmost British Fifth Army where the BEF met the French lines. The strategic goal was to divide the Allies and push the British into the sea. After a lightning barrage the shock troops of the Stosstruppen divisions went over the top and infiltrated the crumbling British Fifth Army. Low clouds prevented any morning aerial activity, but by noon the haze lifted and the Hannover CL.IIIa and Halberstadt CL.II and CL.IV of

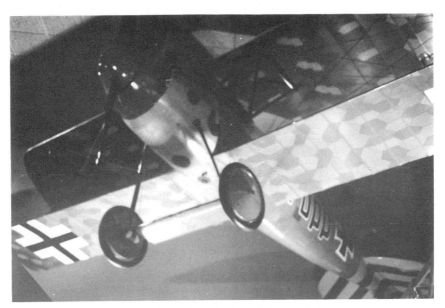

Albatros D.Va preserved at the National Air and Space Museum, showing the camouflage fabric developed by Germany late in the war. **(Author photo)**

the Schlasta dove into the assault. Flying at 300 feet they scoured the battlefield, strafing the British tommies with machine gun and hand grenade. In four-plane formations they infiltrated, like Stosstruppen of the air, up to ten miles to harass artillery units and disrupt the enemy retreat, gaining the accolade "Sturmflieger." The armored Junkers J.I infantry cooperation planes also followed the advance closely, searching out white cloth panels laid down by the troops for recognition. Fokker triplanes and Albatros D.Va's from 35 Jastas flew impeccable protective cover above the Sturmflieger and Infanterieflieger. Some Jastas attacked the balloon line to blind the British artillery while others searched out enemy planes. The Jagdgeschwader generally flew top cover at altitudes of 12,000 feet to maintain aerial superiority.

The British were completely surprised and overwhelmed on the ground and in the air. The Third and Fifth Brigades of the RFC attached to the Third Army and Fifth Army of the BEF immediately requested reinforcement. British fighters flew repeated missions strafing enemy ground troops, but they could not significantly stop the progress of the Stosstruppen. There were no Tommies left to take advantage of the aerial support. Major Sholto Douglas commanding No. 84 Squadron within Fifth Brigade sent his S.E.5a flights out to drop 20 lb. Cooper bombs on the approaching Germans while he sent mechanics ahead on motorcycles to determine how close the collapsing front was to their airfield. An Albatros strafed one of the motorcycles, and when the mechanic returned fire with his rifle the Albatros went silent and surprisingly glided into a ditch with a dead engine. When the mechanic reported this victory along with the danger of being overrun by German infantry, No. 84 Squadron refueled its planes, destroyed its hangars, and relocated to another airfield 15 miles further west. Such former British airstrips soon became the new fields of German Jastas as the battle progressed.

For the first three days of the assault German air power ruled. Casualties were surprisingly light as most of the fighter activity for both sides was directed at the ground. British squadrons were in hasty retreat and had to change their flying fields several times. The integrity of the Fifth Army had collapsed, and in some places only vicious strafing by the British fighter planes prevented major breakthroughs. The British lost many fighters in these low level attacks for which they were poorly suited. When reinforcements from 9th Wing and the wings of adjacent armies came into the battle, German air casualties rose and their air superiority slipped away. Massive patrols of up to sixty British aircraft began to appear. German Gotha bombers of *Bombengeschwader 5* (*Bogohl 5*) put a dent in the RFC replacements and hampered its patrol en masse capability by dropping 12,000 kg. of bombs on the large airfield at Doullens the night of March 26. That same day the French sent the Groupement Ménard up from Champagne into the Amiens sector to squelch German air power and join in attacks on German infantry. This combat group under Battalion Chief Victor Ménard consisted of a fighter wing and a day bombing wing: the Escadre de Combat No. 1 comprised thirteen fighter escadrilles of SPAD XIII and Caudron R XI, and the Escadre de Bombardement de jour No. 17 comprised nine escadrilles of Breguet XIV B2. This group flew eighty planes at a time to attack enemy troop concentration and crossings of the Somme and Crozat Canal. The momentum of the initial Kaiserschlacht offensive ground to a halt on March 28 barely ten miles from Amiens. Although the Germans made remarkable advances, destroying one British army and crippling another, they did not break the Anglo-French line. Having failed to achieve his strategic goals, Ludendorff called off the ground offensive April 4. He would try again somewhere else.

On April 9, Hindenburg and Ludendorff shifted their offensive to the Lys. Blasting the Portuguese divisions at Neuve Chapelle, the Stosstruppen again made remarkable advances and threatened Ypres itself. After the first day's haze lifted, local German air superiority again proved valuable but eventually faded as before. British fighters made constant attacks on ground targets, as on April 9 when General Haig issued his "backs to the wall" order that "there must be no retirement." British squadrons flew repeated ground attack sorties for the entire day until the crisis came under control. Only when ground strafing was no longer critically required for infantry support did Allied squadrons resume normal patrols at high altitude to reassert their aerial dominance. The Germans made another thrust on April 25. This time sixteen *Schlachtstas* led the infantry advance into No-Man's-Land, covered overhead by fourteen Jastas including *JG III* and *Jagdgruppen 6* and *10*, while a dozen other Jastas covered the flanks. This temporary concentration of force assured the successful taking of Kemmel Hill without loss of a single German plane. During the whole month of April, German flyers shot down 232 Allied planes, but the Allied ability to replace these losses eventually tore down German dominance over the battlefield.

The Allied planes were not only greater in numbers, but by this point in the war were superior in quality. Highly maneuverable Sopwith Camels or fast S.E.5a's equipped nearly every British fighter squadron. The twin gunned 200 hp. SPAD XIII re-equipped most of the French pursuit escadrilles. Two British squadrons sported a new Sopwith Dolphin type with twin Vickers guns and a spare Lewis mounted on the back-staggered top wing near the pilot's head. The French fighter escadrilles all eventually upgraded to SPAD XIII, but four of those that hadn't yet were flying the Morane Saulnier A1, a remarkably modern

Captain Eddie Richenbacker, leader of the US 94th "hat-in-the-ring" squadron, with his speedy SPAD XIII. (NASM)

high-wing monoplane. David Putnam, an American still flying for France in the Lafayette Flying Corps, scored a dozen victories with this vixen of a plane. This extremely maneuverable craft was ahead of its time in design, but unfortunately suffered from an inherent weakness of its wooden monoplane wing.

Manfred von Richthofen lamented this swing of the pendulum in fighter quality. He reported that the Albatros D.Va had seen its day, and his wickedly maneuverable Fokker Triplanes were simply too slow to catch a fleeing S.E.5a or SPAD. "If German industry does not soon supply us with a considerable number of single-seater planes of much better quality than our present ones," he wrote, "it will soon be impossible to fly on the Western Front." Casualties increased to about one-seventh of each squadron per month, and one of these losses was the master himself. On April 21 the flying circus was embroiled in a massive dogfight, typical for this period of the war. One Camel piloted by a rookie at the front fell out of the "fur ball" when he lost altitude due to wild maneuvering. Von Richthofen followed him down, with another Camel on his tail. Captain Roy Brown, flight leader of 209 Squadron RAF, stalked the red triplane as it pursued the rookie. Flying low over the Australian trenches

Herman Göring led JG I late in 1918 after Von Richthofen's death. He flew an all-white Fokker D.VII F. (NASM)

near the Somme, the Red Baron closed on the young Camel pilot. As he took aim, so did Brown, and so did an Australian machine gunner on the ground. Bullets and tracers crisscrossed the sky. An instant later, the red triplane went into a dead stick glide down into an embankment. A single bullet had penetrated the Ace-of-Aces' body.

Equally as earth-shaking, the British Parliament on April 1, 1918, united the RFC and RNAS air services into the Royal Air Force (RAF), a new independent military arm completely separate from the Army or Navy. It was the world's first air force, under its own command with its own government ministry, and was not beholden to any other military arm. After the Gotha bomber raids on London, the cabinet had commissioned Lieutenant General Jan Smuts to develop a plan to defend England from air raids. He returned with an overall recommendation for the establishment of a unified air force with its own Air Ministry. This had much popular approval. With the creation of the RAF, Major General Hugh Trenchard no longer reported to

General Haig, but to the politically scheming air minister, Lord Rothermere. Trenchard knew he could never get along under this structure and resigned.

Unwilling to let the "Father of the Royal Air Force" leave the RAF, the government asked Trenchard to lead a special strategic bombing unit called the Independent Force of the RAF. Formed on May 13, this force was composed of five bomber squadrons previously from the 41st Wing and 83rd Wing of the Eighth Brigade. Day bombers equipped three squadrons: No. 5 with D.H.4, No. 99 with D.H.9, and No. 104 with some of each. For night work, No. 100 Squadron flew the F.E.2b and No. 216 flew the ex-RNAS Handley Page O/100 and O/400 twin-engined bombers.

The Independent Force started out bombing the sources of war materiel from its base near Nancy in May, and dropped more bombs in that month than the entire British forces had dropped in the past six months of the war. In June they dropped 70 tons on the near side of the Rhine river and in July, 85 tons. The activity caused the Germans to increase the 400 interceptor fighters in the home defense Kampfeinsitzerstaffel (Kest) to 600. The size of the Independent Force doubled in August and eventually came up to strength with 120 aircraft when a squadron of the Liberty engined D.H.9A (No. 110) for day bombing and three more squadrons of Handley Page O/400 night bombers came on line.

The French created their own version of an air force with the First Air Division (Division Aérienne) on May 14. General Maurice Duval, who headed all French aviation at the front, took command of this huge mobile force designed to seize air supremacy rapidly wherever control of the air was threatened. This air force combined the Group Ménard (later called the 1st Brigade) and the Group Féquant (the 2nd Brigade) and two night bombing escadre groups. With concentration of pursuit aircraft, day bombers, and night bombers under one unified command, the Division Aérienne was a powerful striking force independent from army cooperation requirements. Barely a week old, it went into immediate use when Germany surprise attacked along the French front.

While all the French and British air services were busy dealing

Royal Artillery officers, part of a kite balloon section, don parachute harness at Gosnay, France, on May 2, 1918.

with the battles around Amiens, the German armies fell upon the lightly defended Chemin des Dames on May 27. Two entire *Jagdgeschwader*, the *JG I* and *JG III*, had secretly moved into carefully prepared airfields overnight. *Jastas 6* and *11* had just re-equipped with the new Fokker D.VII and more of the new Fokkers were on their way. Five additional Jastas (*Jasta 22, 50, 63, 66,* and *81*) grouped together as *Jagdgruppe 5* for the offensive. These German fighting units achieved complete mastery of the air, shooting down all French aircraft in their path and clearing the skies above the advancing Stosstruppen. When top cover was no longer needed, the Jastas flew low level attacks alongside the Schlachtstaffels to disrupt the enemy retreat.

Advanced elements of the Division Aérienne flew from Amiens into the airfields around Fère-en-Tardenois, but soon evacuated them as Stosstruppen over-ran the town. German troops advanced so rapidly that they destroyed or captured 200 French planes on the ground. More French air resistance arrived on May 30, finally forcing the German Jastas into a defensive posture. *JG I* flew top level patrols hunting enemy intruders while *Jagdgruppe 5* flew near ground level to protect its own troops and army cooperation planes. The offensive drove toward Paris at an alarming rate, extending closer to the French capital than at any other time since the Battle of the Marne in 1914. Only by throwing American troops in front of this onslaught at Belleau Wood and Chateau Thierry was the German drive halted on June 6.

A hastily organized German offensive north of Compiegne failed to make much headway in the second week of June. Then both sides paused to regroup after the exhausting battles. The German Gotha bombers took on new roles during these summer offensives. After May, they ceased all strategic bombing attacks on England in order to focus attention on Paris. During the continued German offensives in the early summer, the Gothas often flew three missions a night to harass Parisians, break up railroad lines and destroy ammo dumps. By war's end the Gothas had dropped 30 tons of bombs on Paris, just about a third as many as had been used in raids on England.

Across the front in the quiet Toul sector, the American bombers got off to a bad start. On June 10, six Breguet XIV's of the 96th Aero Squadron took off on a night bombing mission ignoring the severe overcast weather and strong winds at upper altitudes. The commander of the 96th, Major Harry Brown, led the mission himself because he felt it too dangerous to send his men out alone. The planes could not locate their primary targets, got lost on the way back to the front, and landed behind German lines when their fuel ran out. All were captured by the Germans, most with planes intact. A German flyer dropped a note on an American airfield addressed to the head of the U.S. air service saying, "We thank you for the fine airplanes and equipment which you sent us, but what will we do with the Major?" Upon receiving this message, Mitchell made an entry in his diary, "We did not reply about the major as he was better off in Germany at that time than he would have been with us."

At the end of June, the American First Pursuit Group (containing the 94th, 95th, 27th, and 147th Aero Squadrons) flew fifty-two Nieuport 28 planes from the quiet Toul sector 140 miles to the point of the Chateau Thierry salient. Three American observation squadrons of the 1st Corps Observation Group (1st, 24th, and 88th Aero Squadrons) followed. As the pursuit squadrons of the VIth French Army were decimated in the previous month and the Division Aérienne was occupied elsewhere in the Champagne region, the American squadrons were the only fighter squadrons at Chateau Thierry. Opposing these rookies were none other than the cream of the German *Luftstreitkräfte*: two German flying circuses, both *JG I* and *JG III*, served with the German *VIIth Army* along with ten other Jastas in two more Jagdgruppen. *JG II*, now under the command of the ace Hauptmann Rudolf Berthold (44 victories), was stationed at Coincy and four more Jagdgruppen were available with the flanking armies. A total of 46 Jastas, well over half of all the fighter aircraft in the German air service, were preparing for the next offensive out of the Chateau Thierry salient.

The American airmen immediately went head to head with the top flying circuses of the *Luftstreitkräfte*. The Salmson 2A2 planes of the 1st and 12th Aero Squadrons flew infantry contact patrols for the U.S. 2nd Division's attack on Vaux while the American fighters mixed it up with the Richthofen Circus. Fokker formations twenty to thirty planes strong forced the Americans to adopt new tactics. Observation planes flew in flights of four to provide their own protection while three pursuit flights provided more distant protection. Billy Mitchell stepped each flight 4,000 feet above and one mile deeper into enemy territory than the next flight to create a large fan barrage. When encountering a German formation, the first American flight splintered the enemy group as the next American flight entered the battle in succession. According to Mitchell's plan, "the last formed organization wins the fight."

On July 14, American reconnaissance photos indicated that the Germans were about to launch a major attack. Then just after midnight on July 15, the sky lit up with gunfire signaling the start of the Second Battle of the Marne. Colonel William "Billy" Mitchell, commander of U.S. aviation at the front, took to the air in a Nieuport 28 to see for himself what was happening. Flying along the Marne at low altitude in the darkness, he spotted German troops flooding across the river on pontoon bridges just a few miles east of Chateau-Thierry. "It seemed the whole German Army," wrote Mitchell, "simply hurled itself at our part of the lines...." Upon landing he ordered his entire force to bomb and strafe these bridges immediately and relentlessly. The American fighters and observation aircraft as well as two French Breguet XIV escadrilles dropped 45 tons worth of small 10kg and 20kg bombs on the bridges and machine gunned hundreds of German troops. German Halberstadt CL.II's on infantry contact duty and Fokker D.VII's of the flying circuses tried to break up these attacks.

Billy Mitchell had caught the Germans off guard with a brilliant strategic maneuver. He then called upon the British 9th Brigade at Saintes to send its four squadrons of D.H.9 day bombers against the enormous German supply dumps at Fère-en-Tardenois. At noon on July 16, 35 bombers under the protection of two squadrons of S.E.5a's, two squadrons of Sopwith Camels, and the U.S. First Pursuit Group bombed the main German supply base for the salient. The German Jastas retreated to protect Fère-en-Tardenois, shooting down 12 British bombers, but left their bridgeheads on the Marne unprotected. Inferior numbers of Allied aircraft in this sector succeeded in disrupting the German ground offensive both at its head and at its rear by this clever strategy. The coup de grace came on July 18 when the U.S. 1st and 2nd Divisions in concert with the French Moroccan Division smashed through the German lines at Villers-Cotterets. The Second Battle of the Marne ended in Allied victory, and the first wave of German retreats began. General Pershing promoted Billy Mitchell to Chief of Air Service of the First Army. Mitchell summed up the month saying, "I felt that our work at Chateau-Thierry had been remarkable."

BLACK DAYS FOR THE *LUFTSTREITKRÄFTE*

Further north, the British army prepared for its own offensive.

Clerget rotary-powered Sopwith Camel with whitewash squadron markings of No. 65, RFC.

They maintained complete secrecy before the assault to keep from tipping off the Germans. General Sir John Monash forbade forward scouting probes into enemy lines before the battle, forcing his Australian Corps to rely completely on aerial photographs for tactical information. The British Mark V tanks secretly moved into position for their attack just three miles behind the front. Handley Page O/400's bombed the German lines to drown out the sound of the noisy tank movements and draw German aerial attention elsewhere. During the first hours of August 8, lumbering tanks made their final advance to jump off points, protected by a lone bomber who cleared away just before the great artillery barrage erupted at 4:20 a.m. The Battle of Amiens had begun. The great British tank offensive forced the German armies back from all they had achieved in the spring offensives in what was truly the "Black Day of the German Army." Allied air power in this sector was overwhelming. The British force contained 800 aeroplanes, about half of which were

189

Captain G.H. Lewis, DFC, in his No. 40 Squadron S.E.5a, Summer 1918. White "N" was No. 40 Squadron marking.

fighters, plus a thousand French planes on the flanks versus only 365 German planes, only a third of which were fighters.

All Allied fighters were assigned to coordinated ground strafing for the first day. One squadron of Armstrong Whitworth F.K.8's and a Sopwith Camel squadron had trained together with the tank corps for months before the attack and proved their worth at the time of the assault. These planes laid smoke screens ahead of the tanks to cover their advance, strafed anti-tank artillery and performed important liaison with the tanks. The initial breakthrough was so successful that General Salmond commanding the RAF at the front switched his emphasis from ground support to bombing the Somme bridges to cut off the German retreat. But the day bombers and their escort met stiff resistance from Fokker D.VII's of the Jastas and failed to disrupt movement across the Somme. Losses for the day were the highest of the war with 144 Allied planes lost or damaged in combat, and 86 casualties. The German air service in this sector lost only 30 planes. Reinforcements came into the conflict on both sides. Jagdstaffeln rushed in, reinforcing the Germans. Ninety more RAF planes entered, concentrating 70 per cent of

Sopwith Camel night fighter with twin overwing Lewis guns and underwing landing flares, on Home Defense duty, No. 44 Squadron, RFC, England.

the RAF fighter force into this sector. Fighters patrolled in large stepped formations spanning the full range of altitudes and layers of combats broke out above key objectives. The emphasis for August 10 was to bomb the railroad junctions and rail yards to block counterattack. Again the day bombers and their escorts had to fight their way through the Jastas and suffered heavily. The RAF lost 847 planes during the month of August, but their offensive efforts were instrumental in supporting the most significant British victory of the war.

While the British pressed on toward the Hindenburg Line, the Allies planned a new offensive along the American front. After American successes at Chateau Thierry, General John "Black Jack" Pershing concentrated his divisions along the St. Mihiel salient and created the American First Army on August 10. The First Army controlled its own front and operated independently under American command. The segment of the front it acquired from the French was a triangular salient bowing into French territory south of Verdun, cutting the Meuse River with its apex

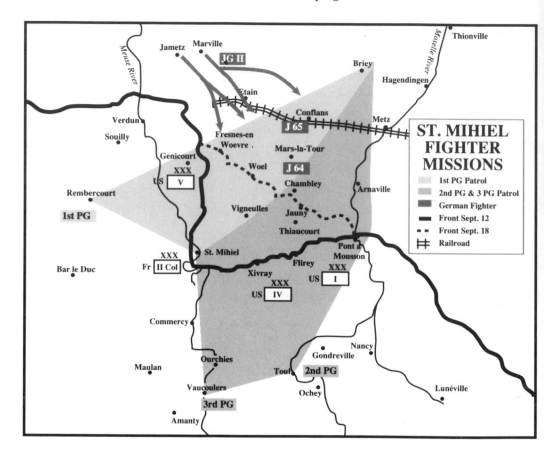

at St. Mihiel. Pershing planned to cut this salient off at its base, shorten the length of the front, and remove its threat to Verdun with the first major offensive by the unified American Expeditionary Force.

Billy Mitchell's Air Armada

Colonel Billy Mitchell, the Chief of Air Service for the First Army, immediately set off with plans to support the great offensive. Knowing that the element of surprise was essential, he used the air service to maintain secrecy while the American forces entered their positions. Mitchell ordered dummy hangars and fake aircraft built to confuse the German high altitude photography planes. Fighter aircraft patrolled constantly over their own territory to safeguard against enemy reconnaissance planes. They flew in patrols of two or three planes and did not cross beyond the enemy balloon line to minimize enemy suspicions of impending attack. When one American fighter pilot fell into German hands just four days before the offensive, all fighters were kept back from offensive patrols until the moment the offensive began. Meanwhile, the reconnaissance planes sortied deep into the salient obtaining critically important photographs on which the attack plans were made. On September 10, Mitchell made a lone patrol in his SPAD XVI. Crossing the salient at low altitude, Mitchell observed the German preparations to withdraw. He immediately presented this to General Pershing and convinced him to attack without delay in order to catch the Germans off guard.

In order to achieve the most effective victory, Mitchell wanted to wrest complete air superiority and maximize air support for the first major American offensive. He assembled the largest concentration of air power during the war. His U.S. Air Service had grown immensely, and Mitchell brought 28 American squadrons into action along the St. Mihiel front. Three observation squadrons were assigned to each army corps, of which I Corps and IV Corps on the right would attack from the south while the 26th Division of V Corps on the left of the salient would attack from the northwest. Six of these observation squadrons flew fast new Salmson 2A2's (having discarded their obsolete Sopwith 1½ Strutters, A.R. 2's and SPAD XI's), while three came on line with the new American built Liberty DH-4 (the 135th, 8th and 50th Aero Squadrons). The First Army headquarters retained two day observation squadrons (91st and 24th with Salmson 2A2's) and one night observation squadron

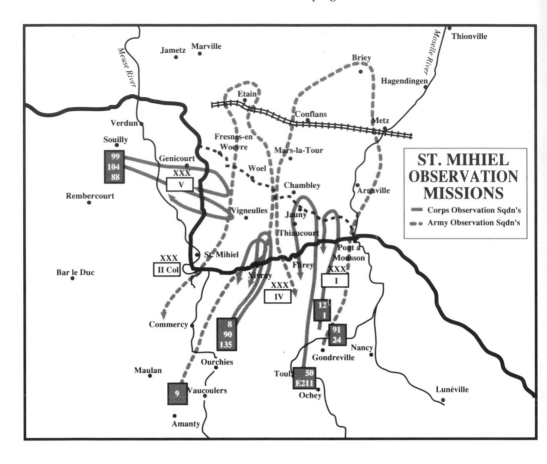

**ST. MIHIEL
OBSERVATION
MISSIONS**

Corps Observation Sqdn's
Army Observation Sqdn's

(the 9th flying Breguet XIV A2's) for obtaining strategic information deep behind enemy lines. For attaining air superiority over
the battlefield, Major B.M. Atkinson commanded the First
Pursuit Wing made up of the 2nd Pursuit Group, the 3rd Pursuit
Group, and the 1st Day Bombardment Group. Of the eight
fighter squadrons in this wing only the 103rd Aero Squadron,
the old Lafayette Escadrille, was a veteran. Of the 1st Day

DH-4 Bombers of US 11th Aero Squadron, 1st Day Bombardment Group. Crewmen hold maps and photos of the latest target. Seven of their DH-4's were lost during the St. Mihiel Offensive. **(NASM)**

Bombardment Group only the Breguet XIV B2 bombers of 96th Aero Squadron had front-line experience. The other two squadrons (the 11th and 20th Aero Squadrons) were newly formed with Liberty DH-4 aircraft. While this eleven squadron wing protected the main American forces attacking from the south, the 1st Pursuit Group with its four veteran squadrons from Chateau Thierry supported the 26th Division in attacking from the northwest. All told the U.S. Air Service on this sector contained 609 planes, 108 of which were the new American built Liberty DH-4.

Besides the American airmen, Mitchell worked out a multi-national plan in which forces of all the Allies took part on a grand scale. He meticulously coordinated strategies with all units involved and proved himself an excellent leader with the aircraft of four nations at his command. The French offered him temporary control of the 42 squadrons of their Division Aérienne. One brigade, a mobile tactical force of 142 SPAD fighters and 90 Breguet XIV bombers with 75 Caudron R XI escort gun-ships, set up on each side of the salient. A night bombing escadre with two squadrons of French Farman F.50

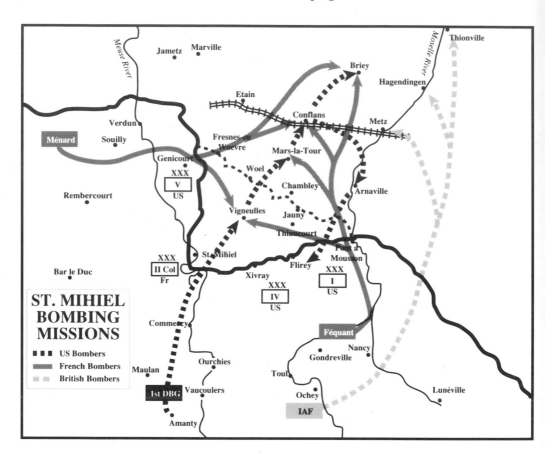

ST. MIHIEL BOMBING MISSIONS

- ▪▪▪ US Bombers
- ▬▬ French Bombers
- ▪▪ British Bombers

bombers and three of Italian Caproni Ca 33 bombers also supported Mitchell's efforts. Additionally, four French pursuit squadrons supported Mitchell's First Pursuit Wing, and twelve French observation escadrille served the French and American ground troops in the sector. To top it off, Hugh Trenchard allocated eight squadrons of the IAF night bombers to cooperate with Mitchell for his air campaign. With the American, French,

Italian, and British units, Billy Mitchell had at his disposal 696 fighters, 366 reconnaissance planes, 323 day bombers, and 91 night bombers, totaling 1,476 aircraft and 20 observation balloons. The German force initially opposing this armada was estimated between 200 and 300, of which only one third were fighters.

On the night before the attack, British Handley Page O/400 bombers of the Independent Force bombed targets as distant as Metz and Thionville while French night bombers attacked aerodromes and targets within the St. Mihiel salient. After the artillery barrage signaling the start of the offensive had peppered the German lines in the early hours of September 12, the first dawn patrols took off. Due to low clouds and miserably rainy weather, the plan for large multi-tiered formations was scrapped, and squadrons performed their assignments in small independent flights. Mitchell assigned one-third of his total force to ground attack missions. The SPAD XIII's of the American and French Pursuit Groups went in at low altitude to strafe the German infantry in their trenches and retreated along the roads deeper in the salient. The 103rd Aero Squadron of Bill Thaw's 3rd Pursuit Group were the first to use their bombs on motor trucks and troop concentrations. Each plane of the fourteen plane formation carried four 20 lb. Cooper bombs that they released from an altitude of under 300 feet for a telling effect. Of the American bombers, only the Breguet XIV's of the 96th Aero Squadron were assigned to bomb enemy troops and other tactical targets on the first day. As the day progressed they switched to bombing the town of Buxieres, then bombed a troop center at Buxerulles, and lastly dropped 1,150 kg. of bombs on the main objective of Vigneulles at the base of the St. Mihiel salient. The rest of the First Day Bombardment Group wasted their abilities flying barrage patrols above the 2nd Pursuit Group. While the main attacks in the south occupied the German defenders, the 1st Pursuit Group thundered down from the north to split and overwhelm the German Jasta. The whole group flew at barely 100 feet altitude in a novel maneuver for a formation of that size. Deeper into the salient, the first brigade of the French Division Aérienne attacked at full strength with bombers and pursuit aircraft from the south. A half hour before

Results of American aerial bombardment and directed artillery, on the German occupied town of Vaux. **(NASM)**

it left the battle zone the other brigade of the Division Aérienne attacked from the north. By the time the second brigade was ready to head for home, the first brigade returned after refueling. Deeper still, the British bombers attacked railroad stations and bridges across rivers at the base of the St. Mihiel salient with high explosives to prevent both reinforcement and retreats. With this combination of punches, Mitchell could "hit first from one side of the salient, then from the other, just as a boxer gives a right hook and a left hook successively to his opponent."

The first day of the St. Mihiel offensive ended with a number of triumphs. The salient was successfully conquered by American troops converging upon Vigneulles, with the support of 400 tanks and Billy Mitchell's 1,476 plane armada. Mitchell's "Air Blitz" split the German Jasta and seized complete air supremacy, drawing great praise from Pershing. The young Arizonan Frank Luke of the 27th Aero Squadron shot down his first of many German balloons and set off on a streak of destruction that virtually eradicated German balloon observation between St. Mihiel and Verdun.

Two days into the offensive, *Jagdgeschwader II* arrived with four Jastas (*Jasta 12, 13, 15,* and *19*) of Fokker D.VII's led by Freiherr Oscar von Boenigk. These reinforcements, including the great aces Georg von Hantelmann (25 victories) and Josef Veltjens (35 victories), challenged Allied aerial dominance. On September 14, German fighters attacked a large formation of French Breguet XIV's from Groupe de Bombardement GB 4 on its way to bomb the railroad station at Conflans-Jarny. They shot down seven French planes, but not before the bombers and their escort of Caudron R XI three-seaters from Escadrille R 46 shot down eight of the Germans. The First Day Bombardment Group also met trouble September 14, when it flew its first mission as a full three squadron bombardment group. The red nosed Fokkers of *JG II* intercepted the squadrons on their way to bomb Conflans. Seven DH-4's of the 11th Aero Squadron fought off 15 Fokkers but lost two planes from their "V" formation. Only the arrival of a flight of SPAD's saved them. Two days later *Jasta 19* put the 96th Aero Squadron out of action when it shot down four Breguets, three of them in flames at the hands of twenty-five victory ace Leutnant Oliver von Beaulieu-Marconnay. For the remaining days of the offensive, the DH-4's alone bombed the marshaling yards at Anaville, and Longuyon and the bridges across the Moselle river. On September 18, *Jasta 12* finished off the 11th Aero Squadron. Of the six DH-4 that bombed Mars-la-Tour, only one remained as the sole survivor of the squadron. The other five were shot down in a vicious battle with Hermann Becker (23 victories) and his Staffel, three falling in flames. The Independent Force under "Boom" Trenchard also encountered growing resistance as they nightly bombed the towns of Conflans, Longuyon, and Metz. Although the Independent Force dropped 32 tons of bombs on Metz during the campaign, September 15 was the worst night when several of the big Handley Page O/400 bombers were lost over that town. In general, *JG II* had a very successful week. It put two American bomber squadrons out of action, scored 89 victories with the loss of only 10 of its Fokker D.VII pilots. The presence of *JG II* neutralized much of the Allied control of the air over St. Mihiel, but it was too little too late.

Overall, the Allied victory at St. Mihiel was a roaring success. American airmen destroyed sixty enemy aircraft, twelve balloons, dropped 75 tons of explosives, interdicted the movement of enemy troops into and out of the salient, and scouted the progress of the offensive continuously. Only 40 casualties were suffered by the USAS. The bombing units got the worst of it. "Black Jack" Pershing sent congratulations to Billy Mitchell saying, "The organization and control of the tremendous concentrations of Air Forces, including American, French, British and Italian units, which has enabled the Air Service of the First Army to carry out so successfully its dangerous and important mission, is as fine a tribute to you personally as is the courage and nerve shown by your officers a signal proof of the high morale which permeates the service under your command.... I am proud of you all." The next step for Mitchell was to secretly usher his entire U.S. Air Service across the Bar le Duc to the other side of Verdun for the next offensive. This was particularly difficult because JG I, the old Richthofen Circus now led by Hermann Goering, arrived at Metz on September 20. Mitchell spirited his units to camouflaged airfields near Verdun during the night. American planes were not allowed to fly over their new sector of the front, and American observers rode with French pilots to accustom them to the new terrain in the Meuse-Argonne. Only 831 planes (646 American and 185 French and Italian) were involved due to the attrition of damaged aircraft and difficulty obtaining trained replacements.

The Americans went over the top in the Meuse-Argonne offensive on September 26. The 1st Pursuit Group under Major Harold Hartney was assigned to low level patrol and ground attack while the 2nd and 3rd Pursuit Groups each flew top cover with patrols at medium and high altitude bands. At 5:45 a.m. pairs of SPAD XIII from the 1st Pursuit Group simultaneously attacked each German Drachen balloon site using the techniques developed by "balloon busters" Luke and Wehner. Four balloons and eight low flying enemy aircraft were successfully destroyed on the first day. Higher up, the 2nd Pursuit Group accounted for another seven German planes. To oversee the aerial activity, General Billy Mitchell flew another of his lone patrols across the battle front. On his way back over Avocourt he observed a severely deadlocked traffic jam of American supply vehicles behind the V Corps lines. These trucks would have been sitting ducks had any German Schlachtstas spotted them. Mitchell immediately ordered the 1st Day Bombardment Group to attack Dun-sur-Meuse, a major German rail junction across from Verdun, to draw German attention and Jastas away from the V Corps dilemma. This ploy succeeded in safeguarding the stalled American supply train. It also crippled German reinforcements coming through Dun-sur-Meuse, and drew enemy fighters away from the center of the American advance. It cost the 96th Aero Squadron one dead while the 20th Aero Squadron lost five of its seven DH-4 bombers in battle against *Jasta 12*.

The 1st Pursuit Group continued low level patrols for the remainder of the campaign. The group set up forward flying fields close to the front lines from which Frank Luke and others pounced on another eight Drachen balloons to blind the Germans of their immediate artillery observation. On patrol they flew below 2,000 feet to drop light bombs on columns of enemy troops, strafe trenches, locate enemy artillery positions, and protect the "doughboys" from attacks by German Schlachtstas. In doing so, Hartney's group sustained only eleven casualties in the first four days of battle, while accounting for half of the 66 German planes credited to U.S. aero squadrons. Much of this success may be attributed to Captain "Eddie" Rickenbacker, the commander of the 94th Aero Squadron who was well on his way to becoming America's ace-of-aces. Rickenbacker routinely conducted his patrols with the flight staying in close formation near the ground while he stood watch above and behind them, the best tactic for surprising low level enemy patrols without being surprised oneself.

The other pursuit groups followed a different tactic. At their assigned upper altitude bands, the 2nd and 3rd Pursuit Groups conducted mass patrols concentrated along the ground troop's axis of attack. They patrolled high above their own troops to discourage enemy reconnaissance planes, and penetrated 10 km ahead of the troops to clear the air space for their own observation planes. The corps observation aircraft in this operation

Frank Luke, Jr., Arizona cowboy, balloon buster, and the second highest ranking ace of the USAS. **(NASM)**

generally flew without close fighter escort. They performed their duties singly or in tight groups of three or four. The planes had to negotiate jagged ravines to reconnoiter the complex terrain of the Argonne forest. Casualties among observers were great and replacements difficult to obtain, so many of the squadrons' ground officers stepped out of their roles as armorers and radio technicians to become gunner-observers.

As the American forces drove tenaciously up the Meuse River into the Argonne forest, one battalion of the 77th Division outdistanced its regiment and became cut off. The 1st Battalion of the 308th Infantry was outflanked and surrounded while clearing machine gun nests in the dense thickets of the Argonne. The terrain was so rugged and densely wooded that neither the German nor the American headquarters had a clear picture of where this "Lost Battalion" was. The 50th Aero Squadron searched the ravines and finally located the tiny 70 yard long defensive pocket. The battalion commander Major Charles Whittlesey sent messages to the rear by carrier pigeon since the fierce German ground fire prevented the DH-4 planes from reading any ground panels he laid out. While the army attempted counterattacks to relieve the Lost Battalion for five days, the isolated unit relied solely on supplies dropped from the air by the courageous airmen of the 50th Aero Squadron. The DH-4 crews flew daring low runs into the pocket through storms of machine gun and small arms fire to maintain contact and attempt to parachute supplies to the struggling survivors on the ground. The most valiant crew, Flight Commander Harold "Dad" Goettler and his observer Lt. Erwin Bleckley, flew two missions into the gauntlet on October 6. They succeeded in dropping enough ammunition, medicines, chocolate, and carrier pigeons to sustain the Lost Battalion until its ultimate rescue, but they paid the ultimate sacrifice for their heroism. Goettler and Bleckley never returned from their final mission. Both were honored with the Congressional Medal of Honor.

Throughout October and early November, the combined Allied armies pushed the German army back along its supply routes. Difficult fighting continued all along the front as Allied aviators struggled to continue their control of the air above the battlefield. The rapidity of the German retreats in some areas and the increasingly bad weather put a damper on air activity as old airfields were lost to advancing enemies and new airfields became seas of mud in the rain. Allied flyers pressed onward in great numbers, keeping the Germans off balance. Kogenluft von Hoeppner wrote, "The enemy was attacking simultaneously along practically the entire front. We could no longer concentrate all our forces at a given point to gain air superiority. We were numerically inferior everywhere."

CONCLUSION

The bloodiest war in European history ended at the eleventh hour of the eleventh day of the eleventh month of the final year of fighting. The night before, word went out to all air squadrons that they'd be grounded for the day pending a major event. An excited orderly awoke Lieutenant Colonel Louis Strange at 2:00 a.m. with the remarkable news that hostilities would cease that day, but Strange was too war weary after fighting to respond in kind. Strange recalls, "... I turned over and went to sleep again, dimly wondering why I could not wake myself up enough to become enthusiastic about it, and what on earth we were going to do with ourselves in the morning without a war." When he finally rose at dawn, he found not a single aircraft on the field—all were gone to witness the conclusion of the war from the air. One pilot returning from a long morning flight crossed the foggy front lines to see a sudden blur of colored lights from Very pistols firing up at him from all along the front. At first he thought he was in the midst of a nightmare until he realized it must be the celebration over the war's end. Down on the American front, Captain Eddie Rickenbacker put down the phone in the squadron mess. The room had fallen silent and all eyes were on him. Before he could speak, the proof came as gunshots and wild cheers erupted from miles around. The men of the 94th Aero Squadron burst out of the mess to join in the elation. The war was over.

René Fonck

If there was one man who was an ace of aces, that man was Frenchman René Paul Fonck (1894-1953). He was a warrior and an aviator without equal, and he made sure everyone knew it. A braggart, he endeared himself to few and spent most of his time both on the ground and in the air alone. Officially acknowledged as the Allied Ace of Aces with 75 confirmed victories, Fonck may have downed more unconfirmed planes than von Richthofen. He reported 52 additional victories that were never verified, but many of these claims are quite plausible. Fonck claimed "120 victories of which I, myself, am certain."

Born in the Vosges in 1894, he was fascinated with aviation and idolized the great pioneers of flight. The guns of August drew him immediately into the army where he served as a construction engineer for five months before getting into flight training. By the middle of 1915, Fonck was already flying above the trenches in a Caudron G III observation plane. He was increasingly engaged in aerial combats as the air war heated up, and by August 1916 Fonck received his first confirmed victory when his observer shot down a Rumpler. After a repeat performance, Fonck proved he was suited for pursuit work. During "Bloody April" 1917 he transferred to Escadrille Spa 103, part of the famous "Storks" of Brocard's elite Groupe de Combat 12.

Flying SPAD VII and later SPAD XIII fighters, Fonck's victory list grew. So did his collection of medals: the Medaille Militaire, the Legion of Honor, the British Military Cross, the Belgian Croix de Guerre, and the French Croix de Guerre with 28 palms. Introspective and brooding, Fonck plotted out his personal attack strategies and then performed them. Prone to explosive outbursts of temper on the ground, Fonck was cool in battle. He perfected each of his attacks, counting bullets used per victory, and evaluating his own performance. He reveled in destroying Boche planes, and challenged himself to destroy them more efficiently. Whereas most aces rejoiced if they scored a double kill in one day, doubles and triples were common for Fonck. After twice achieving six victories in a single day, he described himself as a "virtuoso" of the deadly aerial concert. His fastest score occurred August 14, 1918, when he shot down three planes in ten seconds.

Fonck never became the commander of a fighter unit. His talent lay in improving his own combat abilities, not in leading others into combat. He liked solo missions where he could "perform those little coups of audacity which amused me." Fonck studied deflection shooting and analyzed his enemy's tactics. He used deception and cloud cover to the maximum to stalk his prey. An exceptional marksman, Fonck dispatched his victims with as little as five bullets.

Surviving the war, Fonck promoted aviation with exhibition flying. He hoped to be the first to cross the Atlantic with a plane designed by Igor Sikorsky, but Charles Lindbergh beat him just days before Fonck's plane was ready for the attempt. He served as inspector of fighter aircraft for the French Air Force up to the outbreak of World War II. Fonck retired to a quiet life and lived in Paris until his death in 1953.

Mick Mannock

Nothing ever came easy for Great Britain's top ace Edward "Mick" Mannock—not in life, and not even in death. Born in 1887, Mannock was the son of an Army man who soon abandoned his family. From the age of 12 Mannock lived in grinding poverty, working long hours at hard labor to provide for his mother and 4 brothers and sisters. At 24, in 1912, Mannock took a job with an English telephone company in Turkey. As Mannock's luck would have it Turkey joined Germany in 1914 in declaring war against Great Britain. Mannock was a prisoner of war in Turkey before the first shot was fired! It was as a POW that Mannock's eyesight, never good, worsened without proper medical care.

In 1915 Turkey repatriated Mannock because of his poor physical condition. Mannock immediately joined the Royal Army Medical Corps. In the next year Mannock joined the Royal Engineers as a "tunnel rat" saying, "I intend to...blow the bastards up. The higher they go and the more pieces that come down, the happier I shall be." Obviously possessing the requisite fighting spirit, Mannock's next stop was the RFC. Passing the rudimentary physical examination (Mannock was blind in one eye) in August 1916, Mannock was sent on to Hendon for flight training in late 1916. Mannock received his commission in April

1917 and was assigned to No. 40 Squadron. He flew the Nieuport 17 in offensive patrols and bomber escorts—some of the most mortally dangerous of all air jobs. Mannock's success as an air fighter did not come easily or naturally, either one—it was a hard won victory. For two months after his arrival at Squadron 40 he had no kills. There was talk among his squadron mates that Mannock was "yellow," and suffering from cold feet. Mannock himself admitted, "Now I can understand what a nervous strain flying is. However cool a man might be, there must always be more or less of a tension on the nerves under such trying conditions.... When it is considered that seven out of ten forced landings are practically write-offs and 50% are cases where the pilot is injured, one can quite understand the strain of the whole business." When confronted by his captain, G.L. Lloyd in May 1917, Mannock said, "Of course, I've been very frightened against my will— nervous reaction. I have now conquered this physical defect, and having conquered myself, I will now conquer the Hun. Air fighting is a science. I have been studying it, and I have not been unduly worried about getting Huns at the expense of being reckless. I want to master the tactics first. The present bald-headed tactics should be replaced by well-thought-out ones. I cannot see any reason why we should not sweep the Hun right out of the sky."

In the next year Mannock racked up 73 kills, becoming Great Britain's ace of aces. He developed an implacable hatred of the Germans and was never so happy as after a kill, having sent the "German vermin to hell in flames." Yet, as a poor Irish boy, he despised much of the elitist political and social system of Britain and alienated many of his own superiors with his radical socialist leanings. Mannock was rude to General Plumer when he wanted to congratulate Mannock on his DSO. He wrote of Hugh Trenchard, "Talked bilge. Don't like him. Too schoolmastery." But, he took his responsibility to his pilots seriously. In March 1918 Mannock was promoted to flight commander in the new No. 74 Squadron flying the S.E.5a. A new recruit wrote, "...he looked after me just like a big brother. It was wonderful to be in his Flight....Every member had his special thought and care." Mannock went from squadron to

squadron in 1918 teaching his motto to fledgling flyers: "Always above, seldom on the same level, never underneath."

Mannock's last months of life were haunted by nightmares of airplanes in flames. Dreams of death dogged his days. Mannock swore he would blow his brains out rather than burn alive in a blazing plane. In July 1918 he replaced Billy Bishop as commander of No. 85 Squadron. Returning from a leave to recover from influenza and still in low spirits, Mannock offered to go up with Donald Inglis, a rookie pilot, to get his first kill. Mannock got a Hun two-seater. Inglis got home. Mannock went down in flames, to an unknown grave. A flyer in Mannock's squadron reported simply, "When he died every man in the squadron wept." But even in death Mannock was haunted—by a ghost from the past. It was Mannock's long missing father who accepted his Victoria Cross, awarded posthumously, from King George V.

Eddie Rickenbacker

Danger was Eddie Rickenbacker's business. America's ace of aces with 26 victories, Rickenbacker raced cars as a teenager, making a good living at it until he decided to pursue a new career—flying airplanes. Alas, when Rickenbacker attempted to join the American Aero Reserves, the officer in charge rejected him as too old (over 25) and too ignorant (no college degree). Furthermore, Rickenbacker's distinguished background as a racecar driver worked against him! The recruiting officer

commented, "We don't believe that it would be wise for a pilot to have any knowledge of engines and mechanics. Airplane engines are always breaking down, and a man who knew a great deal about engines would know if his engine wasn't functioning correctly and be hesitant about going into combat." Instead, Rickenbacker joined the army in May 1917 and chauffeured the top military brass. One day he came upon Billy Mitchell whose car had broken down, repaired it in a snap, and revealed his interest in flying. Billy Mitchell pulled some strings for his new driver and got Rickenbacker into flight training at the new American school at Issoudun.

Rickenbacker finally arrived at the 94th Aero Squadron in March 1918, ready for action. In company with the great Raoul Lufbery and Doug Campbell, he made the first patrol over enemy lines by an American trained fighter squadron, even though guns hadn't yet been installed on their new planes. Rickenbacker's personal battle with airsickness complicated his transition to combat flying. But Rickenbacker adjusted quickly; he swiftly learned the science of aerial combat from his mentor Lufbery. By June, Rickenbacker, flying his Nieuport 28, achieved five kills, becoming the second new ace of the squadron. Rickenbacker took a cold and calculating approach to aerial warfare, "...I was an automaton behind the gun barrels of my plane. I never thought of killing an individual but of shooting down an enemy plane...nothing more than scientific murder." After five kills Rickenbacker was felled by a serious mastoid infection that required surgery. He was in and out of the hospital all summer with fevers and an ear abscess. Rickenbacker returned fully to action in September 1918 and was named commander of the Hat-in-the-Ring squadron, the top scoring squadron of the U.S. Air Service. In less than 2 months Rickenbacker scored 21 more victories, flying a SPAD XIII appropriately marked with the number "1." For his achievements, Rickenbacker received the DSC, Croix de Guerre, and, after a long wait, the cherished Congressional Medal of Honor.

After the war Rickenbacker continued to live life on the edge. He founded the Rickenbacker Motor Company that soon went bankrupt. Rickenbacker ran the Indianapolis Speedway for a time, then moved on to Eastern Airlines as president. In 1941 Rickenbacker barely survived a plane crash in Atlanta. After a two year convalescence, Rickenbacker went to work for the Army in the Second World War. He toured bases, sharing his experience of wartime flying with fledgling flyers. On one such mission Rickenbacker's plane crash landed in the Pacific Ocean. He spent 24 days stranded in the shark-infested sea in a life raft with no water and no food, save 3 oranges. Of course he survived this last endurance challenge; no shark could finish the man who beat the Flying Circus. Rickenbacker died in 1973, at the age of 82.

Frank Luke, Jr.

The Army might seem an odd choice for a boy dubbed "too happy-go-lucky" in his high school yearbook. But this free spirit named Frank Luke accomplished much in his short time on earth. Luke, son of German immigrants, was raised in the wild, wild West of turn-of-the-century Arizona. But the wide-open southwest desert was not enough for him; Luke wanted to ride the sky. When America went to war in 1917, Frank began his one year odyssey into the heavens. In September of that year he rode from work in the little desert mining town of Globe straight to Tucson to enlist in the U.S. Air Service. He was soon learning about aeronautics in Austin, Texas, and after two months went on to Rockwell Field in San Diego, California, where he was selected to be a fighter pilot. In 1918 Luke received his commission as a Second Lieutenant and was shipped off to France in March.

The second half of Luke's year in the Air Service began with intense flight training at Issoudun. Upon graduation he served as a ferry pilot, learning the subtle characteristics of the latest aircraft. In August 1918 Luke joined Major Harold Hartney's 27th Aero Squadron. On August 16, after just two weeks at the front, he dropped out of formation without permission and later returned with his first victory claim. This cast him as a bragging, hothead rookie in the eyes of his jealous veteran squadron mates, but Hartney never doubted this grinning self-confident firebrand. Hartney later said, "Man, how that kid could fly! No one, mind you, no one, had the sheer contemptuous courage that boy possessed.... We had ... excellent pilots and ... good shots but the perfect combination ... was scarce. Frank Luke was that perfect combination."

Shunned by his fellow flyers, Frank Luke became close friends with another loner, Joseph Wehner. Both men were questioned about their German ancestry, and Wehner was twice arrested by suspicious intelligence officers. Luke also made friends with the greatest French squadron of aces, Les Cicognes (The "Storks"), whose airfield was just a few miles away. Driven to make himself "known, or go where most of them go," Luke took to conducting lone patrols. He often broke away from his aggravated flight leaders on "joy-rides" to seek the enemy and gain respect.

Luke's opportunity came when he began his balloon busting campaign. His flight leader Lt. Jerry Vasconcelles of Colorado called balloons "the toughest proposition a pilot has to meet." Luke developed a hatred of these floating sausages when he saw how they directed the German artillery right into the American trenches, causing the greatest and most grotesque casualties. On September 12 he went after a German balloon on his own. After chasing off three enemy planes and flying through an iron curtain of shrapnel and explosive shells, Luke flamed the hydrogen gas bag on the third pass. He nursed his bullet-riddled and shrapnel-shredded SPAD XIII back to his own field, but not without first landing by an American observation balloon company to get signed witness reports proving his victory. His squadron mates were now believers who cheered him on with "Get 'em Arizona" and "Ride 'em cowboy" as his successes mounted.

Frank Luke was riding high. Now his balloon busting missions were officially condoned, with requests coming down from army headquarters. Luke developed a master strategy to surprise the balloons at sunset, attacking them low while his wingman Wehner protected him from above. In this way, Luke scored a double on September 14, a triple the next day, and two more balloons the following day. Each time his plane was so damaged from combat that a new one was requisitioned. Wehner himself flamed several balloons and shot down a Fokker D.VII. The 27th Aero Squadron had two new aces to revel in for the moment, but that night the wily Germans placed a crack fighter squadron on balloon protection duty. On the evening of September 18, Luke and Wehner fell into the trap. Luke successfully fought through the barrage by destroying two Fokkers, a Halberstadt, as well as two more balloons within minutes. His elation crashed when he found that his friend Joe Wehner had been shot down.

Frank Luke lost all concentration and interest after the loss of his friend and protector. He was sent on one week's leave to Paris to recover, but returned after just a couple days filled with vengeance. He resumed his attack on the balloon line from a forward airfield. Once again he lost a wingman and went AWOL for a day as a result. On his return he was grounded, but scoffingly took off anyway and scored more victories. He spent that evening away with his French ace friends at the Storks. Upon his return the morning of September 29 he was reprimanded and confined to his tent ... but Luke had other plans. He stole away with his SPAD to the forward airfield near Verdun. Orders for his arrest chased him there by telephone. By chance he bumped into the Group Leader Maj. Hartney at the field, told him he was after more balloons, and took off again. Frank Luke's last

message dropped to the ground was "Watch 3 Hun balloons on the Meuse." If he returned, he would face court-martial for his disobedience.

In the sky, Luke achieved his revenge. Going up the line of trenches he disposed of three enemy balloons, the last of his 18 confirmed victories in as many days. Pursued by eight Fokkers (civilian witnesses say he downed two of them as well), and wounded by heavy anti-aircraft fire, he was forced down behind the lines in the town of Murvaux. He strafed every field-gray uniform he saw prior to his crash, then fled across a cemetery to a stream. The posse approached. It all happened so quickly—the victories, the dogfight, the crash, the chase, and now the final showdown. There was no question of surrender, for as Luke had told a friend the day he left Phoenix, "one thing will not happen, I'll never be taken prisoner." As a cool September breeze blew back his blond hair, he steadied himself, glared at his pursuers, and drew his trusty Colt .45 automatic. Another German fell to Frank's deadly aim, and then another. Each shot was returned by a hail of bullets from the platoon of riflemen gunning for him. With no ammunition left, Frank raised his Colt for the last time and drew the last hail of fire.

When news arrived back at the 27th Aero Squadron's field that Frank was Missing in Action after destroying three enemy balloons, Luke's commander Capt. Alfred Grant stopped writing the request for Luke's court-martial, and began a recommendation for the Distinguished Service Cross. Two months after the war ended and the truth of Frank's last day could be obtained, this same commander requested that the Congressional Medal of Honor be awarded, the first ever to an air fighter. This cowboy from Arizona, who had been a thorn in the side of many a commanding officer, was awarded the highest honor of his nation. With 21 victories (of which 14 balloons and four aircraft were confirmed) 21 one year old Frank Luke, Jr. became the second highest scoring ace of the United States in World War I.

Back home in Arizona, Frank Luke, Sr. never saw his son become a man. He never saw his boy's grave in the Romagne Military Cemetery in France, one white cross among thousands. He did see all of the medals issued posthumously— the Congressional Medal of Honor, the Distinguished Service Cross with oak leaf cluster, the Margarita Fisher Medal for Valor, the Aero Club Medal for Bravery, the Italian Croce di Guerre. He did see the memorials to his namesake: Luke Air Field in Hawaii, the tiny town of Lukeville, Arizona, Luke Monument in Phoenix. Yet it is a heartbroken father's tearful good-bye that echoes forever: "He was such a darn lively kid."

Flying High
Altitude Effects on Men and Machines

Lt. John Grider wrote in his diary *Warbirds*, "There were five of us and we ran into five Fokkers at 15,000 feet. We both started climbing of course—and they out climbed us. We climbed up to 20,500 feet and couldn't get any higher. We were practically stalled and these Fokkers went right over our heads and got between us and the lines. ... Gosh, it's unpleasant fighting at that altitude. The slightest movement exhausts you. Your engine has no pep and splutters; it's hard to keep a decent formation, and you lose 500 feet on a turn. The Huns came in from above and it didn't take us long to fight down to 12,000 feet. ... "

His experience demonstrates the effects of high altitudes on the men and machines which fought in W.W.I. All but a very few were open cockpit aircraft. The crew was exposed to less oxygen and extremely low temperatures at elevated altitudes. Some high flying bombers carried liquid oxygen in bottles for the crew to use, but most smaller craft did not carry any such equipment. Aircrew cannot spend more than ten minutes at 20,000 feet before risking hypoxia and unconsciousness. Ambient temperatures drop about 20°C every 6,000 feet, and the wind-chill factor from sitting behind the propeller thrust amplifies that to sub-zero temperatures even on a warm day. Airmen gathered flying clothing to protect them from the cold, acquiring hip length fur lined flying boots and warm flight suits, scarves and helmets. Heat from the engine and radiator offered some additional warmth for one of the crew.

Aircraft lose performance as they climb in altitude. Engine horsepower at 14,000 feet drops to 60% of its rating due to lack of oxygen. Special control of carburetion restored some, but not much, of this loss. Air pressure at 18,000 feet is half that at sea level, reducing the lift of the wings and the thrust of the propeller. The plane's top speed is reduced while the minimum speed required to maintain level flight increases, thus reducing the maneuvering options available to the pilot as he nears the plane's ceiling. Any turning maneuver reduces the amount of lift provided by the wing and results in an immediate loss of altitude. At the higher altitudes, this loss in height is greater and occurs more easily with less sharp maneuvers.

As a result of all these factors, most dogfights started out high after each side attempted to gain a height advantage, and quickly dropped several thousand feet during the fight. Once at lower altitudes, height losses due to maneuvering were less drastic and the fighting planes could use their climbing capabilities to best advantage. Some vicious fights bottomed out nearly at ground level where fire from the infantry became as deadly as the dogfight. Such may have been the case for Manfred von Richthofen on his last flight.

The First Battle of Britain

After Britain's preemptive strike against the Zeppelin sheds in Dusseldorf in 1914, the German offensive escalated in 1915. Airships dropped bombs on several civilians in raids on coastal towns in England. In March, Paris was the target. And, by May, a raid on London killed seven. Captain Peter Strasser, commander of the German Naval Airship Division, was the major proponent for the use of airships in war. Strasser was convinced that England could be crushed through air power. The vision of armadas of airships setting London ablaze was not just science fiction to him. Soon airships raided in squadron strength of four and five. The last raid of 1915, in October, was one of the deadliest, with almost 200 casualties. And Britain still had no effective air defense.

The year 1916 had a bloody opening. Strasser believed that large multi-ship raids were the key to victory. The first raid of the year, on England, killed 70. Finally Britain's government responded to the public's outcry. Entire aircraft squadrons were assigned to intercept airships. The "blackout" program became the order of the day in most English cities. German raids continued throughout 1916, but airships began showing their vulnerability. Able to raid effectively only in good weather and with a full moon, the airships increasingly fell prey to engine problems and British AAA. Then the British discovered the power of the incendiary bullet to pierce the airship's gas cell, and turn the target into a fireball. This invention, dubbed the "invention of the devil" by the Germans, literally sent the dream of victory over Britain by Zeppelin up in smoke. September 1916 marked a turning point in the first battle of Britain. Nineteen airships participated in the largest raid of the war, and a million Londoners watched as one airship, pierced by incendiary bullets, exploded in the sky above them. The tide of the Zeppelin war had turned. While German leaders refused to believe a mere bullet could bring down an airship, the irrefutable evidence remained: Six airships shot down in flames by intercepting aircraft in less than three months!

Germany was on the strategic defensive throughout 1917. Gotha bombers became active in May. Airships executed only seven raids in the entire year, compared to 24 in 1916. They focused on reconnaissance missions. Strasser concentrated on developing better defensive systems, namely the "safety-in-height" concept. Airships raided at an altitude far above the ceiling attainable by aircraft. Everything else—speed, comfort, bomb load—was sacrificed to achieve record altitudes. But, again, the first attack in October 1917 with the new "height-climber" Zeppelins was a complete disaster. Eleven airships flew into a gale over England. Only one airship completed its bombing mission and returned home safely. The others either crash-landed, were captured, or shot down. 1917 ended as dismally for the Germans as 1916.

The year 1918 began with a bang—the Great Ahlhorn Explosion. Five airships went up in flames in their sheds at Ahlhorn, Germany's largest Zeppelin base, in an accidental hydrogen gas explosion. This disaster spurred German military leaders to withdraw support from the airship campaign. Bombing aircraft had proved more efficient. Only Strasser continued to support the use of airships. And even Strasser admitted that raids would not achieve military victory, but should continue due to their "nuisance value." The final airship raid of the war was also Strasser's last. On August 5, at the helm of L70, Strasser led a five-airship raid on England. L70 never made it, but was attacked and brought down in flames. The loss of Strasser, the driving force behind the Zeppelin raids, paralyzed the navy airship division. It was the last Zeppelin raid. Shortly thereafter even all reconnaissance missions by airships were banned as well. This marked the end of airship operations in World War I.

A distinctly separate phase of the First Battle of Britain involved the great German bombing aircraft. The large Gotha bombers of *Kagohl 3*, deadly offspring of the still-born *Brieftauben Abteilung Ostende*, began raiding England from bases around Ghent, Belgium, in the summer of 1917. Renamed *Bogohl 3*, this "English Squadron" comprised six Bombenstaffeln (Bosta), and conducted raids of ten to twenty planes over London and southern England. The largest single raid consisted of 43 aircraft, while the deadliest caused 162 deaths. Giant Zeppelin Staaken R.VI bombers of squadron *Riesenflugzeug Abteilung* 501 later joined the strategic force and flew night raids both independently and in conjunction with the Gothas.

British response to these assaults differed from the Zeppelin defense. No magic bullet could flame a Gotha, so entire squadrons of the newest and best fighters with veteran RFC pilots drawn from the Western Front using novel night interception tactics were required. The German bomber assaults were finally brought to an end in May of 1918 after sixty Gotha losses. The remaining *Bostas* went to serve along the French front in the Second Battle of the Marne.

In the First Battle of Britain Zeppelins killed 557 people, injured 1358 and caused 3 million pounds sterling material damage on the Allied side. In as many raids as the Zeppelins, just over fifty, the German bombers added a further 836 Britons killed, nearly 2,000 injured, and 1.5 million pounds sterling in damage. The public outcry for protection caused the British military to station 12 RFC squadrons and enough men to outfit a full division on the Western Front. On the German side, 500 airshipmen died. Twenty airships went down with the loss of all hands. Zeppelin warfare proved to be a grand experiment that failed in the face of other aerial alternatives. Yet the Zeppelin threat prompted the development of aerial interceptors, night flying, civil defense organizations, ship-borne fighters and aircraft carriers. Zeppelin warfare advanced aerial navigation, strategic bombing and high altitude engines. And, while the First Battle of Britain was history's first air campaign against an enemy's economic centers far from the battlefield, the Zeppelin was the wrong vehicle. As Winston Churchill wrote, "I rated the Zeppelin much lower as a weapon of war than almost anyone else. I believed that this enormous bladder of combustible and explosive gas would prove to be easily destructible. I was sure the fighting aeroplane, rising lightly laden from its own base, armed with incendiary bullets, would harry, rout, and burn these gaseous monsters."

CHAPTER VIII

Conclusion

The last year of the war in the air demonstrated the best abilities of all nations involved. The air services played a valuable and necessary role in every action. Their presence significantly affected the successes of the ground troops both materially and morale-wise. Offensives were planned with information obtained by the airplane, attacks were supported and sustained with a significant measure of air supremacy, and defensive action was not secured without aerial support. Air forces gained respect and autonomy as military leaders and civilian authorities realized the importance of air power. Great Britain was the first nation to officially form an independent military arm, the Royal Air Force. All the nations' air services matured and developed distinct qualities and characteristics during the Great War.

The Germans opened the last year of the war with their spring offensives, concentrating the best and brightest for an integrated combined arms attack, hoping for victory. When this failed they relied on their best advantages to gain control of the air—a new Fokker fighter design, successful ground attack tactics, and the redirection of strategic bomber forces to serve the immediate needs of the army in the field. The Germans fully understood that they were fighting at an inferior strength and that their Amerikaprogramm had fallen short of its mark. The *Luftstreitkräfte* had grown to a force of 3,668 aircraft prior to the spring offensives but fell to 2,590 aircraft in the field by August. The German air service included 81 fighter Jastas, 38 ground attack

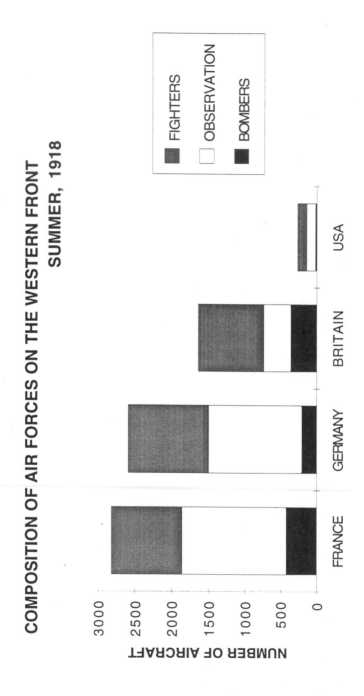

COMPOSITION OF AIR FORCES ON THE WESTERN FRONT
SUMMER, 1918

FIGHTERS
OBSERVATION
BOMBERS

NUMBER OF AIRCRAFT

3000
2500
2000
1500
1000
500
0

FRANCE
GERMANY
BRITAIN
USA

Staffels, 26 bombing Staffels, and 153 artillery and reconnaissance flying units. The industrial output of aircraft and the flow of trained pilots from the schools could not keep up with the growing losses during consecutive seasons of the offensive. By the Armistice 3,128 German aircraft (and 546 balloons) had fallen in combat with 6,840 flyers killed in action. German flyers shot down 4,865 planes and 614 balloons while antiaircraft fire accounted for another 1,588. Germany had 363 flyers with five or more victories. Manfred von Richthofen had 80 victories officially confirmed and was the top ace of all nations.

The Allied counterattacks beginning in the summer of 1918 turned the tide and led to the ultimate defeat of the Central Powers. By the time of the Armistice the French Aéronautique Militaire was a force of 3,556 aircraft equipping 80 fighter escadrilles, 52 bombing escadrilles, and 126 reconnaissance escadrilles. The majority of the fighters and bombers were grouped into the Division Aérienne to achieve local air supremacy by concentration of force. France suffered over 7,200 air casualties representing 40 per cent of all the flyers it trained. Its victory claims totaled 2,049 enemy aircraft destroyed plus 1,079 probables and 357 observation balloons flamed. The originator of the term, France produced 158 "aces." René Fonck was the highest scoring French ace with 75 confirmed victories.

The British amalgamated their air forces into the Royal Air Force which fielded 1,576 front line aircraft in 99 squadrons on the Western Front at the conclusion of hostilities. This number includes all RAF squadrons serving along the British front in France and the squadrons allocated to the Independent Air Force for strategic bombing. Nearly as many squadrons were scattered throughout the Mediterranean and the rest of Europe, from Palestine to Macedonia to the Home Establishment, or serving with the fleet. British casualties at the front throughout the course of the war totaled 16,623 of whom 6,166 were killed. A remarkable number of aces, 784, arose in the British flying services, with the top ranked being Mick Mannock at 73 victories followed by Billy Bishop at 72.

The American air services learned on-the-job how to fight a modern air campaign in 1918, and performed very well relative to the size of its forces actually in action. At home, however,

American aircraft manufacture fell below expectations. As a result the USAS purchased the majority of its aircraft from the French. Billy Mitchell was a leading critic of this scandalous industrial performance in which only a handful of Liberty planes arrived at the front after inordinate expenditure and delay. The U.S. Air Service had 740 planes in 45 squadrons at the front on November 11, 1918; several had barely come into service in the closing month of the war. Another 600 planes were spread across eight U.S. Marine Corps squadrons and two dozen U.S. Naval Air Stations along the coasts of Europe. The U.S. Air Service lost 289 aircraft in combat with the deaths of 169 airmen while accounting for 756 aircraft and 76 balloons destroyed. A total of 118 American aces came out of the war. Most of these aces served solely in the USAS, but a third scored their victories while serving the air forces of Britain and France. Captain Eddie Rickenbacker of the USAS was America's top ace with 26 victories.

LESSONS LEARNED

Winning the world's first air campaign involved a complex mixture of many factors. As in the ground campaign—numbers, organization, strategies, tactics, supply, morale, men, and materiel were all critical to success. The campaign in the skies, however, brought a new dimension to traditional warfare. The first steps required of all the aviation arms was a definition of purpose and the determination of goals. Since nothing like this campaign had occurred before, air services had to develop their own agenda as they discovered their own strengths and weaknesses. Such introspection encountered immediate resistance from officers with either antiquated beliefs or unrealistic expectations, both inside and outside the air service. Serving the obvious needs of the armies in the field took initial creativity but quickly became routine. To truly exercise the power of the new aviation arm required leadership, wisdom, and commitment.

Through the course of the war the air services grew and matured into air forces. Those services of France and Germany remained within the army command but achieved semi-autonomous status during the war with special ministries in the government and a high level reporting structure. The British RAF became the first fully autonomous air force mainly because of the strategic implications of air power. The British populace witnessed the effects of air power first hand as victims of strategic bombing. They at once realized that the English Channel was no longer the impenetrable barrier it had been in past wars. The British Isles were vulnerable to air attack and a non-traditional military arm was required for defense. As well, Britons desired to turn the tables by strategically bombing Germany with their new air force.

In fact, strategic bombing was not very productive in the first air war. The airships and planes of the time could not carry the necessary explosive tonnage to be significantly effective. The crippling of industry and generation of mass hysteria never came about the way both sides had hoped. Bombing London may have actually been counter-productive in that it gave civilians that much more reason to win rather than quit, and it sensitized them to be ready to handle the next Battle of Britain. On the other hand, air raid sirens frequently interrupted work in British factories, and several squadrons of aircraft and thousands of men were withdrawn from the war zone to defend England which reduced British strength along the Western Front. When Allied aircraft bombed targets in the German homeland, morale dropped in the German workforce, munitions plants on the Rhine experienced delays when forced to relocate, and rail traffic slowed due to the bombers overhead. Germany began in 1914 with the intent of bombing England and never really gave up on the idea of strategic air offensive until its great Zeppelin proponent, Peter Strasser, was killed. The Gotha bombers only stopped when they were urgently recalled to the western front in the 1918 offensives. France pursued strategic bombing in 1915 but rejected it later in place of more tactical uses of bombing. The RNAS used their bombers to harass submarine bases in Belgium and the Independent Force targeted industry in the Saar and on the Rhine. America never began strategic bombing on its own but was very aggressive with a small force at an operational and tactical level, bombing the lines of communication leading from the front to the German supply centers. The seed was planted, however, and it bore deadly fruit in the coming decades.

At the front, all nations struggled for aerial supremacy. The balance of power swung wildly from side to side during the air campaign. Industrialism, technology, and doctrine played as great a role as the military tactics and materiel. Theories of air power affected the structure of the air forces of the First World War. Major General Hugh Trenchard stressed the air offensive and tailored the British RFC and RAF with the highest percentage of fighter planes (55 per cent) of all the major powers. While other nations maintained at least half their force as reconnaissance aircraft, Trenchard devoted less than a quarter of his force to army cooperation types. And while the *Luftstreitkräfte* followed basically defensive doctrines, Trenchard pushed the battle zone over the German lines and drove aerial ascendancy through offensive doctrine and élan. His aim was to provide the means for accomplishing Allied missions while denying the enemy the same ability. Strategic bombing of distant economic sites came second to the destruction of the enemy army in the field and control of the air. The strategies developed by Trenchard and his disciple American General William Mitchell form the basis of aerial doctrine today.

Aerial supremacy shifted several times due purely to the introduction of new types of aircraft. The airplane was a weapon dependent on the latest technology, and this technology developed radically as the war progressed. Aircraft speeds increased during the war from barely 60 mph to over 138 mph, service ceilings were raised from 7,000 feet to above 22,000 feet, synchronized machine gun fire escalated from an interrupted 100 rounds per minute to a buffered 1,000 rounds per minute, and bomb loads were lifted from tiny hand held grenades to loads greater than a ton! New ideas revolutionized all aspects of military aviation, changing the conduct of warfare in the process. New classes of aircraft carried special equipment to perform novel missions. The Fokker D.VII, Germany's last threat to Allied aerial ascendancy, was so feared that the peace treaty specified it be surrendered to the Allies.

Organization, strategy and tactics interacted with the evolution of aircraft designs and focused the strengths of each nation.

THE SHIFTING BALANCE OF POWER

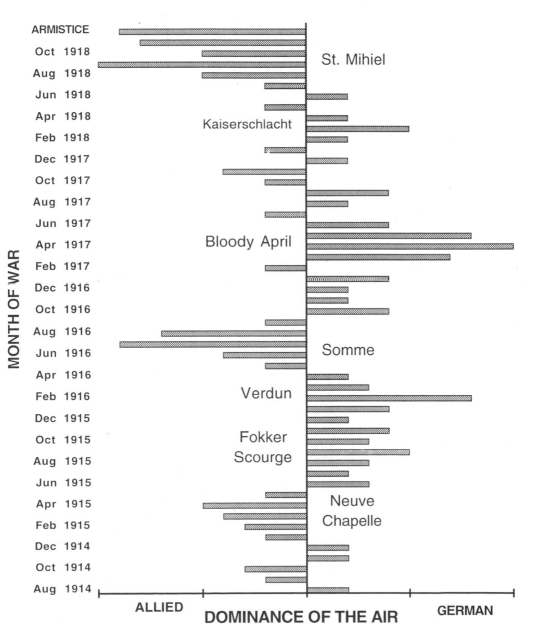

France developed the best day bomber of the war with the Breguet XIV and switched from strategic bombing to focus on tactical bombing in 1918. Germany and Britain had the best night bombers in 1918 with the Gotha and Staacken bombers and the Handley-Page O/400 respectively, thus retaining their strategic bombing organizations. Germany produced superior ground attack planes in the armored Junkers and light Hannoveranners which played into their offensive Stösstruppen tactics. The evolution of the fighter plane directly influenced the development of fighter tactics that drove the reorganizations of all combat plans.

The First World War was as much a war of attrition in the air as it was on the ground. Losses in the air placed great stresses on the aircraft manufacturing industry and on the training of flyers. France took the lead early in the mass production of aircraft and especially of aircraft engines, supplying her Allies as well as equipping her own large air force. Britain took more than a year to bring her aircraft industry into action, but ended the war producing large numbers of top quality planes. The German aircraft industry was limited in resources and therefore had to be very selective. They instituted intelligent programs like the Aldershof competitions to bring together the ideas and knowledge of private industry, the military leadership, and the flyers at the front. Superior designs came out of German firms, but were never built in large enough numbers to satisfy the needs of the front. All the countries struggled with the trade-off of specializing on proven aircraft types for mass production and encouraging many new designs to anticipate the advancement of military technology at the front. Shooting down more enemy aircraft did not necessarily provide lasting aerial dominance if the other side had more plentiful reserves. The German Jagdstaffels had their greatest successes and the Allies their bloodiest losses in April 1917. Though struggling to maintain their force that month, the Allies drew upon their greater industrial output and manpower resources to eventually replace these losses and squelch German aerial dominance.

With increased complexity of air operations, quality of training had to increase apace with the quantity of flyers being trained. Deaths by accidents rivaled the number killed in combat, and much of this related to training. Shifts in the balance of air power frequently followed the level of training received by the average rookie pilot at the front. As many aircraft were required by schools as were in combat, further taxing the production of planes.

The Allies ultimately won the campaign in the air by taking advantage of all of these elements to tip the balance of power in their favor. The offensive policies of innovative leaders like Trenchard and Mitchell, the superior numbers of trained men and machines eventually available, the superior output of Allied industrial capacity, the inter-allied cooperation to share resources and strengths, the development of competitive to superior equipment, and aggressive strategies and tactics, all peaked in the closing battles which ended the first campaign in the sky.

World War I was a watershed for the development of airpower and the history of aerial warfare. The airplane and its uses in war evolved more in the 52 months of World War I than in the 52 years that followed it. The basic concepts, technologies, organizations, strategies and tactics devised in World War I became the dogma of air power today. History's first air campaign dramatically changed the face of war forever.

Guide for the Interested Reader

Books of Interest

The First World War in the air spawned a school of literature. Virtually every top ranking ace wrote a first person narrative account of his experience, many first published in the middle of the war because of widespread personal popularity. Manfred von Richthofen's *Red Knight of Germany* (New York: 1969), Billy Bishop's *Winged Warfare* (New York: 1967), Eddie Rickenbacker's *Fighting the Flying Circus* (New York: 1965), René Fonck's *Ace of Aces* (New York: 1967), Willy Coppens' *Flying in Flanders* (New York: 1971) best exemplify these "white knuckle" recitation of events. Bare bones training, engine troubles, crash landings, miraculous maneuvers, and kills, kills, kills. Greenhill Books recently reprinted a comprehensive series of books in this vein, including: *Recollections of an Airman* (Novato, CA, and London: 1989) by Louis Strange, *Flying Fury* (Vista, CA, and Hertfordshire, England: 1987) by James McCudden, and *An Air Fighter's Scrapbook* (Novato, CA, and London: 1990) by Ira Jones. After the war many lesser known aces published their personal accounts based on diaries and letters. Several are noteworthy for the depth of insight and moving eloquence shared about their revolutionary occupation. *Warbirds* (London: 1966), edited by Elliott White Springs, *Sagittarius Rising* (New York: 1970) by Cecil Lewis, and Arch Whitehouse's many books like *Heroes of the Sunlit Sky* (Garden City, NY: 1967) are all must-reads. Detailed and well-written biographies and autobiographies are plentiful. Excellent examples include *Memoirs of World War I* (New York: 1960) by Billy Mitchell, *Knight of Germany* (London: 1985) about Oswald Boelcke written by Johannes Werner, and *Trenchard* (New York: 1962) by Andrew Boyle.

Books about the great aces abound, such as *They Fought For the Skies* (New York: 1958) by Quentin Reynolds, *The Canvas Falcons* (New York: 1970) by Stephen Longstreet, and Fred Oughton's *The Aces.* (New York: 1960). Norman Franks, Frank Bailey, Russell Guest, and Christopher Shores compiled a list of every American and French ace, complete with biographical sketches and victories in *Over the Front* (London: 1992). They did the same for British and Commonwealth aces in *Above the Trenches* (London: 1990), and for the German aces in *Above the Lines* (London: 1993). These volumes are a treasure trove of information. Dr. Martin O'Connor presents personal research in *Air Aces of the Austro-Hungarian Empire 1914-1918* (Mesa, AZ: 1986). Another classic book of the aces is *Air Aces of the 1914-1918 War* (Fallbrook, CA: 1964), edited by Bruce Robertson.

For general histories of the war in the air, there are several excellent selections currently available. *The First Air War* (New York: 1991) by Lee Kennett is a comprehensive survey of World War I aviation. *Sky Battle: 1914-1918* (New York: 1970) by David Cooke and *Aces High* by Alan Clark (New York: 1973) provide an overview of the aerial conflicts of the Western Front. John Morrow's *The Great War in the Air* (Washington, D.C.: 1993) emphasizes the supply side of the air campaign with detailed data on production and the first military industrial complex. An overall introduction to the war era is offered in the book *Legend, Memory, and the Great War in the Air* by Dominick Pisano et al (Seattle: 1992) which complements the latest WWI exhibit at the National Air and Space Museum.

Many interesting texts are readibly accessible on specific aspects of the first aerial campaign. *The Zeppelin in Combat* (Seattle: 1980) by Douglas Robinson is a detailed account of the Zeppelin campaign with orders of battle and cross-section diagrams. *Airshipwreck* (New York: 1978) by Len Deighton and Arnold Schwartzman offers extraordinary tragic photographs while *Zeppelin Adventures* (London: 1986) by Rolf Marben is a compilation of firsthand recollections by airship crewmen. Arch

Whitehouse's *Zeppelin Fighters* (New York: 1966) describes in exciting detail the British fighter pilots who won the first Battle of Britain. United States involvement is chronicled in *America's First Eagles* (Mesa, AZ: 1983) by Lucien Thayer, and James Hudson's *Hostile Skies* (Syracuse, NY: 1968). The U.S. Air Force also prepared a multi-volume set entitled *U.S. Air Service in World War I*. Alex Imrie's many texts on German operations include *Pictorial History of the German Army Air Service* (Chicago: 1971) and *German Fighter Units 1914-May 1917* (London: 1978). Charles Christienne includes hard to find information on France's World War I air service in *A History of French Military Aviation.* (Washington D.C.: 1986). John Angolia and Clint Hackney, Jr. describe decorations and give capsule biographies in *The Pour le Mérite and Germany's First Aces* (Friendswood, TX: 1984). Richard Hallion examines *The Rise of Fighter Aircraft* (Annapolis: 1984). Strategic bombing of England is examined in *The Sky on Fire* (New York: 1976) by Raymond Fredette and the bombing of Germany is covered in Neville Jones' *The Origins of Strategic Bombing* (London: 1973). Prewar aviation history is highlighted in John Villard's *Contact!* (New York: 1968). *The Smithsonian Book of Flight* (Washington, D.C.: 1987) by Walter Boyne and C.D.B. Bryan's *The National Air and Space Museum, Volume 1, Air* (New York: 1982) include sections on both the prewar era and the First World War. *Wilbur and Orville* (New York: 1987) by Fred Howard and *One Day at Kitty Hawk* (New York: 1975) by John Walsh explore the dawn of aviation and the lives of the Wright brothers.

Nearly as popular as books on the aces are books on the aircraft themselves, most with prolific illustrations and photographs valuable to modelers and hobbyists. Kenneth Munson's books are the most succinct and cover sufficient scope including the photographic *Aircraft of World War I* (Doubleday, New York: 1968), and the split view color illustrations in the series including *Fighters 1914-19, Bombers 1914-19, Flying Boats and Seaplanes, Pioneer Aircraft*, all by Macmillan Publishing (New York: 1968 to 1971). J.M. Bruce of the Imperial War Museum began a series of *Fighters: Warplanes of the First World War* (Garden City, NY: 1972) that sadly doesn't seem to have gone past volume five. Arms and Armour Press have published several series of photographic collections including *Vintage Warbirds* and *Vintage Aviation Fotofax*. Individual aircraft are highlighted in various profiles such as *Bristol Fighter in Action* (Carrollton, TX: 1993), *De Havilland DH-4* (Washington, DC: 1984), and *The Martinsyde Elephant* (Surrey, England: 1967). The Jane's annual publications are valuable sources. A reprint by Military Press compiling several annual editions is called *Jane's Fighting Aircraft of World War I* (New York, NY: 1990).

Journals give excellent insight into narrowly defined and interesting subjects. *Over the Front* is a fine quarterly journal of the League of World War I Aviation Historians edited by well known professional and amateur writers. It provides personal narrative and valuable amateur historical research. *Cross and Cockade International* from England follows a similar format. *World War One Aero* offers details on aircraft technology and restoration ideas. Ray Rimell's *Windsock International* is aimed at the aeromodeller but is packed with historical data and even paint chips to recreate the color schemes of the period.

Wargames

Biplanes fighting against triplanes in face to face battles in the clouds has been a most popular topic for gamers and hobby enthusiasts. Board games of varying degrees of detail and simulation quality have proliferated from nearly every game producer. An article in a recent issue of *Wargamer* magazine reviewed 17 of these simulations. Most recently published is 3W's game *The American Aces* (1994), which presents American experiences across all fronts of World War I from Caporetto to Dunkirk, with capsule biographies, O.B.'s for specific air actions, and aircraft performance specifications for planes that were flown by or fought against American aces. Another 3W game is the highly acclaimed multi-player board game *Aces High* (second edition 1993), an air wargame with realistic aircraft movement, maneuvers and realistic missions. Another title currently available is *Knights of the Air* (1987) by the Avalon Hill Game Company which gives the player a feel for the dynamics of climb, dive, and speed interaction. Avalon Hill's *Richthofen's War* (1972) is a classic of the genre. The popular games *Fight in the Skies* (1968) and *Dawn Patrol* (1982) by TSR Publications, Inc. spawned a society and a journal for gamers interested in WWI. *Wings* (second edition 1993) by Yaquinto won the award for best game of the year at the 1981 Origins national gaming convention and has been reprinted by Excalibre Games. A non-board game using illustrated books for two players to maneuver is *Ace of Aces* (1980, 1986) by Nova Games. *Wings Over France* (1991) by Lambourne Games focuses on the squadron level aspect of fighting the Bloody April campaign with a good feel for the management of attrition and the workload of a combat squadron. The first Battle of Britain is highlighted in the *Strategy and Tactics* magazine game *Zeppelin* (1993) by Decision Games. For miniatures gaming, *Hostile Aircraft* (1994) from Goblintooth Enterprises includes rules and two metal planes to start a collection. Computer flight simulators have also capitalized on the fascination with First World War era combat with several mostly solitaire format games. *Red Baron* (1991) by Dynamix/Sierra, *Wings of Glory* (1994, Origins), and *Dawn Patrol* (1994, Empire) are flight simulator based programs and include historical booklets.

Films

The first action classics of silent film centered on the dramatic air battles of the Great War. The 1927 film *Wings* with actress Clara Bow won Hollywood's first Academy Award for best motion picture. *Hell's Angels* made in 1930 by Howard Hughes and *The Dawn Patrol* starring Douglas Fairbanks, Jr. used a host of war surplus aircraft including the Pfalz D.XII now on display in the Smithsonian National Air and Space Museum.

Museums and Living History Museums

From Weeks Museum in Florida, through Harold Warp's in Nebraska, to the Museum of Flight in Seattle, numerous museums across North America contain some planes or artifacts of interest regarding First World War aviation, but the following stand out for particular emphasis on WWI. The National Air and Space Museum (part of the Smithsonian Institute) in Washington, D.C. recently revamped its First World War exhibit. This remarkable collection of classic planes from fighters to bombers is displayed and includes ace Ray Brooks' SPAD XIII. Besides the room of WWI planes, the exhibits on Lighter Than Air, Trainers, Pioneer Aircraft, and Air Mail also contain significant related subjects—and don't forget the restoration going on at the

Garber Facility in Maryland. In Dayton, Ohio (the sight of the Liberty DH-4 production), is the United States Air Force Museum. Of special note is the only surviving Caproni bomber like that flown by La Guardia, the SPAD XVI flown by Billy Mitchell, the Caquot balloon, the Medal of Honor exhibit, an S.E.5, a replica of George Vaughn's Camel, and much more. Mesa, Arizona, is the site of the Champlin Fighter Aces Museum with up-close views in the World War I hangar of over a dozen exacting replica fighters and two extremely rare originals: the Pfalz D.XII and the Aviatik D.I Berg. Canada's rich collection at the National Aviation Museum in Ottawa, Ontario includes the only A.E.G. G.IV bomber, a Curtiss HS-2L flying boat, Sowrey's Zeppelin killing B.E.2c, and the remains of Barker's Sopwith Snipe.

Europe is filled with museums, cemeteries, and battlefield memorials relating to the Great War in the air. The Musée de l'Air at Le Bourget, France, is the most famous air museum with a huge collection of WWI planes. England is scattered with air museums. The Imperial War Museum's airfield at Duxford and the RAF Museum at Hendon are good starting points. Italy has a Caproni museum in Milan as well as its national collection near Rome. Germany has an original Fokker, a Rumpler C.IV, and a Taube in its Science and Technology Museum in Munich. Russian, Austrian, and Czech designs are displayed in the National Technical Museum in Prague. A truly rare gem is the little known Royal Army Museum in Brussels, Belgium, with over fifteen planes that flew above that city in WWI.

The thrill of seeing and hearing these planes once again in flight has attracted many a visitor to the Rhinebeck Aerodrome in Rhinebeck, New York. Begun by Cole Palen, this living museum flies a World War I air show every summer weekend with top quality replicas powered by original engines. The Owls Head Transportation Museum in Maine also flies replicas of WWI and pioneer aircraft several times a year. Old Warden Aerodrome in Bedfordshire, England, flies both original and replica planes of the Great War. Original WWI era planes and scale replicas often appear at annual air meets like the Experimental Aircraft Association in Oshkosh, Wisconsin. Such living history museums capture the awesome excitement of the world's first aerial campaign.

APPENDIX

LEADING ACES OF THE FIRST WORLD WAR (Western Front)

ACE	UNIT	VICTORIES
Britain		
Major Edward C. Mannock	40, 74, 85	73
Major William A. Bishop	60, 85	72
Major Raymond Collishaw	10N, 203	60
Major James T.B. McCudden	29, 56	57
Captain Anthony W. Beauchamp-Proctor	84	54
France		
Capitaine René P. Fonck	Spa103	75
Capitaine Georges M.L.J. Guynemer	MS3, N3, Spa3	53
Lieutenant Charles E.J.M. Nungesser	N65, V116, Spa65	43
Capitaine Georges F. Madon	N38, Spa38	41
Lieutenant Maurice Boyau	N77, Spa77	35
Belgium		
2/Lieutenant Willy Coppens de Houthulst	6me, 1re, 9me	37
Adjutant André de Meulemeester	1re, 9me	11
2/Lieutenant Edmond Thieffry	5me, 10me	10
America (USAS)		
Captain Edward V. Rickenbacker	94th	26
Lieutenant Frank Luke, Jr.	27th	18
Major Gervais Raoul Lufbery	N124, 94th	16
Captain George A. Vaughn, Jr.	84 RAF, 17th	13
Captain Elliott White Springs	85 RAF, 148th	12
Lieutenant Field E. Kindley	148th	12
Lieutenant David E. Putnam	MS156, Spa138, 139th	12
Americans in Foreign Services		
Captain Frederick W. Gillet	79 RAF	20
Captain Wilfred Beaver	20 RFC	19
Captain William C. Lambert	24 RAF	18
Captain August T. Iaccaci	20 RAF	17
Captain Paul T. Iaccaci	20 RAF	17
Captain Oren J. Rose	92 RAF	16
German		
Rittmeister Manfred von Richthofen	*2, 11, JG I*	80
Oberleutnant Ernst Udet	*15, 11, 4*	62
Oberleutnant Erich Löwenhardt	*10*	54
Leutnant Werner Voss	*2, 5, 10*	48
Hauptmann Bruno Loerzer	*26, JG III*	44

Representative Aircraft Types of the First Air Campaign

Year	Aircraft	Nation	Role	Type	Crew	Engine	Speed	Span	Ceiling	Weapon	Bomb Load
1914	Blériot XI-2	France	Recon	Monopl	2	80 hp Gnôme rotary	66 mph	33' 11"	3,280'	none	none
1914	Henry Farman HF.20	France, Brit.	Recon	Pusher	2	80 hp Gnôme 7A rotary	61 mph	51'	9,022'	none	none
1914	Maurice Farman VII	France	Recon	Pusher	2	70 hp Renault	59 mph	51'	13,123'	none	none
1914	B.E.2a	Britain	Recon	Biplane	2	70 hp Renault	70 mph	35'	9,500'	none	100 lbs.
1914	AVRO 504B	Britain	Recon, Bombing	Biplane	2	80 hp Gnôme	62 mph	36'	12,000'	none	4x 16 lbs.
1914	Rumpler Taube	Germany	Recon	Monopl	2	100 hp Argus	59 mph	45' 11"	8,500'	none	none
1914	Albatros B.II	Germany	Recon	Biplane	2	100 hp Mercedes D.I	65 mph	42'	9,843'	none	none
1915	Caudron G IV A2	France	Recon	Biplane	2	2x 80hp LeRhône 9C rotaries	83mph	56' 5"	14,108'	1x Lewis	249 lbs.
1915	Maurice Farman XI	France	Recon	Pusher	2	100 hp Renault	66 mph	53'	12,467'	1x Hotchkiss or Lewis	18x 16 lbs.
1915	Morane Saulnier L	France	Recon, Fighter	Monopl	2	80 hp Gnôme rotary	71 mph	36' 9"	13,123'	1x Hotchkiss or Lewis	none
1915	Voisin 3 LA	France	Bomber	Pusher	2	120 hp Salmson Canton-Unné radial	62 mph	48' 5"	10,000'	1xm.g. or 47mm canon	100 lbs.
1915	Vickers F.B.5	Britain	Recon, Fighter	Pusher	2	100 hp Gnôme rotary	70 mph	36' 6"	9,000'	1x Lewis	none
1915	B.E.2c	Britain	Recon	Biplane	2	90 hp RAF 1a	72 mph	37'	10,000'	personal arms	4x 25lbs.
1915	DFW B.I	Germany	Recon	Biplane	2	100 hp Mercedes D.I	75 mph	46'	9,843'	personal arms	none
1915	Rumpler C.I	Germany	Recon	Biplane	2	160 hp Mercedes D.III	95 mph	39' 10 "	16,568'	1x Parabellum	none
1915	Fokker E.I	Germany	Fighter	Monopl	1	80 hp Oberursel	82 mph	28'	10,000'	1x LMG.08	none
1916	Nieuport XI	France	Fighter	Sesquipl	1	80 hp Le Rhône 9C rotary	97 mph	24' 9"	15,092'	1x Hotchkiss or Lewis	none
1916	Morane Saulnier N	France	Fighter	Monopl	1	80 hp Le Rhône 9C rotary	89 mph	26' 9"	13,123'	1x Hotchkiss or Lewis	none
1916	Voisin 5 LA.S	France	Bomber	Pusher	2	150 hp Salmson Canton	65 mph	48' 5"	11,485'	1x m.g. or 37mm canon	132 lbs.
1916	Bréguet-Michelin 4B2	France	Bomber	Pusher	2	220 hp Renault 12	86 mph	57' 8"	14,108'	1x Hotchkiss or Lewis	40x 16 lbs.
1916	Sopwith 1 1/2 Strutter	Britain	Recon, Bomber	Biplane	2	130hp Clerget 9B rotary	102 mph	33' 6"	13,000'	1x Lewis + 1x Vickers	260 lbs.
1916	Airco D.H.2	Britain	Fighter	Pusher	1	100 hp Gnôme rotary	93 mph	28' 3"	14,500'	1x Lewis or Vickers	none
1916	F.E.2b	Britain	General	Pusher	2	120 hp Beardmore in-line	81 mph	47' 9"	9,000'	2x Lewis	3x 112 lbs
1916	Albatros C.III	Germany	Recon	Biplane	2	160 hp Mercedes D.III	87 mph	38' 5"	11,155'	1x Spandau + 1x Par'um	198 lbs.
1916	Fokker E.III	Germany	Fighter	Monopl	1	100 hp Oberursel U I	87 mph	30' 10"	11,500'	1x LMG.08	none.

Year	Aircraft	Nation	Role	Type	Crew	Engine	Speed	Span	Ceiling	Weapon	Bomb Load
1916	Albatros D.II	Germany	Fighter	Biplane	1	160 hp Mercedes D.III	108 mph	27' 11"	17,060'	2x Spandau	none
1917	Dorand AR 1	France	Recon	Biplane	2	190 hp Renault	94 mph	43' 7"	18,045	1x Vickers + 1 Lewis	181 lbs.
1917	Nieuport XVII	France	Fighter	Sesquipl	1	110 hp Le Rhône 9J rotary	109 mph	27'	17,390'	1x Lewis and/or Vickers	none
1917	SPAD VII	France	Fighter	Biplane	1	180 hp Hispano 8-Ab	127 mph	25' 7"	21,500'	1x Vickers	none
1917	Voisin 8 LA.P	France	Bomber	Pusher	2	220 hp Peugeot 8Aa	82 mph	61' 8"	14,107'	1x Hotchkiss	396 lbs.
1917	R.E.8	Britain	Recon	Biplane	2	150 hp RAF 4a	102 mph	42' 7"	13,500'	1x Vickers + 1x Lewis	2x112 lbs.
1917	Bristol Fighter F2B	Britain	Fighter, Recon	Biplane	2	275 hp Rolls-Royce Falcon III	123 mph	39' 3"	18,000'	1x Vickers + 1x Lewis	none
1917	Sopwith Pup	Britain	Fighter	Biplane	1	80 hp Le Rhône 9C rotary	111 mph	26' 6"	17,000'	1x Vickers	none
1917	Sopwith Triplane	Britain	Fighter	Tripe	1	130 hp Clerget 9B rotary	116 mph	26' 6"	20,000'	1x Vickers	none
1917	Airco D.H.5	Britain	Fighter	Biplane	1	110 hp Le Rhône 9J rotary	102 mph	25' 8"	16,000'	1x Vickers	4x 25 lbs.
1917	Sopwith Camel	Britain	Fighter	Biplane	1	130 hp Clerget 9B rotary	108 mph	28'	18,500'	2x Vickers	4x 20 lbs.
1917	Airco D.H.4	Britain	Bomber, Recon	Biplane	2	250 hp Rolls-Royce Eagle III	117 mph	42' 5"	16,000'	1x Vickers + 1x Lewis	4x 112 lbs.
1917	Hanriot HD.1	Belgium	Fighter	Biplane	1	120 hp Le Rhône 9Jb rotary	114 mph	28' 6"	19,685'	1x Vickers	none
1917	Curtiss H.12	USA, Britain	Flying Boat	Biplane	4	2x 275 Fp Rolls-Royce Eagle I	93 mph	92' 8"	10,800'	4x Lewis	460 lbs.
1917	Curtiss JN-4D	USA	Trainer	Biplane	2	90 hp Curtiss OX-5	75 mph	43' 7"	11,000'	none	none
1917	DFW C.V	Germany	Recon	Biplane	2	200 hp Benz Bs.IV	96 mph	43' 6"	20,997'	1x Spandau + 1x Parabellum	none
1917	Albatros D.III	Germany	Fighter	Biplane	1	175 hp Mercedes D.IIIa	109 mph	29' 8"	18,045'	2x Spandau	none
1917	Fokker Dr.I	Germany	Fighter	Tripe	1	110 hp Oberursel UR.II rotary	102 mph	23' 8"	20,013'	2x Spandau	none
1917	Pfalz D.III	Germany	Fighter	Biplane	1	160 hp Mercedes D.III	103 mph	30' 10"	17,060'	2x Spandau	none
1917	Halberstadt CL.II	Germany	Escort, Attack	Biplane	2	160 hp Mercedes D.III	103 mph	35' 4"	16,732'	1x Spandau + 1x Parabellum	stick-grenades
1917	Junkers J.I	Germany	Ground Support	Biplane	2	200 hp Benz Bz.IV	96 mph	52' 6"	9,000'	1x Spandau + 1x Parabellum	stick-grenades
1917	**AEG G.IV**	**Germany**	**Day Bomber**	**Biplane**	**3**	**2x 260hp Mercedes D.IVa**	**90mph**	**60'**	**12,123'**	**2x Parabellum**	**772 lbs.**
1917	Gotha G.IV	Germany	Night Bomber	Biplane	4	2x 260 hp Mercedes D.IVa	87 mph	77' 9"	21,325'	4x Parabellum	1,100 lbs.
1918	Salmson 2A2	France, USA	Recon	Biplane	2	260 hp Salmson Canton-Unné racial	115 mph	38' 8"	20,505'	1x Vickers + 2 Lewis	none

Year	Aircraft	Nation	Role	Type	Crew	Engine	Speed	Span	Ceiling	Weapon	Bomb Load
1918	SPAD XIII	France, USA	Fighter	Biplane	1	234 hp Hispano 8-BEc	138 mph	26' 6"	22,500'	2x Vickers or Marlins	none
1918	Morane Saulnier AI	France	Fighter	Monopl	1	150 hp Gnôme 9N monosoupape	137 mph	27' 11"	22,965'	2x Vickers	none
1918	Caudron R XI A3	France	Bomber Escort	Biplane	3	2x 220 Hispano-Suiza 8B	114 mph	58' 9"	19,521'	5x Lewis	265 lbs.
1918	Bréguet XIV	France, USA	Bomber, Recon	Biplane	2	1x 310 hp Renault 12-Fcy	110 mph	47' 3"	19,030'	1x Vickers + 2 Lewis	660 lbs.
1918	D.H.9A	Britain	Recon, Bomber	Biplane	2	400 hp Liberty 12	123 mph	30' 3"	16,750'	1x Vickers + 2x Lewis	4x 112 lbs.
1918	S.E.5a	Britain	Fighter	Biplane	1	200 hp Wolseley Viper	120 mph	26' 7"	19,500'	1x Vickers + 1x Lewis	none
1918	Sopwith Snipe	Britain	Fighter	Biplane	1	230 hp Bentley B.R.2 rotary	121 mph	30'	19,500'	2x Vickers	none
1918	Handley Page O/400	Britain	Night Bomber	Biplane	4	2x 360hp Rolls-Royce Eagle VIII	98'	100'	8,500'	5x Lewis	8x 250 lbs.
1918	Liberty DH-4	USA	Bomber, Recon	Biplane	2	416 hp Liberty 12A	125 mph	42' 5"	15,800'	2x Marlin + 2x Lewis	450 lbs.
1918	Nieuport 28	USA	Fighter	Biplane	1	170 hp Gnôme 9N rotary	122 mph	26' 9"	16,995'	2x Vickers	none
1918	LVG C.VI	Germany	Recon	Biplane	2	200 hp Benz Bz.IV	106 mph	42' 8"	21,325'	1x Spandau + 1x Parabellum	none
1918	Rumpler C.VI	Germany	Recon	Biplane	2	240 hp Maybach Mb.IV	109 mph	41' 2"	23,944'	1x Parabellum	none
1918	Albatros D.Va	Germany	Fighter	Biplane	1	175 hp Mercedes D.IIIa	116 mph	29' 8"	20,505'	2x Spandau	none
1918	Fokker D.VII	Germany	Fighter	Biplane	1	175 hp Mercedes D.IIIa	118 mph	29' 4"	19,685'	2x Spandau	none
1918	Fokker D.VIII	Germany	Fighter	Monopl	1	110 hp Oberursel UR.II rotary	115 mph	26' 3"	20,669'	2x Spandau	none
1918	Zeppelin Staaken R.VI	Germany	Night Bomber	Biplane	7	4x 260hp Mercedes C.IVa	81mph	138' 3"	12,467'	8x Parabellum	4,409 lbs.

KEY TO ABBREVIATIONS:

TYPE:
Monopl = monoplane wing configuration
Sesquipl = sesquiplane "V-strutter" wing configuration
Biplane = biplane wing configuration
Tripe = triplane wing configuration
Pusher = pusher airframe design

NOTES:
YEAR represents the year that most were in service. Such types may have been introduced in the previous year.

ORDER OF BATTLE

RAF Order of Battle, 1918

IX Brigade (Headquarters)

9th Wing
squadron No. 32 (S.E.5a), 73 (Camel), and three day bomber squadrons

51st Wing
squadron No. 1 (S.E.5a), 43 (Camel and Snipe), 54 (Camel)

54th Wing
squadron No. 151 (Camel) night fighters

eight additional squadrons including the 82nd Wing

I Brigade

1st Corps Wing
seven observation squadrons including: 2, 5, 10, 16 and 91st Wing

10th Army Wing
squadron No. 19 (Dolphin), 40 (S.E.5a), 64 (S.E.5a), 203 (Camel)

II Brigade

2nd Corps Wing
thirteen observation squadrons including: 6, 21, 42, 46, 53

11th Army Wing
squadron No. 29 (S.E.5a), 70 (Camel), 74 (S.E.5a), 79 (Dolphin)

65th Wing
squadron No. 17 USAS (Camel), 148 USAS (Camel)

III Brigade

12th Corps Wing
nine squadrons including: 8, 12, 13, 59 and 90th Wing

13th Army Wing

squadron No. 3 (Camel), 56 (S.E.5a) 60 (S.E.5a), 87 (Dolphin)

V Brigade

15th Corps Wing
seven observation squadrons including: 4, 15

22nd Army Wing
squadron No. 23 (Dolphin), 24 (S.E.5a), 41 (S.E.5a), 65 (Camel), 80 (Camel), 84 (S.E.5a), 201 (Camel), 209 (Camel)

X Brigade

81st Corps Wing
seven observation squadrons

80th Army Wing
squadron No. 2 AFC (S.E.5a), 4 AFC (Snipes), 92 (S.E.5a)

61st Wing

squadron No. 204 (Camel), 210 (Camel), 213 (Camel)

Independent Air Force (VIII Brigade)

41st Wing (day)
squadron No. 55 (D.H.4), 99 (D.H.9), 104 (D.H.9), 110 (D.H.9A)

83rd Wing (night)
squadron No. 100 (F.E.2b), 216 (HP O/100), 97 (HP O/400), 215 (HP O/400), 115 (HP O/400)

88th Wing
mobilized later

Home Establishment (Home Defense of British Isles):

Twelve Squadrons

235

Observation squadrons flew
D.H.9A, D.H.9, D.H.4, R.E.8, and
Armstrong-Whitworth F.K.8. Other
RAF squadrons in Palestine, Meso-
potamia, Italy, Macdonia, and else-
where plus numerous

Naval Air Stations along coast and
units stationed with the Fleet

Australian Flying Corps
In France

squadron No. 2 AFC (S.E.5a), 3
AFC (R.E.8 and Brisfits), 4
AFC (Snipes)

In Palestine
squadron No. 1 AFC (Brisfits
and various types including
one HP O/400)

Canadian Air Force
two squadrons forming in
England

BELGIAN Order of Battle, 1918

1re Group de Chasse:
9me (Hanriot HD-1), 10me (SPAD
VII), 11me (Sopwith Camels).

Observation Escadrilles:
2me (Bréguet XIV), 3me (Bréguet
XIV),

4me (SPAD XI), 5me (SPAD XI),
6me (SPAD XI), 7me (Maurice
Farman 11bis)

Night Bombing
8me (Farman F60)

Depot Escadrille
1re (various types)

AMERICAN USAS Order of Battle, 1918

First Army Command

1st Corps Observation Group
1st (Salmson), 12th (Salmson),
50th (DH-4)

3d Corps Observation Group
88th (Salmson), 90th (Salmson)

4th Corps Observation Group
8th (DH-4), 135th (DH-4),
168th (DH-4)

5th Corps Observation Group
99th (Salmson), 104th
(Salmson)

7th Corps Observation Group
258th (Salmson)

1st Army Observation Group
9th (Breguet 14), 24th
(Salmson), 91st (Salmson),
186th (Salmson)

1st Pursuit Group:

27th (SPAD 13), 94th (SPAD
13), 95th (SPAD 13), 147th
(SPAD 13), 185th (Camel)

1st Pursuit Wing:
2nd Pursuit Group (SPADs)
13th, 22th, 49th, 139th
3rd Pursuit Group (SPADs)
28th, 93th, 103th, 213th
1st Day Bombardment Group
11th (DH-4), 20th (DH-4), 96th
(Breguet 14), 166th (DH-4)

Second Army Command

6th Corps Observation Group
354th (DH-4)

2nd Day Bombardment Group
163rd (DH-4)

4th Pursuit Group
25th (S.E.5a), 141st (Camel)

Attached to British 65th Wing
17th (Camel), 148th (Camel)

and 17 Balloon Companies

FRENCH Order of Battle, 1918

Division Aérienne

Groupement Ménard, 1st Brigade

Escadre 1er (Chasse)
GC 15
Spa37, Spa81, Spa93, Spa97
GC 18
Spa48, Spa94, Spa153,
Spa155
GC 19
Spa73, Spa85, Spa95, Spa96
Escadre 12 (Bombardement jour)
GB 5
Br117, Br120, Br127
GB 6
Br66, Br108, Br111
GB 9
Br29, Br123, Br129, RXI239,
RXI240

Groupement Féquant, 2me Brigade

Escadre 2 (Chasse)
GC 13
Spa15, Spa65, Spa84, Spa88
GC 17
Spa77, Spa89, Spa91,
Spa100, Spa174
GC 20
Spa68, Spa99, Spa158,
Spa159, Spa16
Escadre 13 (Bombardement jour)
GB 3
Br107, Br126, Br128
GB 4
Br131, Br132, Br134, RXI246

Groupement Bloch, strategic photo-mapping

Br220, Br45, R46

**Escadre 11 (Bombardement nuit)
(flying Farman F5C and Voisin 10)**

GB 1
GB 7
GB 8
GB 2
GB 18 (Italian bombing unit
flying Caproni Ca3)
GB10

I Army Command
Spa102, Spa171
GC 14
Spa75, Spa80, Spa83, Spa86,
Spa166

II Army Command
Spa23

III Army Command
Spa79

IV Army Command
Spa156
GC 12
(Storks) Spa3, Spa26, Spa67,
Spa103, and Spa167,
Spa173
GC 21
Spa98, Spa157, Spa124,
Spa163, Spa164, and US
103rd Aero Sqdn.
GC 22
Spa38, Spa87, Spa92,
Spa152, Spa169

V Army Command
Spa76
GC 16
Spa78, Spa112, Spa151,
Spa168

VI Army Command
Spa62
GC 23
Spa82, Spa158, Spa160,
Spa161, Spa170

VII Army Command
Spa49

VIII Army Command
Spa90
GC 11
Spa12, Spa31, Spa154,
Spa165, Spa170

X Army Command
Spa69

Army and Corps Observation
forty observation escadrilles flying Br XIV A2

forty-eight Salmson 2A2 escadrilles

twenty-nine SPAD XVI and XI escadrilles

two additional escadrilles of Caudron R XI for observation escort

five escadrilles of Voisin Bn2

two escadrilles of Caproni Ca33

three escadrilles of Farman F50

Urban defense units
Spa57, Spa124, Spa461, Spa462, Spa463, Spa464, Spa313, Spa314, Spa315

Other theaters
six escadrilles de chasse

GERMAN Order of Battle, 1918

Jagdgeschwader

JG I Richthofen
Jasta 11, Jasta 4, Jasta 6, Jasta 10 (flying Fokker D.VII and D.VIII)

JG II
Jasta 12, Jasta 13, Jasta 15, Jasta 19 (flying Fokker D.VII)

JG III
Jasta Boelcke, Jasta 26, Jasta 27, Jasta 36 (flying Fokker D.VII)

JG IV **(Bavarian)**
Jasta 23b, Jasta 32b, Jasta 34b, Jasta 35b (flying Fokker D.VII and Pfalz D.XII)

sixty-nine further *Jastas*
(flying Fokker D.VII, Pfalz D.IIIa, Albatros D.Va, Pfalz D.XII, Fokker D.VIII)

ten *Kampfeinsitzerstaffel* (*Kest*) **for home defense (later reformed as** *Jasta 82* **through** *90*)
(flying D types including the Siemens-Schuckert D.III and D.IV, and LFG Roland D.VI)

Bombengeschwader **(each with three Bostas of Gotha G.IV and G.V):**
Bogohl 1, Bogohl 2, Bogohl 4, Bogohl 5, Bogohl 6, Bogohl 7, Bogohl 8 (Bavarian)

Bogohl 3 **"England Geschwader"**

Bosta 13, Bosta 14, Bosta 15, Bosta 16, Bosta 17

Riesenflugzeug Abteilung
R500, R501 (Zeppelin Staaken)

thirty-one *Flieger Abteilung* **observation squadrons**
(flying C type aircraft)

ten *Flieger Abteilung Lb* **for photographic reconnaissance**
(flying C types for army cooperation)

fifty-seven *Flieger Abteilung (A)* **artillery cooperation units**
(flying C types for artillery cooperation)

five *Flieger Abteilung (A) Lb* **for photo mapping**
(flying Rumpler C.VI "Rubild" and C.VII)

thirty-seven *Infanterieflieger*
(flying C and J types for close infantry and artillery support)

thirty-eight *Schlachtstaffeln* **for ground assault**
(flying Halberstadt CL.II, CL.IV, and Hannover CL.IIIa)

five *Marine-Feldjagdstaffel*

six *Flieger Abteilung Pascha* **in the middle east**

fifty-six *Feldluftschiffer Abteilung* **plus 186 balloon companies**

Bibliography

Angolia, John. *The Pour le Merite and Germany's First Aces.* Friendswood, TX: Hackney Publishing Company, 1984.

Archer, Wesley. *Death In The Air.* London: Greenhill Books, 1985.

Bakcr, David. *Billy Bishop: The man and the aircraft he flew.* London: Outline Press, 1990.

Baker, David. *Richthofen: The man and the aircraft he flew.* London: Outline Press, 1990.

Balfour, Harold. *An Airman Marches.* London: Greenhill Books, 1985.

Baynes, Ernest. *Animal Heroes of the Great War.* New York: The MacMillan Company, 1925.

Béraud-Villars, Jean. *Notes of a Lost Pilot.* Hamden, Conn: Archon Books, 1975.

Bewsher, Paul. *Green Balls.* London: Greenhill Books, 1986.

Biddle, Charles. *Fighting Airman: The Way of the Eagle.* New York: Ace Books, Inc., 1968.

Bishop, Wm. *Winged Warfare.* New York: Ace Books, 1967.

Bishop, William Arthur. *The Courage of the Early Morning.* New York: David McKay Co., 1966.

Bott, Alan. *An Airman's Outings with the RFC, June-December 1916.* London: Greenhill Books, 1986.

Bowen, Ezra. *Knights of the Air.* Alexandria, Va.: Time-Life Books, 1980.

Boyle, Andrew. *Trenchard.* New York: W.W. Norton & Company Inc., 1962.

Boyne, Walter. *The Smithsonian Book of Flight.* Washington, D.C.: Smithsonian Books, 1987.

Bruce, J.M. *Warplanes of the First World War, Fighters.* Garden City, NY: Doubleday and Company, Inc., 1972.

Bryan, C.D.B. *The National Air and Space Museum, Volume 1, Air.* New York: Bantam Books, 1982.

Burlingame, Roger. *General Billy Mitchell, Champion of Air Defense.* New York: McGraw-Hill Book Company, Inc., 1952.

Cameron, Lou. *Iron Men with Wooden Wings.* New York: Belmont Productions, Inc. 1967.

Carisella, P.J., and James W. Ryan. *The Black Swallow of Death.* Boston, MA: Marlborough House, Inc., 1972.

Chant, Chris. *The Illustrated History of the Air Forces of World War I & World War II.* Seacaucus, NJ: Chartwell Books, Inc., 1979.

Chant, Christopher. *The Military History of the United States, World War I.* New York: Marshall Cavendish, 1992.

Chant, Christopher. *The Military History of the United States, Border Wars and Foreign Excursions.* New York: Marshall Cavendish, 1992.

Christienne, Charles, and Pierre Lissarague. *A History of French Military Aviation.* Washington D.C.: Smithsonian Institution Press, 1986.

Churchill, Winston S. *The World Crisis.* New York: Charles Scribner's Sons, 1927.

Clark, Alan. *Aces High, The War in the Air over the Western Front 1914-1918.* New York: G.P. Putnam's Sons, 1973.

Cobby, A.H. *High Adventure.* Melbourne, Australia: Kookaburra Technical Publications, 1981.

Colvin, Fred H. *Aircraft Mechanics Handbook.* New York: McGraw-Hill Book Company, Inc., 1918.

Cooke, David. *Sky Battle 1914-1918.* New York: W.W. Norton & Company, 1970.

Coppens, Willy. *Flying in Flanders.* New York: Ace Books, 1971.

Crouvezier, Gustave. *L'Aviation pendant la Guerre.* Paris et Nancy: Librairie Militaire Berger-Levrault, 1916.

Cuneo, Ernest. *Life with Fiorello.* New York: The MacMillan Company, 1955.

Davis, Burke. *The Billy Mitchell Affair.* New York: Random House, 1967.

Deighton, Len, and Arnold Schwartzman. *Airshipwreck.* New York: Holt, Rinehart and Winston, 1978.

de Vries, Col. John A. *Taube, Dove of War.* Temple City, CA: Historical Aviation Album, 1978.

Dupuy, Trevor. *The Military History of World War I, Summation: Strategic and Combat Leadership.* New York: Franklin Watts, 1967.

Eder, Jack (ed.) *Let's Go Where The Action Is !* Knightstown, IN: JaaRE Publishing, 1984.

Eells, George. *The Life That Late He Led.* London: W. H. Allen, 1967.

Elliott, Lawrence. *Little Flower: The Life and Times of Fiorello La Guardia.* New York: William Morrow and Company, 1983.

Finne, K. N. *Igor Sikorsky: The Russian Years.* Washington, D.C.: Smithsonian Institution Press, 1987,

Fitzsimmons, Bernard. (ed) *Warplanes and Air Battles of World War I.* New York: Beekman House, 1973.

Flammer, Philip. *The Vivid Air.* Athens, GA: University of Georgia Press, 1981.

Fokker, Anthony, and Bruce Gould. *Flying Dutchman*. New York: Henry Holt and Co., 1931.

Fonck, Rene. *Ace of Aces*. New York: Ace Books, 1967.

Franks, Norman; Frank Bailey, and Russell Guest. *Above the Lines*. London: Grub Street, 1993.

Franks, Norman, and Frank Bailey. *Over the Front*. London: Grub Street, 1992.

Fredette, Raymond. *The Sky on Fire*. New York: Harcourt, Brace, Jovanovich, 1976.

Funderburk, Thomas. *The Fighters*. New York: Grosset & Dunlap, 1965.

Genet, Edmund. *An American for Lafayette, The Diaries of E.C.C. Genet, Lafayette Escadrille*. Charlottesville: University Press of Virginia, 1981.

Gibbons, Floyd. *The Red Knight of Germany*. New York: Bantam Books, 1959.

Gilbert, James. *The Great Planes*. New York: Grosset & Dunlap, Inc. 1970.

Goodspeed, D.J. *Ludendorff: Genius of World War I*. Boston: Houghton Mifflin Company, 1966.

Gray, Peter, and Owen Thetford. *German Aircraft of the First World War*. Garden City, NY: Doubleday & Company, 1970.

Grey, C. G. ed. *Jane's All The World's Aircraft 1919*. New York: Arco Publishing Company, 1969.

Grinnell-Milne, Duncan. *Wind In The Wires*. New York: Ace Books, 1968.

Hall, Norman S. *The Balloon Buster*. Garden City, NY: Doubleday, Doran & Co, 1928.

Hallion, Richard. *Rise of the Fighter Aircraft 1914-1918*. Annapolis, MD: Nautical & Aviation Publishing Company of America, 1984.

Hart, Liddell. *The Real War*. Boston: Little, Brown and Company, 1930.

Harvey, W. J. *Rovers of the Night Sky*. London: Greenhill Books, 1984.

Howard, Fred. *Wilbur and Orville*. New York: Knopf, 1987.

Hylands, Dennis. *Werner Voss*. Berkhamsted, Great Britain: Albatros Productions, Ltd., 1986.

Hylands, Dennis. *Georges Guynemer*. Berkhamsted, Great Britain: Albatros Productions, Ltd., 1987.

Immelmann, Franz. *Immelmann: The Eagle of Lille*. London: Greenhill Books, 1984.

Imrie, Alex. *Pictorial History of the German Army Air Service 1914-1918*. Chicago: Henry Regnery Co., 1971.

Imrie, Alex. *German Fighter Units 1914-May 1917.* London: Osprey Publishing, 1978.

Jablonski, Edward. *Warriors with Wings, the story of the Lafayette Escadrille.* Indianapolis: The Bobbs-Merrill Company, Inc., 1966.

Jones, H.A. *Over the Balkans and South Russia, 1917-1919.* London: Greenhill Books, 1987.

Jones, Ira. *An Air Fighter's Scrapbook.* London: Greenhill Books, 1990.

Jones, Neville. *The Origins of Strategic Bombing.* London: William Kimber, 1973.

Kahnert, M.E. *Jagdstaffel 356.* London: Greenhill Books, 1985.

Karl, Frederick. *William Faulkner: American Writer.* New York: Weidenfeld & Nicolson, 1989.

Kennett, Lee. *The First Air War 1914-1918.* New York: The Free Press, 1991.

Kennett, Lee. *A History of Strategic Bombing.* New York: Charles Scribner's Sons, 1982.

Kilduff, Peter. *Richthofen.* New York: John Wiley & Sons, Inc., 1993.

Lawson, Don. *Great Air Battles.* New York: Lothrop, Lee & Shepard Co., 1968.

Lewis, Cecil. *Sagittarius Rising.* New York: The MacMillan Company, 1970.

Limpus, Lowell, and Burr Leyson. *This Man La Guardia.* New York: E.P. Dutton & Company, 1938.

Livesey, Anthony. *Great Battles of World War I.* New York: Macmillan Publishing Company, 1989.

Lomax, Judy. *Women of the Air.* New York: Dodd, Mead & Company, 1987.

Longstreet, Stephen. *The Canvas Falcons.* New York: The World Publishing Company, 1970.

Marben, Rolf. *Zeppelin Adventures.* London: Greenhill Books, 1986.

Manners, William. *Patience and Fortitude.* New York: Harcourt, Brace, Jovanovich, 1976.

Maurer, Maurer. *The U.S. Air Service in World War I.* Washington, D.C.: The Albert F. Sompson Historical Research Center, Maxwell AFB Alabama, The Office of Air Force History, Headquarters USAF, 1979.

Mason, Herbert. *The United States Air Force.* New York: Mason/Charter, 1976.

McCudden, James. *Flying Fury.* London: Greenhill Books, 1987.

McKee, Alexander. *The Flying Aces.* New York: Lancer Books, 1962.

"McScotch". *Fighter Pilot.* London: Greenhill Books, 1985.

Bibliography

Mason, Herbert. *High Flew the Falcons*. Philadelphia: J. B. Lippin-cott Co. 1965.

Mead, Peter. *The Eye in th Air: History of Air Observation and Recon-naissance for the Army, 1785-1945*. London: Her Majesty's Sta-tionery Office, 1983.

Mitchell, William. *Memoirs of World War I*. New York: Random House, 1960.

Mondey, David, and Michael J.H. Taylor. *The Guinness Book of Air-craft: Records, Facts, and Feats*. Middlesex: Guinness Publ. Ltd., 1988.

Moolman, Valerie. *Women Aloft*. Alexandria, VA: Time-Life Books, 1981.

Morrow, John. *The Great War In The Air: Military Aviation from 1909 to 1921*. Washington: Smithsonian Institute Press, 1993.

Morrow, John. *German Air Power in World War I*. Lincoln, NE: Univ. of Nebraska Press, 1982.

Munson, Kenneth. *Pioneer Aircraft 1903-14*. London: Blandford Press Ltd. 1969.

Munson, Kenneth. *Fighters 1914-19*. New York: MacMillan Pub-lishing Company, 1969.

Munson, Kenneth. *Bombers:Patrol and Reconnaissance Aircraft 1914-19*. New York: MacMillan Publishing Company, 1968.

Munson, Kenneth. *Aircraft of World War I*. Garden City, NY: Dou-bleday & Company, Inc. 1968.

Musciano, Walter. *Eagles of the Black Cross*. New York: Ivan Obolensky, Inc. , 1965.

Neumann, Georg Paul, Maj. *The German Air Force in the Great War*. London: Holden and Stoughten Ltd., 1920.

Nitske, W. Robert. *The Zeppelin Story*. New York: A.S. Barnes and Company, 1977.

O'Connor, Martin. *Air Aces of the Austro-Hungarian Empire 1914-1918*. Mesa, AZ: Champlin Fighter Museum Press, 1986.

Oakes, Claudia. *United States Women in Aviation through World War I*. Washington, D.C.: Smithsonian Institution Press, 1978.

Oughton, Frederick. *The Aces*. New York: G. P. Putnam's Sons, 1960.

Parkinson, Roger. *Tormented Warrior*. New York: Stein and Day Publishers, 1978.

Phelan, Joseph. *Aeroplanes and Flyers of the First World War*. New York: Grosset & Dunlap Publishers, 1973.

Pisano, Dominick; Thomas Dietz, Joanne Gernstein, and Karl Schneide. *Legend, Memory and the Great War in the Air*. Seattle: University of Washington Press, 1992.

Postma, Thijs. *Fokker: Aircraft Builders To The World*. London: Jane's Publishing Co. 1979.

Raleigh, Walter Alexander, Sir, and Henry Albert Jones. *The War in the Air; Being the Story of the Part Played in the Great War by the Royal Air Force*. Oxford: The Clarendon Press, 1922 and 1937.

Revell, Alex. *James McCudden VC*. Berhamsted, Great Britain: Albatros Productions, Ltd., 1987.

Reynolds, Quentin. *They Fought For The Sky*. New York: Bantam Books, 1958.

Richthofen, Manfred von. *The Red Baron*. New York: Ace Books, 1969.

Rickenbacker, Eddie. *Fighting the Flying Circus*. New York: Doubleday & Company, 1965.

Rickenbacker, Eddie. *Rickenbacker*. Englewood Cliffs, NJ: Prentice-Hall, Inc., 1967.

Roberts, E. M. *A Flying Fighter*. London: Greenhill Books, 1988.

Robertson, Bruce, ed. *Air Aces of the 1914-1918 War*. Fallbrook, CA: Harleyford Publications, Aero Publishers, 1964.

Robinson, Douglas. *The Zeppelin In Combat*. Seattle: University of Washington Press, 1980.

Rosher, Harold. *In The Royal Naval Air Service*. London: Greenhill Books, 1986.

Rossano, Geoffrey, ed. *The Price of Honor*. Annapolis, MD: Naval Institute Press, 1991.

Rowe, Josiah. *Letters from a World War I Aviator*. Boston: Sinclaire Press, 1986.

Schneider, Dorothy and Carl. *Into the Breach*. New York: Viking Penguin, 1991.

Schroder, Hans. *A German Airman Remembers*. London: Greenhill Books, 1986.

Schwartz, Charles. *Cole Porter*. New York: The Dial Press, 1977.

Scott, A.J.L. *Sixty Squadron R.A.F. 1916-1919*. London: Greenhill Books, 1990.

Shores, Christopher. *Above the Trenches*, London: Grub Street, 1990.

Springs, Elliott. *War Birds*. London: Temple Press Books, 1966.

Steinböck, Erwin. *Armament and Equipment of Austo-Hungarian Aircraft*. Graz, Austria: H. Weishaupt Berlag, 1983.

Stokesbury, James. *A Short History of Air Power*. New York: William Morrow and Co., 1986.

Strange, L.A. *Recollections of an Airman*. London: Greenhill Books, 1989.

Sutherland, L. W. *Aces and Kings*. London: Greenhill Books, 1985.

Sweeting, C. G. *Combat Flying Equipment*. Washington: Smithsonian Institute Press, 1989.

Sykes, Claud. *French War Birds*. London: Greenhill Books, 1987.

Terraine, John.*The U-Boat Wars 1916-1945*. New York: G.P. Putnam's Sons, 1989.

Thayer, Lucien H., Lt. *America's First Eagles: The Official History of the U.S. Air Service, A.E.F. (1917-1918)*. Mesa Arizona: Champlin Fighter Museum Press and R. James Bender Publishing, 1983.

Todd, Robert. *Sopwith Camel Fighter Ace*. Falls Church, VA: AJAY Enterprises, 1978.

Udet, Ernst. *Ace of the Iron Cross*. New York: Ace Books, 1970.

Ulanoff, Stanley M., ed. *Fighter Pilot*. Garden City, NY: Doubleday & Company, Inc. 1962.

Ulanoff, Stanley. *Illustrated History of World War I in the Air*. New York: Arco Publ., 1975.

Villard, Henry Serrano. *Contact!* New York: Thomas Crowell Company, 1968.

Voss, Vivian. *Flying Minnows*. London: Arms and Armour Press, 1977.

Wallhauser, Henry. *Pioneers of Flight*. Maplewood, NJ: Hammond Inc., 1969.

Walsh, John. *One Day at Kitty Hawk*. New York: Crowell, 1975.

Werner, Johannes. *Knight of Germany*. London: Greenhill Books, 1985.

Whitehouse,Arch. *Decisive Air Battles of the First World War*. New York: Duell, Sloan and Pearce, 1963.

Whitehouse,Arch. *Heroes of the Sunlit Sky*. Garden City, New York: Doubleday, 1967.

Whitehouse, Arch. *Legion of the Lafayette*. Garden City: Doubleday &Co., 1962.

Whitehouse, Arch. *The Zeppelin Fighters*. New York: Ace Books, 1966.

Woodman, Harry. *Early Aircraft Armament*. Washington, D.C.: Smithsonian Institution Press, 1989.

Index

Volume 1 AMERICAN MILITARY HISTORY: 1775-1902
edited by Maurice Matloff
Volume 2 AMERICAN MILITARY HISTORY: 1902-1985
edited by Maurice Matloff

Originally designed for military professionals, this is the ultimate nuts and bolts approach, with emphasis on tactics and challenges of each era. Contributors to this fundamental text are top military analysts and scholars.

Maurice Matloff was Chief of the General History Branch of the U.S. Army Office of Military History. He also wrote *Strategic Planning for Coalition Warfare, 1941-1942* and *Strategic Planning for Coalition Warfare, 1943-1944.*

VOLUME 1: 6 X 9 • 368 PAGES • 23 ILLUSTRATIONS • 37 MAPS
• 0-938289-72-1 • $29.95HC   0-938289-70-5 • $17.95PB

VOLUME 2: 6 X 9 • 384 PAGES • 36 ILLUSTRATIONS • 18 MAPS
• 0-938289-73-X • $29.95HC   0-938289-71-3 • $17.95PB

THE LITTLE BIGHORN CAMPAIGN
March-September 1876
by Wayne Michael Sarf

The destruction of Custer's command at Little Bighorn by the Sioux and Northern Cheyenne in 1876 has remained one of America's longest lingering controversies. *The Little Bighorn Campaign* penetrates the mysteries of Custer's disaster as well as the broader context of the 1876 campaign against the Sioux.
  The Little Bighorn Campaign is the most comprehensive military study of the movements and battles which led up to and followed Little Bighorn. It also examines the numbers and tactics of both the Army and the Indians.

Wayne Michael Sarf is author of *God Bless You Buffalo Bill: A Layman's Guide to History and Western Film* and numerous articles on the Custer legend.
Distinguished Praise for *The Little Bighorn Campaign*:
• "It is well done, and I like your use of sidebars to illuminate particular points." — Arthur Schlesinger, Jr.
• **MILITARY BOOK CLUB MAIN SELECTION**

6 X 9, 304 PAGES, 50 ILLUSTRATIONS, 5 MAPS • 0-938289-21-7 • $22.95

THE WATERLOO CAMPAIGN, June 1815
by Albert A. Nofi

Albert Nofi has used his many years of research to produce an account of the battle of Waterloo that has all the grandeur and military detail one could want, but which never loses its interest in individual human experience. The events of June 18, 1815, are placed in a broader context as Napoleon invades Belgium to do battle with the British and Prussian armies in a grand strategy to defeat his enemies before they can unite against him.

The Waterloo Campaign also covers individual dramas like the death of the Duke of Brunswick, the reconciliation of Napoleon and his estranged brother, and the tragic loss and miraculous delivery of many ordinary people.

New York educator Albert Nofi is the author of numerous books, including The Alamo and the Texas War for Independence, A Civil War Treasury, and The War Against Hitler.
• MILITARY BOOK CLUB MAIN SELECTION

6 X 9, 333 PAGES, 50 ILLUSTRATIONS, 16 MAPS • 0-938289-29-2 • $24.95

THE SPANISH AMERICAN WAR, 1898
by Albert A. Nofi

The Spanish American War of 1898 is often viewed as a disjointed series of colorful episodes about young Americans who would later become famous, fighting a Spanish colonial army putting up a token resistance. Military commentator and historian Albert A. Nofi presents the war as a coherent military narrative, showing the fusion of the American command's Civil War experience and recent developments in technology. Serious attention is also given to the Spanish forces, the army of an empire in decline, but well-equipped and tactically sophisticated.

• American and Spanish aims, assumptions and strategy
• Maps highlight the most tactically significant engagements
• Military operations in a wider world, 35 years after the Civil War.

Albert A. Nofi is also the author of The Gettysburg Campaign, The Waterloo Campaign, and A Civil War Treasury.

6 X 9, 256 PAGES • 50 ILLUSTRATIONS, 5 MAPS • 0-938289-57-8 • $24.95

THE ANTIETAM CAMPAIGN
August-September 1862
Revised Edition
by John Cannan

On September 17, 1862, over 25,000 men became casualties in the battle of Antietam, the Civil War's single bloodiest day. *The Antietam Campaign* contains some of the best moment-by-moment accounts of Civil War combat at the unit level. Yet this unique study goes beyond simple narrative; the battle of Antietam is placed clearly within the context of the strategic and political situation in the second year of the Civil War, and is seen as part of a larger military campaign.

John Cannan established a reputation among Civil War writers in remarkably short time. His distinctions include four books selected by the Military Book Club. He is the author of *The Atlanta Campaign* and *The Wilderness Campaign*.
• **MILITARY BOOK CLUB SELECTION**

6 X 9, 256 PAGES, 53 ILLUSTRATIONS, 9 MAPS • 0-938289-36-5 • $22.95

THE GETTYSBURG CAMPAIGN
June-July 1863 *Revised Edition*
by Albert A. Nofi

This valuable book is now available in a revised edition with a complete order of battle including strength data and new sidebars. Also included are detailed maps, charts, tables, and an informative Reader's Guide lists journals, museums and the best Gettysburg books available. When the first edition of *The Gettysburg Campaign* appeared in 1985, it was immediately recognized as a classic account of the great conflict and has remained in high demand among book sellers and readers alike. Now the book has been updated to provide one of the most intriguing accounts of the battle.
• **MILITARY BOOK CLUB SELECTION**

6 X 9, 256 PAGES, 50 ILLUSTRATIONS, 9 MAPS • 0-938289-24-1 • $19.95

HITLER'S ARMY
The Evolution and Structure of German Forces
by The Editors of Command Magazine

The most technically sophisticated charts, tables of organization and maps available graphically illustrate the structural evolution of the most intensely-studied army of the twentieth century. An insightful main text shows how the Wehrmacht's structure was increasingly contradictory to the military missions Hitler ordered it to undertake.

- Graphics and text in a new approach to Thrid Reich German Army
- Analytical comparison of U.S. and German armies in World War II
- Luftwaffe field divisions, Waffen-SS units, and foreign volunteers
- German organization and tactics in action of 12 key engagements

Ty Bomba is editor and Chris Perello associate editor of Command Magazine, a journal of conflict simulation with a growing international audience.

6 X 9, 416 PAGES • CHARTS, MAPS, DIAGRAMS • 0-938289-55-1 • $29.95

ROMMEL'S NORTH AFRICA CAMPAIGN
September 1940-November 1942
by Jack Greene and Alessandro Massignani

From 1940 to 1942, some of World War II's greatest legends were born, as Erwin Rommel the "Desert Fox" led his Afrika Korps against the "Desert Rats" of Bernard Montgomery's 8th Army.

Rommel's North Africa Campaign features detailed orders of battle, with German and Italian material available nowhere else. The capabilities of tanks, armor, artillery, aircraft and the vital transport vehicles are covered in depth. The largely unknown story of Rommel's radio-intercept unit is examined, as well as fascinating accounts of Mussolini's Blackshirts, the Young Fascists Division, the Folgore Parachute Division, and the Bersaglieri.

Californian Jack Greene has written *Mare Nostrum: The War in the Mediterranean, War at Sea: Pearl Harbor to Midway.* Bersaglieri veteran Alessandro Massignani has written numerous books and articles on Italy's role in World War II, including *Alpini e Tedeschi sul Don.*

6 X 9, 272 PAGES, 50 ILLUSTRATIONS, 18 MAPS • 0-938289-34-9 • $22.95

HITLER'S BLITZKRIEG CAMPAIGNS
The Invasion and Defense of Western Europe, 1939-1940
by J.E. Kaufmann and H.W. Kaufmann

Hitler's Blitzkrieg Campaigns is a unique compilation of narratives, charts, photographs, diagrams, and maps not previously available in the United States. Many years of meticulous research reveals for the first time in English exactly why the Maginot Line and Eben Emael defenses failed, and exactly how the European armies of the first phase of World War II were organized, equipped, and deployed.

Hitler's Blitzkrieg Campaign represents a major step forward in writing on the battles of 1939 and 1940, with coverage of many aspects of the conflict not generally available to the American reader, and with dozens of maps, diagrams and photographs that even the most die-hard World War II reader has never seen.
- "Fabulous book ... well written and researched." — *The Communiqué*
- **MILITARY BOOK CLUB MAIN SELECTION**

6 X 9, 386 PAGES • 100 PHOTOS, 66 MAPS & CHARTS • 0-938289-20-9 • $29.95

WAR AGAINST HITLER
Military Strategy in the West
edited by Albert A. Nofi

Renowned historian and military commentator Albert A. Nofi brings together for the first time in paperback a series of hard-hitting essays on World War II's most pivotal campaigns. Studies by contributors to the classic military journal *Strategy & Tactics* cover tactics and technology of the battles. Clear, concise and packed with information. Includes maps, charts, and a revised and updated bibliography.

6 X 9, 274 PAGES, 18 MAPS, 34 CHARTS • 0-938289-49-7 • $15.95PB

THE BATTLE OF THE BULGE
Hitler's Ardennes Offensive 1944-1945
by Danny Parker

In late 1944, Germany was preparing to crush the Allies. Despite the shocking blow Hitler delivered, Allied forces recovered to smash the brutal offensive. When it was over, Hitler had spent the last energies of his crumbling empire.

Danny S. Parker is a former research consultant to the Joint Chiefs of Staff on the Battle of the Bulge. He is also the author of *To Win the Winter Sky: The Air War over the Ardennes 1944-1945*.

Distinguished Praise for *Battle of the Bulge:*
• "The numerous rare photos and maps, buttressed by valuable new information, make Parker's book a welcome addition to previous histories of one of the most crucial battles ever fought by Americans." —John Toland, author of *Battle: The Story of the Bulge*
• "An epic treatment..." —James Dunnigan, author of *How to Make War*
• **MILITARY BOOK CLUB MAIN SELECTION**

9 X 12, 320 PAGES, 275 ILLUSTRATIONS, 18 MAPS • 0-938289-040-7 • $34.95

TO WIN THE WINTER SKY
Air War over the Ardennes, 1944-1945
by Danny Parker

As Allied and German armies fought on the ground in the Battle of the Bulge, an equally desperate battle raged in the skies overhead. Those who thought they were thoroughly familiar with Hitler's last offensive will find a wealth of new information here, including exclusive interviews with war-time airmen, over 100 rare photos, the unknown story of German MIAs, Luftwaffe jets and other secret weapons, and the innovations in tactics and technology.

Praise for *To Win the Winter Sky:*
• "The story is well told with all the air and ground accounts meshing into a very smooth narrative. The photos, organizational tables, maps, and charts are a veritable gold mine of information, as are the list of references and bibliography." —*Air Power History*
• **MILITARY BOOK CLUB MAIN SELECTION**

6 X 9, 528 PAGES • 153 ILLUSTRATIONS, 8 MAPS • 0-938289-35-7 • $29.95

THE MIDWAY CAMPAIGN
December 7, 1941-June 6, 1942 *Revised and Expanded Edition*
by Jack Greene

New discoveries and de-classified material have made possible this greatly expanded revision of an earlier work on the Pacific War. The author's gripping narrative begins with detailed maps of American dispositions at Pearl Harbor and the Japanese plan of attack. Similar maps and charts bring exceptional clarity to the campaigns in the Philippines and Malaya, the early carrier raids, the battle of the Coral Sea, and the battle of Midway itself. Detailed charts graphically illustrate the composition of air, land, and naval units.

Greene never loses sight of the grand strategic picture, offering an insightful examination of Japan's aims, assumptions, strengths, and weaknesses, as well as a thought-provoking analysis of the Pacific Ocean as a single grand battlefield.

6 X 9, 256 PAGES, 50 ILLUSTRATIONS, 10 MAPS • 0-938289-11-X • $22.95

MacARTHUR'S NEW GUINEA CAMPAIGN
March-August 1944
by Nathan Prefer

Many World War II scholars consider New Guinea to be the finest example of Douglas MacArthur's operational doctrine, a convincing demonstration of his often-neglected flexibility, and one of the most tactically significant campaigns of the war. This fascinating new book is the only fully up-to-date examination of the ambushes, flank attacks, and combined operations of the New Guinea campaign. Includes specially prepared maps, diagrams of the Japanese bunker system, and complete orders of battle.

6 X 9, 288 PAGES, 6 MAPS, 50 PHOTOGRAPHS • 0-938289-51-9 • $24.95

(All prices subject to change.)
Call **TOLL FREE 1-800-418-6065** to order a catalog or books from Combined Books, Inc., 151 E. 10th Ave., Conshohocken, PA 19428. VISA and MASTERCARD accepted.